SPARKNOTES®

SAT* math WORKBOOK

SPARK PUBLISHING

Spark Publishing
120 Fifth Avenue
New York, NY 10011
www.sparknotes.com

ISBN-13: 978-1-4114-0435-9
ISBN-10: 1-4114-0435-1

Please submit changes or report errors to www.sparknotes.com/errors.

Printed and bound in Canada

10 9 8 7 6 5 4 3

CONTENTS

Introduction: The Math Section 1

Multiple-Choice and Grid-Ins 6

Numbers and Operations 10

Data, Statistics, and Probability . . 52

Geometry. 82

Algebra 141

SAT
Math
Workbook

INTRODUCTION: THE MATH SECTION

SAT MATH SPANS TWO QUESTION TYPES, three timed sections, and four major math topics—that's a lot of stuff. This workbook covers all of it—the basic facts, the crucial score-building strategies, and, that's right, all the math tested on the SAT. So read this book, become an SAT Math guru, and then find yourself a mountain somewhere in Tibet. Up there you can give cryptic advice to awed high school students who've climbed thousands of feet to see you, risking their own deaths at the hands of avalanches and abominable snow-men. Or forego this life of reverence and head off to the college of your choice.

SAT MATH

The truth is that SAT Math isn't harder than the stuff you've already seen in your high school math classes. Whether you've seen it before or not, we cover it all in this book:

- **Numbers and Operations**
- **Algebra (I and II)**
- **Geometry**
- **Data Analysis, Statistics, and Probability**

On the SAT, questions covering these four major math topics are spread across three timed sections and 54 total questions.

- **25-minute section with 20 questions**: all questions are Multiple-Choice.
- **25-minute section with 18 questions**: 8 Multiple-Choice and 10 Grid-Ins.
- **20-minute section with 16 questions**: all questions are Multiple-Choice.

Them's the facts. There's nothing else to know about SAT Math—unless you need directions to Tibet.

KNOWING STRATEGIES VS. KNOWING MATH

There are some test-prep books out there—we won't name names, 'cause we're nice—that claim the SAT only tests your ability to take the SAT and doesn't test any actual knowledge. Well, those test-prep books are written by at least one of the following types of people:

- Liars
- Fools

The fact is, someone who has all the math on the test down cold but doesn't know any of the strategies will almost always do better on the test than some other kid who's studied up on the strategies but doesn't know the Pythagorean theorem.

But who would ever go and study just the strategies or just the math? The whole point is to study both. And we promise you: If you know the math and the strategies, you'll whip both of those hypothetical kids who focused only on one or the other.

THE MATH REFERENCE AREA

The math section on the SAT provides a reference area with the basic geometric formulas and information.

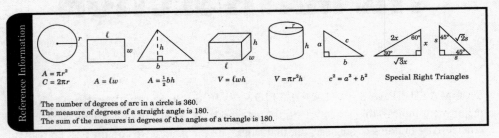

The number of degrees of arc in a circle is 360.
The measure of degrees of a straight angle is 180.
The sum of the measures in degrees of the angles of a triangle is 180.

You might think that the SAT gives you this reference area because it asks lots of questions on these topics. Well, you're right. But the reference area is also a trap. Imagine a lazy student out there named Mike. Mike says to himself, "Why should I study all those formulas if they're just sitting there in the reference area?" Then he goes and takes a nap. On the day of the test, he's sitting there in his seat, sweating under the pressure, flipping maniacally back and forth between the reference area and the test questions, losing time and focus with every flip of the page.

Don't be like Mike. And don't just memorize the formulas. Figure out what they mean. The mathematical facts and rules in the reference area are the *foundation* for almost every geometry question on the test. Know all the formulas in the reference area as if they are tattooed on your body, as if they're part of you. You'll save time. You'll raise your score. You'll have funky mathematical tattoos.

ORDER OF DIFFICULTY

In each group of questions types, questions are ordered by difficulty. The first third of the questions are generally easy, the second third are a little harder, and the last third are difficult. So in the sections that are entirely Multiple Choice, the first third of the section will be easy, the second third medium, and the last third hard. In the section that has both Multiple Choice and Grid-ins, the pattern will start over for each group of questions. Knowing where you are in the order of difficulty can help you in a variety of ways:

- **On Individual Questions.** If you think you've got the answer to an easy question, don't second-guess yourself: You probably do. If you're looking at a difficult question, though, you might want to check your answer just to make sure you haven't fallen into a trap.
- **Overall Strategy.** Unless you're going for a 700 or above, you don't have to worry about answering every question on the test. You can use the order of difficulty to help you focus on answering the questions that you can. You should, for instance, answer every question in the first half of a timed math section. But if you're worried about time, you can probably get by without spending any real time at all on the final two questions.
- **Pacing.** You can also use the order of difficulty to manage your pacing. When you're given 25 minutes to answer 20 math questions in a timed section, you shouldn't just think to yourself that for every five minutes you should answer four questions. It takes more time to answer difficult problems than it does to answer easy problems. So in the early questions, you should be going *faster* than four questions answered per five minutes so that you can save up time to figure out the harder problems.

BETTER, SMARTER, FASTER

Time management separates the students who kick major hindquarters on the Math section from those who merely do okay. If you take two students of equal skill in math, but give one a few extra minutes on an SAT Math section, who's gonna get a better score? The kid with more time.

You might be thinking, "Yeah, but no one's going to get more time." While no proctor is going to come along and give half the room 28 minutes on a section and hold the other half to 25, there is one person who can give you more time on a Math section: you!

Math Shortcuts

On the SAT Math, how much time you spend on a problem depends less on how much math you know and more on how you *approach* the problem. Take a look at the following example:

> Which has a greater area, a square with sides measuring 4 cm or a circle with a radius of the same length?

One student, we'll call him Bob, might solve this problem algebraically: Plug 4 into the formula for the area of a square and then the area of a circle. Area of a square $= s^2$, so the area of this square $= 4^2 = 16$. Area of a circle $= \pi r^2$, so the area of this circle must be $4\pi^2 = 16\pi$. 16π is obviously bigger than 16, so the circle must have a larger area than the square.

But another student, we'll call her Melanie, might choose a faster approach by quickly sketching the square and circle superimposed.

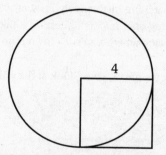

Bob and Melanie know the same amount of math, but because Melanie took the faster approach, she gave herself more time to work on other questions, a distinct advantage. A few more questions like this one, and Melanie will score considerably higher than Bob, even though the two of them know basically the same amount of math.

What Melanie did, essentially, was find a *shortcut*. Though she knew the same math that Bob did, Melanie found a way to answer the question more quickly. This doesn't make Melanie better at math, but it does make her a little bit better at taking the SAT.

The important question is, How can you learn to be more like Melanie? You need to do two things:

- **Be prepared.** You're not going to find a shortcut for a problem *unless* you know how to work it out the "long" way. An ability to find shortcuts is an expression of how *comfortable* you are with the math you know. Familiarity breeds shortcuts. The more you practice and the more you look over the practice tests you take, the better you'll become at finding shortcuts.
- **Be on the lookout.** Be aware that there *are* shortcuts out there just waiting to be found. If you can invest a second to survey the question and think about a faster way, you'll be well served.

This is not to say that you should go into every question searching for a shortcut. A shortcut won't always exist. If you're on some blind quest for a shortcut, it might end up taking *longer* than the obvious long route to solving the problem.

Shortcuts are more common on SAT questions that cover particular SAT math. As we teach you the math you need to rock the SAT, we also point out the shortcuts you need to *really* rock the SAT Math.

SAT CALCULATOR SMARTS

By all means, use a calculator on the test. Bring the biggest, baddest calculator you've got, as long as it fits these specifications from the SAT:

- It isn't a hand-held minicomputer or laptop computer.
- It has no electronic writing pad or pen-input device.
- It isn't a pocket organizer (PDA).
- It doesn't have a QWERTY keyboard.
- It doesn't use paper tape.
- It doesn't make unusual noises (translation: *any* noises).
- It doesn't reqire an electrical outlet.

Any four-function, scientific, or graphing calculator is accepted as long as it doesn't break any of the above rules.

But just because you've got an awesome shiny hammer doesn't mean you should try to use it to pound in thumbtacks. Your calculator will help you on the SAT but only if you use it intelligently.

Every question on the SAT can be solved *without* using a calculator, so you never *need* to start pushing buttons. In fact, on algebra questions involving variables, calculators are absolutely useless. So instead of reaching instinctively for your calculator every time, you should come up with a problem-solving plan for each question. Make sure you understand what the question requires and then decide whether to stick to your no. 2 pencil or to wield your formidable digital axe.

To see an example of what we mean, take a look at the following problem:

If $x = 3$, then what is the value of $f(x) = \dfrac{x^2 - 3x - 4}{11x - 44}$?

(A)   −3
(B)   −1.45
(C)   0
(D)   .182
(E)   .364

A trigger-happy calculator-user might immediately plug 3 in for x and start furiously working the keys. But the student who takes a moment to think about the problem will probably see that the calculation would be much simpler if the function were first simplified. To start, factor the 11 out of the denominator:

$$f(x) = \frac{x^2 - 3x - 4}{11(x - 4)}$$

Then, factor the numerator to its simplest form:

$$f(x) = \frac{(x - 4)(x + 1)}{11(x - 4)}$$

Cancel out, and you get:

$$f(x) = \frac{(x + 1)}{11}$$

Now it's obvious that if you plug the 3 in for x, you get $\dfrac{4}{11}$, which equals .364.

Practical Calculator Rules

There are a few general rules of calculator use on the SAT that it pays to follow:

- Use a calculator for brute-force tasks, such as dealing with decimals.
- If you have to deal with a long string of numbers, do not jump to use your calculator. Instead, look for a way to cancel out some of the terms and simplify. A way will usually exist.
- Avoid using your calculator on fraction problems and on algebra questions with variables.
- Know your calculator before the test. Be comfortable and familiar with it so that you don't waste time fiddling with buttons during the test. This is particularly true of graphing calculators, which have more buttons than 50 Cent has tattoos.
- Make sure your batteries are in good shape. Yes, we sound like your parents. But if your batteries run out during the test, you'll probably have to retake the test and tell your sad story to your entire extended family. That would be ugly.

Above all else, remember: Your calculator is a tool. You wouldn't wildly swing a hammer around, but some students seem to think they can just whip out their calculators and magically solve problems. Those students seldom do all that well on the SAT Math section.

MULTIPLE-CHOICE AND GRID-INS

MULTIPLE-CHOICE QUESTIONS

MC stands for all kinds of things. Rappers. Motorcycles. Master of ceremonies. Even Mariah Carey. On the SAT, MC means good old multiple-choice questions: a question, maybe a graph or a geometric figure, and then five answer choices. About 80 percent of the SAT Math section consists of these little babies. Know how to handle 'em, and you'll be crushing every MC on the block come test day.

For every math multiple-choice question on the test, you have two options:

- Solve the problem directly.
- Use the process of elimination.

In general, solving the problem is faster than going through the answer choices using the process of elimination. Also, in general, if you're at all uncomfortable with the topic, it can be beneficial to try to eliminate answers instead of just solving the question.

Solving the Problem

Solving a problem directly is pretty straightforward as long as you feel comfortable with the math being tested. It's a two-step process.

1. **Read the question**, *but don't look at the answers*. Rephrase the question to make sure you understand it, and devise a plan to solve it.
2. **Solve the problem**. Once you have an answer—*and only then*—see if your answer is listed among the answer choices. By waiting to look at the answer choices until after you've solved the problem, you preempt those nasty SAT traps.

We can't stress enough that if you're trying to solve the problem directly, you should avoid looking at the answer choices until the end. Since trap answers are often the values you would get at the halfway point of the process of working out a problem, if you peek at the answers, you may get tricked into thinking you've solved the question before you actually have.

The Process of Elimination

On every multiple-choice question, the answer is right in front of you. It's just hidden among those five answer choices. This means you can sometimes short circuit the problem by plugging each answer into the question to see which one works. On certain occasions, working backward could actually be a faster method than just solving the problem directly.

Okay, example time:

A classroom contains 31 chairs, some which have arms and some of which do not. If the room contains 5 more armchairs than chairs without arms, how many armchairs does it contain?

(A) 10
(B) 13
(C) 16
(D) 18
(E) 21

If you want to solve the problem directly, you first have to assign variables:

$$\text{Total number of chairs} = 31$$

$$\text{armchairs} = x$$

$$\text{chairs without arms} = y$$

Next, take these variables and translate them into an equation based on the information in the question:

$$31 = x + y$$

$$y = x - 5$$

Then substitute one equation into the other:

$$31 = x + (x - 5)$$
$$31 = 2x - 5$$
$$36 = 2x$$
$$x = 18$$

There you are with the right answer, but it took a bit of time.

What if you plugged in the answers instead? And what if you plugged in intelligently, meaning: First plug in the value **C**.

Since answer choices on the SAT Math always either ascend or descend in value, starting with the middle value means that you'll never have to go through all five choices. For instance, in this question, if you plug in **C** (16) and discover that it's too small a number to satisfy the equation, you can eliminate **A** and **B** along with **C**. If 16 is too big, you can eliminate **D** and **E** along with **C**.

So let's plug in 16 and see what happens:

- The question says that there are 5 fewer armless chairs than armchairs, so if you have 16 armchairs, then you have 11 armless chairs, for a total of 27 chairs.
- Since you need the total numbers of chairs to equal 31, **C** is clearly not the right answer. But because the total number of chairs was too small, you can also eliminate **A** and **B**, the answer choices indicating fewer numbers of armchairs.
- If you then plug in **D** (18), you have 13 normal chairs and 31 total chairs. There's your answer. In this instance, plugging in the answers takes less time and seems easier.

As you take practice tests, you'll need to build up a sense of when working backwards can help you most. But here's a quick do and don't summary to help you along:

- **DO** work backward when the question describes an equation of some sort, and the answer choices are all rather simple numbers.
- **DON'T** work backward when dealing with answer choices that contain variables or complicated fractions.

GRID-INS

Grid-ins cover the same topics and ask the same kind of questions as multiple-choice questions. They just don't have any answer choices. You have to work out the answer yourself and then "grid" it into a special answer-box thingy.

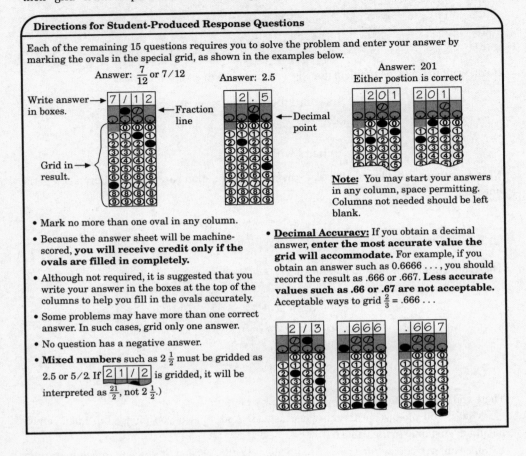

Directions for Student-Produced Response Questions

Each of the remaining 15 questions requires you to solve the problem and enter your answer by marking the ovals in the special grid, as shown in the examples below.

Answer: $\frac{7}{12}$ or 7/12

Answer: 2.5

Answer: 201
Either postion is correct

Write answer in boxes.

Fraction line

Decimal point

Grid in result.

Note: You may start your answers in any column, space permitting. Columns not needed should be left blank.

- Mark no more than one oval in any column.

- Because the answer sheet will be machine-scored, **you will receive credit only if the ovals are filled in completely.**

- Although not required, it is suggested that you write your answer in the boxes at the top of the columns to help you fill in the ovals accurately.

- Some problems may have more than one correct answer. In such cases, grid only one answer.

- No question has a negative answer.

- **Mixed numbers** such as $2\frac{1}{2}$ must be gridded as 2.5 or 5/2. If 2 1/2 is gridded, it will be interpreted as $\frac{21}{2}$, not $2\frac{1}{2}$.)

- **Decimal Accuracy:** If you obtain a decimal answer, **enter the most accurate value the grid will accommodate.** For example, if you obtain an answer such as 0.6666 . . . , you should record the result as .666 or .667. **Less accurate values such as .66 or .67 are not acceptable.** Acceptable ways to grid $\frac{2}{3}$ = .666 . . .

The Grid

As you can see, grid-in instructions are a little intense. Here's a summary:

- **The computer that grades the test can't read anything but the ovals,** so you don't have to write anything in the spaces at the top. However, filling in the spaces at the top might help you to avoid making careless mistakes. So just write it out.

- **The grid cannot accommodate any number longer than four digits, any decimal or fraction that includes more than three numbers, or any negative signs.** Here's another way of looking at that: If the answer you come up with has more than four digits, is a fraction or decimal with more than three digits, or is a negative number, then your answer's wrong.

- **You must express a number as either a fraction or a decimal.** It doesn't matter which you choose.

- **You must transform all mixed numbers to fraction form.** For example, $4\frac{1}{2}$ must be written as $^9/_2$ or 4.5. If you were to try to write $4\frac{1}{2}$, the grading machine would read it as $^{41}/_2$, and you'd lose a point.

- **Sometimes the answer you come to will actually be a range of answers,** such as "any number between 4 and 5." When that happens, you could write in any number that fits the criteria—4.6, 4.2, $^9/_2$. But *no mixed numbers.*

Do Not Work Backward

Since there aren't any answer choices for grid-ins, you can't work backward. To answer these questions, you have to know the concepts and how to solve them directly. Luckily, that's exactly what the rest of this book covers.

NUMBERS AND OPERATIONS

THE SAT ESCHEWS THE SIMPLE AND TIME-HONORED TERM *ARITHMETIC* in favor of the clunky *Numbers and Operations*. Not that it really matters, since both cover the exact same thing, and this gave us the chance to use the word *eschews*, which has nothing to do with teeth or chewing. *Eschew* means "to avoid," and as you know, the SAT tends to eschew simplicity a lot. Hence: Numbers and Operations.

In this chapter, we cover all the Numbers and Operations topics on the SAT. You should know this stuff so well you barely have to think about it, especially since a number of these will resurface in algebra questions.

KNOW YOUR NUMBERS

The SAT loves to throw around terminology about numbers. If you don't know the terminology, you won't know how to answer the question.

- **Whole Numbers.** The set of counting numbers, including zero $\{0, 1, 2, 3, \ldots\}$.
- **Natural Numbers.** The set of all whole positive numbers *except* zero $\{1, 2, 3, 4, 5, \ldots\}$.
- **Integers.** The set of all positive and negative whole numbers, including zero. Fractions and decimals are not included $\{\ldots, -3, -2, -1, 0, 1, 2, 3, \ldots\}$.
- **Rational Numbers.** The set of all numbers that can be expressed as integers in fractions. That is, any number that can be expressed in the form m/n, where m and n are integers.
- **Irrational Numbers.** The set of all numbers that cannot be expressed as integers in a fraction. Examples include π, $\sqrt{3}$, and $1.01001000100001000001\ldots$. A number must be either rational or irrational; no number can be both.
- **Real Numbers.** Every number on the number line. The set of real numbers includes all rational and irrational numbers.

ORDER OF OPERATIONS

PEMDAS is an acronym for the order in which mathematical operations should be performed as you move from left to right through an expression or equation:

- **P**arentheses
- **E**xponents
- **M**ultiplication
- **D**ivision
- **A**ddition
- **S**ubtraction

You may have had PEMDAS introduced to you as "Please Excuse My Dear Aunt Sally." Excuse us, but that's a supremely lame 1950s-style acronym. We prefer "Picking Eminem Made Dre A Star." Whatever. Just remember PEMDAS.

If an equation contains any or all of these PEMDAS elements, first carry out the math within the parentheses, then work out the exponents, then the multiplication, and then the division. Addition and subtraction are actually a bit more complicated. When you have an equation to the point that it only contains addition and subtraction, perform each operation moving from left to right across the equation.

An example will make this easier to get:

$$\frac{(18-3)\times 2^2}{5}-7+(6\times 3-1)$$

First work out the math in the parentheses (following PEMDAS even within the parentheses—always do multiplication before subtraction):

$$\frac{(18-3)\times 2^2}{5}-7+(18-1)$$

$$\frac{15\times 2^2}{5}-7+17$$

Now work out the exponents:

$$\frac{15\times 4}{5}-7+17$$

Then do the multiplication:

$$\frac{60}{5}-7+17$$

Then the division:

$$12-7+17$$

Leaving you with just addition and subtraction. Now work from left to right:

$$5+17$$

And finally:

$$22$$

ODD AND EVEN NUMBERS

Even numbers are numbers that are divisible by 2 with no remainder. Remember that zero is included within this definition.

Even Numbers: . . . , –6, –4, –2, 0, 2, 4, 6, . . .

Odd numbers are numbers that, when divided by 2, leave a remainder of 1.

Odd Numbers: . . . , –5, –3, –1, 1, 3, 5, . . .

Operations and Odd and Even Numbers

For the SAT, you have to know how odd and even numbers act when they're added, subtracted, multiplied, and divided. The chart below shows addition, subtraction, and multiplication because multiplication and division are the same in terms of odd and even.

Addition	Subtraction	Multiplication
Even + Even = Even	Even – Even = Even	Even × Even = Even
Odd + Odd = Even	Odd – Odd = Even	Odd × Odd = Odd
Even + Odd = Odd	Even – Odd = Odd	Even × Odd = Even

If you know how odd and even numbers act when put through any of the four operations, you have a leg up in using the process of elimination. If the numbers in the answer choices are both odd and even, you should be able to use the rules of odd and even numbers to figure out if the answer you're looking for is odd or even. So even if you don't know the exact value of the answer you're looking for, you should be able to eliminate half of the answers based on whether they're odd or even.

THE POSITIVE, THE NEGATIVE, AND THE UGLY

Positive numbers are greater than zero. Negative numbers are less than zero. Zero itself is neither positive nor negative. On a number line, positive numbers appear to the right of zero, and negative numbers appear to the left.

$$\ldots, -5, -4, -3, -2, -1, 0, 1, 2, 3, 4, 5, \ldots$$

In equations and expressions, positive numbers look like normal numbers (for example, 7), while negative numbers have a negative sign in front of them (–7).

Negative numbers can be confusing. It's like you're suddenly told to read from right to left, but all of your instincts tell you to do the opposite. Why are we telling you this? To convince you to concentrate. The SAT Math preys on the careless, and negative numbers are one of the weapons it uses most often.

Negative Numbers and Operations

Negative numbers act differently from positive numbers when you add, subtract, multiply, or divide them.

Adding and Subtracting Signed Numbers

Adding a negative number is like *subtracting* a positive number . . .

$$3 + -2 = 1, \text{ just as } 3 - 2 = 1$$

. . . while subtracting a negative number is the same as *adding* a positive number.

$$3 - (-2) = 5, \text{ just as } 3 + 2 = 5$$

Multiplying and Dividing Negative Numbers

When negative numbers are involved in multiplication and division, they affect whether the outcome is positive or negative. You should know these rules cold.

Multiplying with Negative Numbers	Dividing with Negative Numbers
Positive × Positive = Positive	Positive ÷ Positive = Positive
Negative × Negative = Positive	Negative ÷ Negative = Positive
Positive × Negative = Negative	Positive ÷ Negative = Negative

Here's a helpful trick when dealing with a series of multiplied or divided positive and negative numbers: If there's an even number of negative numbers in the series, the outcome will be positive. If there's an odd number, the outcome will be negative.

The Ugly: Negative Numbers and Parentheses

When negative signs and parentheses collide, well, the heading says it all. The principle is simple: A negative sign outside parentheses is distributed across the parentheses. Take the question $3 + 4 - (3 + 1 - 8) = ?$. Solve this problem by following PEMDAS and first working out the parentheses:

$$3 + 4 - (4 - 8) = 3 + 4 - (-4) = 3 + 4 + 4 = 11$$

When you start dealing with algebra, however, you won't always have like terms, and you won't be able to work out what's in the parentheses. You'll instead have to get rid of the parentheses by distributing the negative sign across it. Why can you do this? Because $3 + 4 - (3 + 1 - 8) = ?$ secretly has multiplication in it. It can also be written as $3 + 4 + (-1)(3 + 1 - 8) = ?$. So every number within the parentheses should be multiplied by -1. But remember that multiplication with a negative number changes the sign of the product. So the simplified expression is $3 + 4 - 3 - 1 + 8 = 11$. Whenever you see a negative sign before parentheses, take a deep breath and be careful of your signs.

Absolute Value

Negative numbers got you down? Absolute value can help. The absolute value of a number is the distance on a number line between that number and zero. Or, you could think of it as the positive "version" of every number. The absolute value of a positive number is that same number, and the absolute value of a negative number is the number without a negative sign.

The absolute value of x is written this way: $|x|$.

$$\text{If } x = 5, |x| = 5.$$
$$\text{If } x = -4.234, |x| = 4.234.$$
$$\text{If } x = 0, |x| = 0.$$

It is also possible to have expressions within absolute value brackets:

$$3 - 2 + |3 - 7|$$

You can't just make that -7 positive because it's sitting between absolute value brackets. You have to work out the math first:

$$3 - 2 + |-4|$$

Now you can get rid of the brackets and the negative sign from that 4.

$$3 - 2 + 4 = 5$$

DIVISIBILITY AND REMAINDERS

The SAT sometimes tests whether you can determine if one number is divisible by another. To check divisibility, you could take the immense amount of time necessary to do the division by hand and see if the result is a whole number. Or you can give yourself a shortcut and memorize this list of divisibility rules:

Divisibility Rules

1. All whole numbers are divisible by 1.
2. All numbers with a ones digit of 0, 2, 4, 6, or 8 are divisible by 2.
3. A number is divisible by 3 if its digits add up to a number divisible by 3. For example, 6,711 is divisible by 3 because $6 + 7 + 1 + 1 = 15$, and 15 is divisible by 3.
4. A number is divisible by 4 if its last two digits are divisible by 4. For example, 80,744 is divisible by 4, but 7,850 is not.
5. A number is divisible by 5 if it ends in 0 or 5.

6. A number is divisible by 6 if it is even and also divisible by 3.

7. There are no rules for 7. It is a rebel.

8. A number is divisible by 8 if its last three digits are divisible by 8. For example, 905,256 is divisible by 8 because 256 is divisible by 8, and 74,513 is not divisible by 8 because 513 is not divisible by 8.

9. A number is divisible by 9 if its digits add up to a number divisible by 9. For example, 1,458 is divisible by 9 because $1 + 4 + 5 + 8 = 18$, and 18 is divisible by 9.

10. A number is divisible by 10 if it ends in 0.

FACTORS

A factor is an integer that divides another integer evenly. If a/b is an integer, then b is a factor of a. The numbers 3, 4, and 6, for example, are factors of 12.

Factorization

Sometimes the SAT requires you to find all the factors of some integer or to just be able to run through the factors quickly. To make this happen, write down all the factors of a number in pairs, beginning with 1 and the number you're factoring. To factor 24:

- 1 and 24 ($1 \times 24 = 24$)
- 2 and 12 ($2 \times 12 = 24$)
- 3 and 8 ($3 \times 8 = 24$)
- 4 and 6 ($4 \times 6 = 24$)

If you find yourself beginning to repeat numbers, then the factorization's complete. After finding that 4 is a factor of 24, the next lowest factor is 6, but you've already written down 6. You're done.

Prime Numbers

Everyone's always insisting on how unique they are. Punks wear leather. Goths wear black. But prime numbers actually are unique. They are the only numbers whose sole factors are 1 and themselves. All prime numbers are positive (because every negative number has –1 as a factor in addition to 1 and itself). Furthermore, all prime numbers besides 2 are odd.

The first few primes, in increasing order, are

$$2, 3, 5, 7, 11, 13, 17, 19, 23, 29, 31, 37, 41, 43, 47, 53, \ldots$$

You don't have to memorize this list, but getting familiar with it is a pretty good idea. Here's a trick to determine if a number is prime. First, estimate the square root of the number. Then, check all the prime numbers that fall below your estimate to see if they are factors of the number. For example, to see if 91 is prime, you should estimate the square root of the number: $\sqrt{91} \approx 10$. Now you should test 91 for divisibility by the prime numbers smaller than 10: 2, 3, 5, and 7.

- Is 91 divisible by 2? No, it does not end with an even number.
- Is 91 divisible by 3? No, $9 + 1 = 10$, and 10 is not divisible by 3.
- Is 91 divisible by 5? No, 91 does not end with 0 or 5.
- Is 91 divisible by 7? Yes! $91 \div 7 = 13$.

Therefore, 91 is not prime.

Prime Factorization

Come on, say it aloud with us: "prime factorization." Now imagine Arnold Schwarzenegger saying it. Then imagine if he knew how to do it. Holy Moly. He would probably be governor of the entire United States.

To find the prime factorization of a number, divide it and all its factors until every remaining integer is prime. The resulting group of prime numbers is the prime factorization of the original integer. Want to find the prime factorization of 36? We thought so:

$$36 = 2 \times 18 = 2 \times 2 \times 9 = 2 \times 2 \times 3 \times 3$$

It can be helpful to think of prime factorization in the form of a tree:

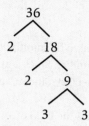

As you may already have noticed, there's more than one way to find the prime factorization of a number. Instead of cutting 36 into 2 × 18, you could have factored it to 6 × 6, and then continued from there. As long as you don't screw up the math, there's no wrong path—you'll always get the same result.

Greatest Common Factor

The greatest common factor (GCF) of two numbers is the largest factor that they have in common. Finding the GCF of two numbers is especially useful in certain applications, such as manipulating fractions (we explain why later in this chapter).

To find the GCF of two numbers, say, 18 and 24, first find their prime factorizations:

$$18 = 2 \times 9 = 2 \times 3 \times 3$$
$$24 = 2 \times 12 = 2 \times 2 \times 6 = 2 \times 2 \times 2 \times 3$$

The GCF is the "overlap," or intersection, of the two prime factorizations. In this case, both prime factorizations contain 2 × 3 = 6. This is their GCF.

Here's another, more complicated example: What's the GCF of 96 and 144? First, find the prime factorizations:

$$96 = 2 \times 48 = 2 \times 2 \times 24 = 2 \times 2 \times 2 \times 12 = 2 \times 2 \times 2 \times 2 \times 6 = 2 \times 2 \times 2 \times 2 \times 2 \times 3 = 2^5 \times 3$$

$$144 = 2 \times 72 = 2 \times 2 \times 36 = 2 \times 2 \times 2 \times 18 = 2 \times 2 \times 2 \times 2 \times 9 = 2 \times 2 \times 2 \times 2 \times 3 \times 3 = 2^4 \times 3^2$$

The product of the "overlap" is $2^4 \times 3 = 48$. So that's their GCF.

MULTIPLES

A multiple is an integer that can divide evenly into another integer. If c/d is an integer, then c is a multiple of d. The numbers 45, 27, and 18, for example, are all multiples of 9. Here's a better example: What are some multiples of 4? The numbers 12, 20, and 96 are all multiples of 4. How do we know? Because:

$$12 = 4 \times 3$$
$$20 = 4 \times 5$$
$$96 = 4 \times 24$$

Also, note that any integer, n, is a multiple of 1 and n because $1 \times n = n$.

Least Common Multiple

The least common multiple (LCM) of two integers is the smallest multiple that the two numbers have in common. The LCM of two numbers is, like the GCF, useful when manipulating fractions. Also similar to the GCF, you can't find the LCM without using prime factorization. For example, what's the least common multiple of 4 and 6? Begin by prime factorizing:

$$4 = 2 \times 2, \text{ and } 6 = 2 \times 3$$

The LCM—get this, it's tricky—is equal to the multiplication of each factor by the maximum number of times it appears in either number. Since 2 appears twice in the prime factorization of 4, it will appear twice (2 × 2) in the LCM. Since 3 appears once, it will appear once. So the LCM of 4 and 6 is 2 × 2 × 3 = 12.

One more example will help. What is the LCM of 14 and 38? Prime factorize:

$$14 = 2 \times 7$$
$$38 = 2 \times 19$$

Since 2 appears a maximum of once in either number, it will appear once in the LCM. Same goes for 7 and 19, making the LCM 2 × 7 × 19 = 266.

KNOW YOUR FRACTIONS

The SAT loves fractions. *Loves* them. The number of questions on the test that covers fractions in some way is nothing short of stupefying. This means you must know fractions inside and out. Know how to compare them, reduce them, add them, and multiply them. Know how to divide them, subtract them, and convert them to mixed numbers. Know them. Love them like the SAT does. Make them your friend on the test, not your enemy.

To begin, here are the basics: A fraction is a part of a whole. It's composed of two expressions, a numerator and a denominator. The numerator of a fraction is the quantity above the fraction bar, and the denominator is the quantity below the fraction bar. For example, in the fraction $^1/_2$, 1 is the numerator, and 2 is the denominator.

Equivalent Fractions

Fractions represent a part of a whole, so if you increase both the part and whole by the same multiple, you will not change the relationship between the part and the whole.

To determine if two fractions are equivalent, multiply the denominator and numerator of one fraction so that the denominators of the two fractions are equal. (This is one place where knowing how to calculate LCM and GCF comes in handy.) For example, $^1/_2 = {}^3/_6$ because if you multiply the numerator and denominator of $^1/_2$ by 3, you get:

$$\frac{1 \times 3}{2 \times 3} = \frac{3}{6}$$

As long as you multiply or divide *both* the numerator and denominator of a fraction by the *same* nonzero number, you will not change the overall value of the fraction.

Reducing Fractions

Reducing fractions makes life simpler. It takes unwieldy monsters like $^{450}/_{600}$ and makes them into smaller, friendlier critters. To reduce a fraction to its lowest terms, divide the numerator and denominator by their GCF. For example, for $^{450}/_{600}$, the GCF of 450 and 600 is 150. So the fraction reduces down to $^3/_4$, since 450 ÷ 150 = 3, and 600 ÷ 150 = 4.

A fraction is in its simplest, totally reduced form if its numerator and denominator share no further GCF (in other words, their GCF is 1). There is no number but 1, for instance, that can divide into both 3 and 4, so $^3/_4$ is a fraction in its lowest form.

Comparing Fractions

Large positive numbers with lots of digits, like 5,000,000, are greater than numbers with just a few digits, such as 5. But fractions don't work that way. While $^{200}/_{20,000}$ might seem like a nice, big, impressive fraction, $^2/_3$ is actually larger because 2 is a much bigger part of 3 than 200 is of 20,000.

In certain cases, comparing two fractions can be very simple. If the denominators of two fractions are the same, then the fraction with the larger numerator is bigger. If the numerators of the two fractions are the same, the fraction with the smaller denominator is bigger.

However, you'll most likely have to deal with two fractions that have different numerators and denominators, such as $^{200}/_{20,000}$ and $^2/_3$. Don't worry. There is an easy comparison tool, which we now reveal: cross-multiplication. Just multiply the numerator of each fraction by the denominator of the other, then write the product of each multiplication next to the numerator you used to get it. Here's the cross-multiplication of $^{200}/_{20,000}$ and $^2/_3$:

$$600 = \frac{200}{20,000} \times \frac{2}{3} = 40,000$$

Since $40,000 > 600$, $^2/_3$ is the greater fraction.

Adding and Subtracting Fractions

Adding and subtracting fractions that have the same denominator is a snap. If the fractions have different denominators, though, you need an additional step.

Fractions with the Same Denominators

To add fractions with the same denominators, all you have to do is add up the numerators:

$$\frac{1}{20} + \frac{3}{20} + \frac{13}{20} = \frac{17}{20}$$

Subtraction works similarly. If the denominators of the fractions are equal, just subtract one numerator from the other:

$$\frac{13}{20} - \frac{2}{20} = \frac{11}{20}$$

Fractions with Different Denominators

If the fractions don't have equal denominators, then before you can actually get to the addition and subtraction, you first have to make the denominators the same. *Then* adding and subtracting will be a piece of cake, as in the example above. The best way to equalize denominators is to find the least common denominator (LCD), which is just the LCM of the two denominators. For example, the LCD of $^1/_2$ and $^2/_3$ is 6, since 6 is the LCM of 2 and 3.

But because fractions are parts of a whole, if you increase the whole, you also have to increase the part by the same amount. To put it more bluntly, multiply the numerator by the same number you multiplied the denominator. For the example $^1/_2 + ^2/_3$, you know you have to get denominators of 6 in order to add them. For the $^1/_2$, this means you have to multiply the denominator by 3. And if you multiply the denominator by 3, you have to multiply the numerator by 3 too:

$$numerator = 1 \times 3 = 3$$
$$denominator = 2 \times 3 = 6$$

So, the new fraction is $^3/_6$. Repeat the same process for the second fraction, $^2/_3$, except this time you have to multiply both denominator and numerator by 2:

$$numerator = 2 \times 2 = 4$$
$$denominator = 3 \times 2 = 6$$

The new fraction is $^4/_6$. The final step is to perform the addition or subtraction. In this case, $^3/_6 + ^4/_6 = ^7/_6$.

Another approach is to skip finding the LCD and simply multiply the denominators together to get a common denominator. In some cases, such as our example, the product of the denominators will actually be the LCD ($2 \times 3 = 6 = $ LCD). But, other times, the product of the denominators will be greater than the LCD. For example, if the two denominators are 6 and 8, you could use $6 \times 8 = 48$ as a denominator instead of 24 (the LCD). There are two drawbacks to this second approach. The first is that you have to work with larger numbers. The second is that you have to take the extra step of reducing your answer. SAT answer choices almost always appear as reduced fractions. Trust us.

Multiplying Fractions

Multiplying fractions is a breeze, whether the denominators are equal or not. The product of two fractions is the product of their numerators over the product of their denominators:

$$\frac{a}{b} \times \frac{c}{d} = \frac{ac}{bd}$$

Want an example with numbers? You got one:

$$\frac{3}{7} \times \frac{2}{5} = \frac{3 \times 2}{7 \times 5} = \frac{6}{35}$$

Canceling Out

You can make multiplying fractions even easier by canceling out. If the numerator and denominator of any of the fractions you need to multiply share a common factor, you can divide by the common factor to reduce both numerator and denominator. For example, the fraction:

$$\frac{4}{5} \times \frac{1}{8} \times \frac{10}{11}$$

To answer this fraction as it is, you have to multiply the numerators and denominators and then reduce. Sure, you could do it, but it would take some time. Canceling out provides a shortcut.

In this case, you can cancel out the numerator 4 with the denominator 8, and the numerator 10 with the denominator 5, which gives you:

$$\frac{4^1}{5^1} \times \frac{1}{8^2} \times \frac{10^2}{11} = \frac{1}{1} \times \frac{1}{2} \times \frac{2}{11}$$

Then, canceling the 2's, you get:

$$\frac{1}{1} \times \frac{1}{\cancel{2}^{1}} \times \frac{\cancel{2}^{1}}{11} = \frac{1}{1} \times \frac{1}{1} \times \frac{1}{11}$$

Canceling out can *dramatically* cut the amount of time you need to spend working with big numbers. When dealing with fractions, whether they're filled with numbers or variables, *always* be on the lookout for chances to cancel out.

Dividing Fractions

Multiplication and division are inverse operations. It makes sense, then, that to perform division with fractions, all you have to do is flip the second fraction and then multiply. Check it out:

$$\frac{a}{b} \div \frac{c}{d} = \frac{a}{b} \times \frac{d}{c} = \frac{ad}{bc}$$

Here's a numerical example:

$$\frac{1}{2} \div \frac{4}{5} = \frac{1}{2} \times \frac{5}{4} = \frac{5}{8}$$

Mixed Numbers

A mixed number is an integer followed by a fraction, like $1^1/_2$. But operations such as addition, subtraction, multiplication, and division can't be performed on mixed numbers, so you have to know how to convert them into fraction form.

Since we already mentioned $1^1/_2$, it seems only right to convert it. The method is easy: Multiply the integer (the big 1) of the mixed number by the denominator, and add that product to the numerator: $1 \times 2 + 1 = 3$ is the numerator of the improper fraction. Now, put that over the original denominator: $^3/_2$ is the converted fraction.

Here's another example:

$$3\,\frac{2}{13} = \frac{(3 \times 13) + 2}{13} = \frac{39 + 2}{13} = \frac{41}{13}$$

We said it once, we'll say it again: Converting mixed numbers is particularly important on grid-in questions, since you can't actually write a mixed number into the grid. If you tried to grid $1^1/_2$, the computer that scores your test will read it as $^{11}/_2$. Ouch!

Complex Fractions

Complex fractions are fractions of fractions.

$$\frac{\frac{a}{b}}{\frac{c}{d}}$$

Here's what you should be thinking: "Ugh." Complex fractions are annoying if you try to take them head on. But you don't have to. Instead, transform them into normal fractions according to this quick step: Multiply the top fraction by the reciprocal of the bottom fraction.

$$\frac{\frac{a}{b}}{\frac{c}{d}} = \frac{a}{b} \times \frac{d}{c} = \frac{ad}{bc}$$

And here's an example using actual numbers:

$$\frac{\frac{1}{3}}{\frac{4}{5}} = \frac{1}{3} \times \frac{5}{4} = \frac{5}{12}$$

DECIMALS

A decimal number is any number with a nonzero digit to the right of the decimal point. But for the SAT, it's more important to know that decimals are, like fractions, a way of writing parts of wholes. If you have to perform any operation on a decimal for the SAT, we highly recommend that you use a calculator. It will save time, and you will make fewer mistakes.

Converting Decimals to Fractions

Even if you use a calculator, you should know how to convert decimals into fractions and vice versa. Both conversions are easy to do.

To convert a decimal number to a fraction:

1. Remove the decimal point and make the decimal number the numerator.
2. Let the denominator be the number 1 followed by as many zeros as there are decimal places in the decimal number.
3. Reduce this fraction.

To convert .3875 into a fraction, first eliminate the decimal point and place 3875 as the numerator:

$$.3875 = \frac{3875}{?}$$

Since .3875 has four digits after the decimal point, put four zeros in the denominator following the number 1:

$$.3875 = \frac{3875}{10000}$$

Then, by finding the GCF of 3875 and 10,000, which is 125, reduce the fraction:

$$\frac{3875}{10000} = \frac{31}{80}$$

To convert from fractions back to decimals, divide the numerator by the denominator.

$$31 \div 80 = 0.3875$$

PERCENTS

Percents are a specific type of fraction. *Percent* literally means "of 100" in Latin, so after you ace the SAT, go to college, drop out to become famous, and eventually amass 75 percent of all the money in the world, you'll then have $^{75}/_{100}$ of the world's money. Awesome.

Until then, you don't have that much money, and you still have to take the SAT (and pay for the privilege). So let's look at an example question:

4 is what percent of 20?

The first thing you have to know how to do is translate this sort of question into an equation. It's actually pretty straightforward as long as you see that "is" is the same as saying "equals," and "what" is the same as saying "x." So if 4 equals x percent of 20, then:

$$4 = x\%(20)$$

Since a percent is actually a number out of 100, this means:

$$4 = \frac{x}{100}(20)$$

Now just work out the math:

$$4 = \frac{20x}{100}$$

$$400 = 20x$$

$$x = 20$$

Therefore, 4 is 20% of 20.

Converting Percents into Fractions or Decimals

Converting percents into fractions or decimals is a crucial SAT skill. If you ever want to multiply or divide a number by a percent, you first have to convert it.

- To convert from a percent to a fraction, take the percentage number and place it as a numerator over the denominator 100. If you have 88 percent of something, then you can quickly convert it into the fraction $^{88}/_{100}$.
- To convert from a percent to a decimal, you must take a decimal point and insert it into the percent number two spaces from the right: 79% equals .79, while 350% equals 3.5.

What Percent of This Word Problem Don't You Understand, Bucko?

SAT word problems often seem to be phrased as if the person who wrote them doesn't know how to speak English. The SAT does this purposefully because it thinks that verbal tricks are a good way to test your math skills. If that makes no sense to you, good. It makes no sense to us either. Here's an example of the kind of linguistic trickery we're talking about:

What percent of 2 is 5?

Because the 2 is the smaller number and because it appears first in the question, you're first instinct may be to calculate what percent 2 is of 5.

But as long as you remember that "is" means "equals," and "what" means "x," you'll be able to correctly translate the word problem into math:

$$x\%(2) = 5$$

$$\frac{x}{100}(2) = 5$$

$$\frac{2x}{100} = 5$$

$$2x = 500$$

$$x = 250$$

So 5 is 250% of 2.

Percent Increase and Decrease

One of the most common ways the SAT tests percent is through the concept of percent increase and decrease.

- **Percent increase**—If the price of a $10 shirt *increases* 10%, the new price is the original $10 *plus* 10% of the $10 original.
- **Percent decrease**—If the price of a $10 shirt *decreases* 10%, the new price is the original $10 *minus* 10% of the $10 original.

One of the classic blunders students make on these questions is to figure out what the 10% increase or decrease is but then, lost in a haze of joy and relief, to forget to carry out the necessary addition or subtraction. SAT traps take advantage of this. Be wary.

> A vintage bowling league shirt cost $20 in the 1990s. But during the 1970s, when the shirt was first made, it cost 15% less. What was the price of the shirt in the 1970s?
>
> (A) $3
> (B) $17
> (C) $23
> (D) $35
> (E) $280

First find the price decrease (remember that 15% = .15):

$$\$20 \times .15 = \$3$$

Now, since the price of the shirt was less back in the 1970s, subtract $3 from the $20 price from the early 1990s:

$$\$20 - \$3 = \$17$$

The answer is **B**. If you only finished the first part of this question and looked at the answers, you might see the $3 at answer **A** and forget to finish the calculation.

Double Percents

Some SAT questions ask you to determine a percent of a percent.

> The original price of a banana in a store is $2. During a sale, the store reduces the price by 25% and Joe buys the banana. Joe then raises the price of the banana 10% from the price at which he bought it and sells it to Sam. How much does Sam pay for the banana?

This question asks you to determine the effect of two successive percent changes. The key to solving it is realizing that each percentage change is dependent on the last. You have to work out the effect of the first percentage change, come up with a value, and then use that value to determine the effect of the second percentage change.

When you're working on a percentage problem that involves a series of percentage changes, you should follow the same basic procedure that we explained for one percentage change, except here you should run through the procedure twice. For the first percentage change, figure out what's the whole, calculate the percentage of the whole, make sure to perform addition or subtraction if necessary, then take the new value and put it through these same steps for the second percentage change.

To answer the example problem, first find 25% of the original price:

$$\frac{25}{100} \times \$2 = \frac{50}{100} = \$.50$$

Now subtract that $.50 from the original price:

$$\$2 - \$.5 = \$1.50$$

Then increase $1.50 by 10%:

$$\frac{10}{100} \times \$1.50 = \frac{15}{100} = \$.15$$

Sam buys the banana for $1.50 + $.15 = $1.65. A total rip-off.

Some students, sensing a shortcut, are tempted to just combine the two percentage changes on double percent problems. This is not a real shortcut. It's more like a dark alley filled with cruel and nasty people who want you to do badly on the SAT.

If you reasoned on the last example problem that the first percentage change lowered the price 25%, and the second raised the price 10%, meaning that the total change was a reduction of 15%, then:

$$\frac{15}{100} \times \$2 = \frac{30}{100} = \$.30$$

Subtract that $.30 from the original price:

$$\$2 - \$.30 = \$1.70$$

We *promise* you that when the SAT gives you a double-percent problem, it will include this sort of wrong answer as a trap among the choices.

RATIOS

Ratios look like fractions and are related to fractions, but they don't quack like fractions. Whereas a fraction describes a part of a whole, a ratio compares one part to another part.

A ratio can be written in a variety of ways. Mathematically, it can appear as $^3/_1$ or as 3:1. In words, it would be written out as the ratio of 3 to 1. Each of these three forms of the ratio 3:1 mean the same thing: There are three of one thing for every one of another. If you have three red alligators and one blue alligator, then you would have a ratio of 3:1 for red alligators to blue alligators. For the SAT, you must remember that ratios compare *parts to parts* rather than parts to a whole. Why do you have to remember that? Because of questions like this:

For every 40 games a baseball team plays, it loses 12 games. What is the ratio of the team's losses to wins?

(A)   3:10
(B)   7:10
(C)   3:7
(D)   7:3
(E)   10:3

The question says that the team loses 12 of every 40 games, but it asks you for the ratio of losses to *wins*, not losses to *games*. So the first thing you have to do is find out how many games the team wins in 40 games:

$$40 - 12 = 28$$

The team wins 28 games for every 40. So for every 12 losses, the team wins 28 games, for a ratio of 12:28. You can reduce this ratio by dividing both sides by 4 to get 3 losses for every 7 wins, or 3:7. Answer **C** is correct. If you didn't realize that the losses to games was a part to whole, you might have just reduced the ratio 12:40 to 3:10, and then chosen answer **A**. And there is no question that on ratio problems, the SAT will include an incorrect *part:whole* answer to try to trip you up.

Proportions

Just because you have a ratio of three red alligators to one blue alligator doesn't mean that you can *only* have three red alligators and one blue one. It could also mean that you have six red and two blue alligators or that you have 240 red and 80 blue alligators. Ratios compare only *relative magnitude*. In order to know how many of each color alligator you actually have, in addition to knowing the ratios, you also need to know how many total alligators there are.

The SAT often asks questions testing your ability to figure out an answer based on the ratio between questions and the total number of all questions:

> Egbert has red, blue, and green marbles in the ratio of 5:4:3, and he has a total of 36 marbles. How many blue marbles does Egbert have?

For each group of 5 red marbles, you have a group of 4 blue marbles and a group of 3 green marbles. The ratio therefore tells you that out of every 12 marbles (since $5 + 4 + 3 = 12$), 4 marbles will be blue.

The question also tells you that you have 36 total marbles, and since the ratio of blue marbles to total marbles will not change *no matter how many marbles you have*, you can solve this problem by setting up a proportion, which is an equation that states that two ratios are equal. In this case, you can set equal 4:12 and x:36, with x standing in for the number of blue marbles that you'd have out of a total of 36. To do math with proportions, it's most useful to set up proportions in fractional form:

$$\frac{4}{12} = \frac{x}{36}$$

Now isolate x by cross-multiplying, and then you can solve:

$$12x = 4 \times 36$$
$$12x = 144$$
$$x = 12$$

EXPONENTS

An exponent is a shorthand way of saying, "Multiply this number by itself this number of times." In a^b, a is multiplied by itself b times. Here's a numerical example: $2^5 = 2 \times 2 \times 2 \times 2 \times 2$. An exponent can also be referred to as a power: 2^5 is "two to the fifth power." Before jumping into the exponent nitty-gritty, learn these five terms:

- **Base.** The base refers to the 3 in 3^5. In other words, the base is the number multiplied by itself however many times specified by the exponent.
- **Exponent.** The exponent is the 5 in 3^5. The exponent tells how many times the base is to be multiplied by itself.
- **Squared.** Saying that a number is *squared* is a common code word to indicate that it has an exponent of 2. In the expression 6^2, 6 has been squared.
- **Cubed.** Saying that a number is *cubed* means it has an exponent of 3. In the expression 4^3, 4 has been cubed.
- **Power.** The term *power* is another way to talk about a number being raised to an exponent. A number raised to the third power has an exponent of 3. So 6 raised to the fourth power is 6^4.

One last word of exponent advice before we get started. We'll explain how to deal with exponents without using your calculator, but most good graphing calculators have a variety of exponent functions. Knowing how to use them could save you time, especially when exponent values get larger and involve fractions or negative numbers.

Common Exponents

It can be very helpful and a real time-saver on the SAT if you can easily translate back and forth between a number and its exponential form. For instance, if you can easily see that 36 = 6^2, it can really come in handy if you're dealing with binomials, quadratic equations, or any number of other areas in algebra.

Here are some lists of common exponents. We'll start with the squares of the first ten integers:

$$1^2 = 1$$
$$2^2 = 4$$
$$3^2 = 9$$
$$4^2 = 16$$
$$5^2 = 25$$
$$6^2 = 36$$
$$7^2 = 49$$
$$8^2 = 64$$
$$9^2 = 81$$
$$10^2 = 100$$

Here are the first five cubes:

$$1^3 = 1$$
$$2^3 = 8$$
$$3^3 = 27$$
$$4^3 = 64$$
$$5^3 = 125$$

Finally, the first few powers of two are useful to know for various applications:

$$2^0 = 1$$
$$2^1 = 2$$
$$2^2 = 4$$
$$2^3 = 8$$
$$2^4 = 16$$
$$2^5 = 32$$
$$2^6 = 64$$
$$2^7 = 128$$
$$2^8 = 256$$
$$2^9 = 512$$
$$2^{10} = 1024$$

Adding and Subtracting Powers

Actually, you can't add or subtract *numbers* with exponents. Instead, work out each exponent to find its value, then add the two numbers. To add $3^3 + 4^2$, work out the exponents to get (3 × 3 × 3) + (4 × 4), and then, finally, 27 + 16 = 43.

But if you're dealing with *algebraic expressions* that have the same bases and exponents, such as $3x^4$ and $5x^4$, then you *can* add or subtract them. For example, $3x^4 + 5x^4 = 8x^4$. Algebraic expressions that have different bases or exponents cannot be added or subtracted.

Multiply and Dividing Powers

Multiplying or dividing exponential numbers or terms that have the same base is so quick and easy it's like a little math oasis. When multiplying, just *add* the exponents together. This is known as the **Product Rule**:

$$3^6 \times 3^2 = 3^{(6+2)} = 3^8$$
$$x^4 \times x^3 = x^{(4+3)} = x^7$$

To divide two same-base exponential numbers or terms, *subtract* the exponents. This is known as the **Quotient Rule**:

$$\frac{3^6}{3^2} = 3^{(6-2)} = 3^4$$

$$\frac{x^4}{x^3} = x^{(4-3)} = x^1$$

Quick and easy. Right?

You want the bad news or the bad news? The same isn't true if you need to multiply or divide two exponential numbers that *don't* have the same base, such as, say, $3^3 \times 4^2$. When two exponents have different bases, you just have to do your work the old-fashioned way: Multiply the numbers out and multiply or divide the result accordingly: $3^3 \times 4^2 = 27 + 16 = 43$.

Raising a Power to a Power

To raise one exponent to another exponent, multiply the exponents. This is known as the **Power Rule**:

$$(3^2)^4 = 3^{(2\times4)} = 3^8$$
$$(x^4)^3 = x^{(4\times3)} = x^{12}$$

Again, easy. Just remember that you *multiply* exponents when raising one exponent to another, and you *add* exponents when multiplying two identical bases with exponents. The SAT expects lots of students to mix these operations up.

Fractions Raised to a Power

To raise a fraction to an exponent, raise both the numerator and denominator to that exponent:

$$\left(\frac{1}{3}\right)^3 = \frac{1}{27}$$

Negative Numbers Raised to a Power

Here's a fact you should already know: When you multiply a negative number by another negative number, you get a positive number, and when you multiply a negative number by a positive number, you get a negative number. Since exponents result in multiplication, a negative number raised to an exponent follows these rules:

- **A negative number raised to an even exponent will be positive.** For example $(-2)^4 = 16$. Why? Because $(-2)^4$ means $-2 \times -2 \times -2 \times -2$. When you multiply the first two –2s together, you get positive 4 because you're multiplying two negative numbers. When you multiply the +4 by the next –2, you get –8, since you're multiplying a positive number by a negative number. Finally, you multiply the –8 by the last –2 and get +16, since you're once again multiplying two negative numbers. The negatives cancel themselves out and vanish.
- **A negative number raised to an odd exponent will be negative.** To see why, just look at the example above, but stop the process at -2^3, which equals –8.

Special Exponents

You need to know a few special types of exponents for the SAT.

Zero

Any base raised to the power of zero is equal to 1. If you see any exponent of the form x^0, you should know that its value is 1. Strange, but true.

One

Any base raised to the power of one is equal to itself: $2^1 = 2$, $-67^1 = -67$ and $x^1 = x$. This fact is important to know when you have to multiply or divide exponential terms with the same base:

$$3x^6 \times x = 3x^6 \times x^1 = 3x^{(6+1)} = 3x^7$$

Negative Exponents

Any number or term raised to a negative power is equal to the reciprocal of that base raised to the opposite power. Uh. Got that? Didn't think so. An example will make it clearer:

$$x^{-5} = \frac{1}{x^5}$$

Here's a more complicated example:

$$\left(\frac{2}{3}\right)^{-3} = \left(\frac{1}{\frac{2}{3}}\right)^3 = \left(\frac{3}{2}\right)^3 = \frac{27}{8}$$

Here's a translation: If you see a base raised to a negative exponent, put the base as the denominator under a numerator of 1 and then drop the negative from the exponent. From there, just simplify.

Fractional Exponents

Exponents can be fractions too. When a number or term is raised to a fractional power, it is called taking the root of that number or term. This expression can be converted into a more convenient form:

$$x^{\left(\frac{a}{b}\right)} = \sqrt[b]{x^a}$$

The $\sqrt{}$ symbol is also known as the radical, and anything under the radical is called the radicand. We've got a whole section devoted to roots and radicals coming right up.

ROOTS AND RADICALS

Here's what you already know: (1) Roots express fractional exponents, and (2) it's often easier to work with roots by converting them into expressions that look like this:

$$x^{\left(\frac{a}{b}\right)} = \sqrt[b]{x^a}$$

Roots and powers are reciprocals. To square the number 3, multiply 3 by itself: $3^2 = 3 \times 3 = 9$. To get the root of 9, $\sqrt{9}$, you have to find the number that, multiplied by itself, will equal 9. That number is 3.

Square roots appear far more often than any other kind of root on the SAT, but cube roots, fourth roots, fifth roots, and so on could conceivably make an appearance. Each root is represented by a radical sign with the appropriate number next to it (a radical without any superscript denotes a square root). For example, cube roots are shown as $\sqrt[3]{}$, fourth roots as $\sqrt[4]{}$, and so on. Roots of higher degree operate the same way square roots do. Because $3^3 = 27$, it follows that the cube root of 27 is 3.

Here are a few examples:

$$\sqrt{16} = 4 \text{ because } 4^2 = 16$$
$$\sqrt[4]{81} = 3 \text{ because } 3^4 = 81$$
$$\sqrt{\frac{1}{4}} = \frac{1}{2} \text{ because } \left(\frac{1}{2}\right)^2 = \frac{1}{4}$$
$$\text{If } x^n = y, \text{ then } \sqrt[n]{y} = x$$

Adding and Subtracting Roots

You can't add or subtract roots. You have to work out each root separately and then add. To solve $\sqrt{9} + \sqrt{4}$, *do not* add the 9 and 4 together to get $\sqrt{13}$. Instead, $\sqrt{9} + \sqrt{4} = 3 + 2 = 5$.

The SAT tests if you remember this rule by including trap answers that *do* add or subtract roots.

Multiplying and Dividing Roots

If you're multiplying or dividing two roots, you can multiply or divide the numbers under the root sign as long as the roots are of the same degree. You can multiply or divide two square roots for instance, but you can't multiply a square root and a cube root.

$$\sqrt[r]{x} \times \sqrt[r]{y} = \sqrt[r]{x \times y}$$
$$\sqrt{8} \times \sqrt{2} = \sqrt{8 \times 2} = \sqrt{16} = 4$$

SEQUENCES

A sequence is a series of numbers that proceed one after another according to some pattern. Here's one:

$$1, 2, 4, 8, 16, \ldots$$

Each number in this sequence doubles the previous number. Once you know the pattern, you can come up with the number after 16, which is 32, the number after that, which is 64, and, if you felt like it, you could keep calculating numbers in the sequence for the rest of your life.

The SAT tests you on three specific types of sequences: arithmetic, geometric, and annoying.

Arithmetic Sequences

An arithmetic sequence is an ordered list of terms in which the difference between consecutive terms is constant. In other words, the same value or variable is added to each term in order to create the next term: If you subtract any two consecutive terms of the sequence, you will get the same difference.[*] An example is 1, 4, 7, 10, 13, . . . , where 3 is the constant increment between values.

The notation of an arithmetic sequence is

$$a_n = a_1 + (n - 1)d$$

For the SAT, you should be able to do three things with an arithmetic sequence:

---

[*] This is the one time in the English language when the phrase "same difference" makes sense.

1. Find the constant interval between terms.
2. Find any term in the sequence.
3. Calculate the sum of the first n terms.

Finding the Constant Interval (a.k.a., Finding *d*)

To find the constant interval, d, just subtract one term in an arithmetic sequence from the next. For the arithmetic sequence $a_n = 1, 4, 7, 10, 13, \ldots, d = 4 - 1 = 3$.

Okay, now here's a slightly more complicated form of this same d-finding question:

> In an arithmetic sequence, if $a_4 = 4$ and $a_7 = 10$, find d.

This question gives you the fourth and seventh terms of an arithmetic sequence:

$$a_n = a_1, a_2, a_3, 4, a_5, a_6, 10 \ldots$$

Since in arithmetic sequences d is constant between every term, you know that $a_4 + d = a_5$, $a_5 + d = a_6$, and $a_6 + d = 10$. In other words, the difference between the seventh term, 10, and the fourth term, 4, is $3d$. Stated as an equation:

$$10 = 4 + 3d$$

Now solve it:

$$3d = 6$$
$$d = 2$$

Finding Any Term in the Sequence (a.k.a., Finding the *n*th Term)

Finding the nth term is a piece of cake when you have a formula. And we have a formula:

$$a_n = a_1 + (n - 1)d$$

where a_n is the nth term of the sequence, and d is the difference between consecutive terms.

So, to find the 55th term in the arithmetic sequence $a_n = 1, 4, 7, 10, 13, \ldots$, plug the values of $a_1 = 1$, $n = 55$, and $d = 3$ into the formula: $a_{55} = 1 + (55 - 1)3 = 1 + 162 = 163$.

Finding the Sum of the First *n* Terms

Finding the sum of the first n terms is also cakelike in its simplicity when you have a formula. And we do:

$$\text{Sum of the first } n \text{ terms} = n\frac{a_1 + a_n}{2}$$

Using the same example, the sum of the first 55 terms would be

$$\text{Sum} = 55\left(\frac{1 + 163}{2}\right) = 55\left(\frac{164}{2}\right) = 55(82) = 4510$$

Geometric Sequences and Exponential Growth

Whereas in an arithmetic sequence the *difference* between consecutive terms is always constant, in a geometric sequence the *quotient* of consecutive terms is always constant. The constant factor by which the terms of a geometric function differ is called the common ratio of the geometric sequence. The common ratio is usually represented by the variable r. Here is an example of a geometric sequence in which $r = 3$.

$$b_x = \frac{1}{3}, 1, 3, 9, 27, 81, \ldots$$

The general form of a geometric sequence is

$$b_x = b_1, b_1 r, b_1 r^2, b_1 r^3, \ldots$$

As with arithmetic sequences, you should be able to perform three tasks on geometric sequences for the SAT:

1. Find r.
2. Find the nth term.
3. Calculate the sum of the first n terms.

Finding r

To find the common ratio of a geometric sequence, all you have to do is divide one term by the preceding term. For example, the value of r for the sequence 3, 6, 12, 24, . . . is $6 \div 3 = 2$.

Finding the nth Term

Want to find the nth term of a geometric sequence? How about a formula to help you on your quest?

$$b_n = b_1 r^{n-1}$$

Here's the formula in action. The 11th term of the sequence 3, 6, 12, 24, . . . is

$$b_{11} = 3(2^{10}) = 3072$$

Finding the Sum of the First n Terms

One final formula. To find the sum of the first n terms of a geometric sequence, use this one:

$$\text{Sum of the first } n \text{ terms} = b_1 \frac{1 - r^n}{1 - r}$$

So the sum of the first 10 terms of the same sequence is

$$3 \frac{1 - 2^{10}}{1 - 2} = 3069$$

Geometric Sequences and Negative Numbers

A geometric sequence is formed when each term is multiplied by some standard number to get the next phrase. So far we've only dealt with circumstances where that standard number was positive. But it can also be negative. Take a sequence that starts with the number 1 and multiplies each term by –2: 1, –2, 4, –8, 16, –32, ... See the pattern? Whenever r is negative in a geometric sequence, the terms will alternate between positive and negative.

Annoying Sequences

Annoying sequences is a technical math term that we just made up. We made it up for one reason: These sequences annoy us, and we think they'll annoy you. Notice, though, that we didn't name them devastating sequences or even difficult sequences. That's because they're neither difficult nor devastating. Just annoying.

In annoying sequences, the SAT makes up the rules. For instance, in the annoying sequence 1, 2, 3, 5, 8, 13, . . . , there isn't any standard change between each term, but there is a pattern: After the first two terms, each term is equal to the sum of the previous two terms.

Annoying sequences most commonly show up in problems that ask you to find terms at absurdly high values of n. Here's an annoying sequence word problem:

> If the first two terms of a sequence are 1 and 2, and all the following terms in the sequence are produced by subtracting from the previous term the term before that, then what is the fiftieth term in the sequence?

The 50th term? How are you, with your busy life and no magic formula, supposed to write out the sequence until you get to the 50th term? Looks like you'll end up going to college in Siberia.

While Siberia *is* nice for one day each year in July, you don't have to worry. Whenever the SAT asks a question involving an insanely high term in a sequence, there's always a trick to finding it quickly. When the term is in an annoying sequence, the trick is usually a repeating pattern that will make the answer easy to find. So start writing out the sequence and look for the pattern. Once you see it, strike:

$$1, 2, 1, -1, -2, -1, 1, 2, 1, -1, \ldots$$

Do you see the pattern? After six terms, this sequence starts to repeat itself: 1, 2, 1, –1, –2, –1, and then it starts over. So if the sequence repeats every six terms, then every sixth term will be a –1: the sixth term, the 12th term, all the way up to the 48th term. And if you know that the 48th term is a –1 and that the sequence starts over on the 49th, then you know that the 49th term will be a 1, and the 50th term will be a 2.

SETS

Set is a fancy math word for a group of questions. Each question in a set is called an *element* or a *member*. The entire number of Hummers Jay-Z owns is a set, and each of the Hummers is an element of the set. A set contains only those things that can fit its definitions. Jay-Z's Ferraris and BMWs can't be in the set of his Hummers. If you have a set that is defined as $(1, 2, \sqrt{7})$, then the only things that can be in that set are $(1, 2, \sqrt{7})$.

Union and Intersection

The union of two sets is a set containing each element found in either set. If set A contains all the birds in the world, and set B contains all the fish in the world, then the union of those sets contains all the birds and all the fish in the world. If set A = (1, 6, 7, 8, 11, 13), and set B = (2, 4, 5, 8), then the union of set A and B is (1, 2, 4, 5, 6, 7, 8, 8, 11, 13).

The intersection of two sets is the element common to each set. The intersection of the set that contains all the fish in the world with the set that contains all the birds in the world is an empty set ( ) because there are no animals that are both fish and birds. The intersection of set A = (1, 6, 7, 8, 11, 13) and set B = (2, 4, 5, 8) is (8), since both set A and set B contain an 8.

The Difficult Set Question

One particular type of set question almost always comes up on the SAT and just as often throws students for a loop. In this type of question, the SAT describes two sets and a few people or things that fit into both sets. Then it asks how many total are in the two sets.

> Of the lions at the zoo, 13 eat zebra meat, 11 eat giraffe meat, and 7 eat both. How many lions are there in the zoo?

This question just *feels* hard. Lots of students who haven't read this book will skip it. But you have read this book, and you'll know the (surprisingly simple) formula for getting it right:

Total = number in set 1 + number in set 2 − number common to set 1 and 2

Once you know the formula, all you have to do is figure out which numbers in the word problem define set 1, which define set 2, and which define the overlap set. After that, just plug in the numbers and do some simple addition and subtraction. So how many lions are there in the zoo?

Total lions = 13 zebra eaters + 11 giraffe eaters − 7 eaters of both

Total Lions = 13 + 11 − 7 = 17

That's it for Numbers and Operations. Ready for some practice? You bet you are.

PRACTICE SET 1:
MULTIPLE CHOICE

1. The number 48 consists of how many distinct prime factors?

   (A) 1
   (B) 2
   (C) 3
   (D) 4
   (E) 5

2. Which of the following fractions is in its simplest reduced form?

   (A) $\frac{17}{136}$

   (B) $\frac{7}{126}$

   (C) $\frac{13}{69}$

   (D) $\frac{11}{121}$

   (E) $\frac{5}{160}$

3. The number 210 is divisible by all of the following integers EXCEPT

   (A) 6
   (B) 8
   (C) 10
   (D) 21
   (E) 35

4. In the arithmetic sequence $(5, 9, 13, 17, \ldots)$, where $n_1 = 5$, what is the value of n_8?

   (A) 29
   (B) 33
   (C) 37
   (D) 41
   (E) 45

5. If $2(5 - 8)^2 + 3(6 + 2) = 7x$, what is the value of x?

   (A) $2^2 + 1$
   (B) $3^2 - 3$
   (C) $2^2 + 3$
   (D) 2^3
   (E) 3^2

6. A master of the secretarial arts types at a rate of 55 words per minute. If there are 330 words per page, how many pages could a master be expected to type in four and a half hours?

    (A) 6
    (B) 12
    (C) 37.5
    (D) 45
    (E) 247.5

$$\begin{array}{r} 3X \\ X6 \\ + XX \\ \hline 12X \end{array}$$

7. In the correctly worked addition problem above, which digit could represent X?

    (A) 2
    (B) 4
    (C) 6
    (D) 8
    (E) 0

8. If b is a positive integer, which of the following equals $3b^4$?

    (A) $\sqrt{81b^{56}}$

    (B) $\sqrt{9b^8}$

    (C) $\sqrt{9b^{16}}$

    (D) $9\sqrt{b^{16}}$

    (E) $b^3\sqrt{9b^4}$

9. If set S consists of all positive prime integers greater than 5 and set T consists of all positive odd integers less than 21, which of the following must be true?

    I.   Set T contains more numbers than set S.
    II.   There are no even numbers in either set S or set T.
    III. All numbers in set S are in set T.

    (A) I
    (B) II
    (C) I and III
    (D) II and III
    (E) I, II, III

10. In the geometric sequence $(4, 12, 36, 108, 324, \ldots)$, where $n_1 = 4$, what is the value of n_9?

    (A) $(2^2)(3^8)$
    (B) $(2^2)(3^9)$
    (C) 2^{36}
    (D) 6^9
    (E) $(2^9)(3^8)$

11. When s is divided by 6, the remainder is 5. What is the remainder when $2s$ is divided by 6?

    (A) 1
    (B) 2
    (C) 3
    (D) 4
    (E) 5

12. 288 is divisible by 2^n. What is the greatest possible value for n?

    (A) 5
    (B) 6
    (C) 7
    (D) 8
    (E) 9

13. z is a multiple of 3, and y is a multiple of 5. a is an even integer divisible by both z and y. Therefore, a could equal which of the following?

    (A) 45
    (B) 62
    (C) 75
    (D) 80
    (E) 90

14. If $-1 < x < 0$, then which of the following MUST be true?

    (A) $x^2 < x^3 < x$
    (B) $x < x^2 < x^3$
    (C) $x^3 < x^2 < x$
    (D) $x^3 < x < x^2$
    (E) $x < x^3 < x^2$

15. When 8^{263} is expanded out, what digit will be in the units (1's) space?

    (A) 8
    (B) 4
    (C) 2
    (D) 6
    (E) 5

16. There are six numbers in a certain arithmetic sequence, the sum of which is 297. If the last number in the sequence is 67, by what constant amount is each number increased in the sequence?

    (A) 3
    (B) 7
    (C) 14
    (D) 30
    (E) 32

17. The first two terms of set A are 2 and 3. The rest of the terms are obtained either by adding the two previous terms together, when the last term is odd, or by subtracting the previous term from the term before it, when the last term is even. What is the mode of set A?

    (A) −3
    (B) −2
    (C) 0
    (D) 2
    (E) 3

18. If $s^m = 64$ and s and m are both integers, what is the LEAST possible value of $s - m$?

    (A) 4
    (B) −4
    (C) −6
    (D) −8
    (E) −12

19. If $4^x = 64^{12}$, what is the value of $(\sqrt[3]{2})^x$?

    (A) 2^{36}
    (B) 2^{24}
    (C) 2^{16}
    (D) 2^{12}
    (E) 2^{6}

20. A geometric sequence consists of five terms, the sum of which is 1023. If the common ratio of the sequence is 4, what is the first term of the sequence?

    (A) −9
    (B) −6
    (C) 3
    (D) 6
    (E) 9

ANSWERS & EXPLANATIONS

1.   **B**

You have the phrase "distinct prime factors," and if you have the definition of all three terms in that large brain of yours, you should have little difficulty with this question:

Distinct—the numbers must be different

Prime—divisible only by 1 and itself

Factor—an integer that divides into another integer evenly

Let's do the prime factorization of 48 and see what we get:

$$48 =$$
$$6 \times 8 =$$
$$2 \times 3 \times 8 =$$
$$2 \times 3 \times 2 \times 2 \times 2$$

The prime factorization of 48 gives you four 2s and a 3. There are five factors (choice **E**) in total, but the stem wanted the number of *distinct* prime factors. This cancels out all the repeated 2s, so the number of distinct prime factors is two (2 and 3). That's choice **B**.

2.   **C**

Talking about simple fractions seems vaguely cruel, but we promise not to make fun of the simple fraction in front of its city cousins. Simple fractions are fractions that can't be reduced any more. Four of the answer choices can be reduced. Your goal is to find the one that can't.

Take a first pass through the answer choices and see whether there are any obvious choices for further reduction. **E** springs to mind because the 5 in the numerator could easily go into the 160 in the denominator. This fraction can actually be reduced, but why? It's enough to realize that it *can* be reduced. Once you determine that, cross it out and move on.

The remaining answer choices all have prime numbers in their numerators. This is good news because it means you only have to use your calculator and try to divide the lower number (denominator) by the upper number (numerator).

For **A**, you punch in 136/17 = 8. Because this is a whole number, this fraction can be reduced. Cross out **A** and keep chugging.

B: 126/7 = 18. Nope.

C: 69/13 = 5.307 something. **C** can't be reduced. It's your answer.

3. **B**

The wording in the question is different, but the methods you use to solve it are exactly the same as the previous question. In question 2, we took the denominators and tested to see whether they were divisible by the numerators in order to determine whether the fraction could be reduced. On question 3, the same process is being done, only this time the number we're testing remains the same (210).

Take a moment and look at questions 2 and 3. They show how math terms can be switched around to pose essentially the same question. This is why you need to know the *terms*, not just have a passing familiarity with them. Anything less than true understanding can get you in a bind on a tough question.

Luckily, this isn't a tough question: You know that because it's only the third. Trusting the heavy math lifting to your calculator, we can start with **A** and see that it divides into 210 evenly:

A: 210/6 = 35. You can look down and cross out both **A** and **E** with this information.

B: 210/8 = 26.25. Nothing clean about that .25. **B** is your nondivisible culprit.

4. **B**

You can tackle sequence questions by going all algebraic and setting up a nifty little formula to solve them. Although this method would certainly impress the members of your school's Variable Lovers Club, it's not the smartest path on the SAT. The main reason it's a bad idea is that all the distractors are set up to trap students who do all the math. You play right into the SAT's hands by tackling a question in this manner. This doesn't mean you won't get it right. It just means you run a much greater risk of getting it wrong because the incorrect answer choices are all designed to catch people who make a mistake working the algebra.

So go low-tech instead. *Write stuff out.* You should write work down on every question, every time, and solve the questions on paper, not in your head. For this sequence question, take 15 seconds to write out:

$n1$	$n2$	$n3$	$n4$	$n5$	$n6$	$n7$	$n8$

Now place the numbers given to you in the stem underneath:

$n1$	$n2$	$n3$	$n4$	$n5$	$n6$	$n7$	$n8$
5	9	13	17				

As you can see, 4 is added to each number in the sequence. Finish up the list, and you have your answer. Furthermore, you know it's right *and* you can come back and check your work very easily if you have the time at the end of the section. Those last two points are just as important as the first one.

$n1$	$n2$	$n3$	$n4$	$n5$	$n6$	$n7$	$n8$
5	9	13	17	21	25	29	33

B is 33.

5. **B**

Before jumping into PEMDAS, take a look at the answer choices. None of them are actual integers. They all have some arithmetic work that needs to be done before they can be determined. Sometimes there's a reason for this, such as the equation can't be solved completely and has to remain in a seemingly unfinished state. This time, though, the answer choices are like this simply to bust your chops and make you use knowledge of exponents correctly.

Before we jump into the answer choices, let's solve that equation. It's all about order of operations. Start with parentheses, then exponents, then multiplication and division, and finally addition and subtraction:

$$2(5-8)^2 + 3(6+2) = 7x$$
$$2(-3)^2 + 3(8) = 7x$$
$$2(9) + 3(8) = 7x$$
$$18 + 24 = 7x$$
$$42 = 7x$$
$$6 = x$$

Where's a 6 when you need it? It's at **B** because $3^2 - 3 = 9 - 3 = 6$.

6.   **D**

Here's a chatty little problem with all sorts of embedded facts:

How fast a master types: 55 words/minute

Number of words on a page: 330 words

Number of hours of typing: 4.5 hours

The main thing working to your advantage on this question is that it is question 6. This makes it an easy problem. If it were question 20, you could expect none of the numbers to divide evenly, and all sorts of horrid improper fractions would need to be carried from one part to the next to solve it.

We'll get to some nasty questions later. For now, though, let's get some points where the getting is good. If a master types at 55 words/minute, and there are 330 words/page, then the amount of time it would take to type one page is

$$\frac{330 \text{ words/page}}{55 \text{ words/minute}} = 6 \text{ minutes for each page}$$

In an hour, then, a master of the secretarial arts could type 10 pages because:

$$\frac{60 \text{ minutes/hour}}{6 \text{ minutes/page}} = 10 \text{ pages/hour}$$

With 4.5 hours to type, the typist could complete:

$$(10 \text{ pages/hour})(4.5 \text{ hours}) = 45 \text{ pages}$$

That's **D**.

7.   **B**

There might be a way to solve this algebraically, but why bother? The answer is literally right in front of you. Granted, there are four wrong answer choices clouding up the issue, but instead of racking your brain and coming up with the right solution, just hit the answer choices and start seeing which ones work and which don't.

The best place to start is along the right side of the equation. You have X + 6 + X = X. Start plugging in answer choices to see whether they work. If they don't work there, they won't work on the left side of the question. You can cross them out immediately and not worry about the second part.

Choice **E** is a prime candidate for elimination because 0 + 6 + 0 = 6, not 0. (That's the units digits of the stem.) Because we've started on that end, might as well try 8 next:

$$X + 6 + X = 6$$

8 + 6 + 8 = 22, not 28. A 2 is not an 8, no matter what a politician might say. **D** is out.

Choice **C**:

$$X + 6 + X = 6$$

$$6 + 6 + 6 = 18$$

No 6 at the end here, either.

Choice **B**:

$$X + 6 + X = 6$$

$$4 + 6 + 4 = 14$$

Bingo. This works here. Let's put a 4 in the tens place and see whether it all works out.

$$\begin{array}{r} 34 \\ 46 \\ + 44 \\ \hline 124 \end{array}$$

Your calculator will confirm that this is correct. **B**'s the answer. See? It was right there in front of you all the time.

8.   **B**

The easy questions are behind you now, and you are in the Medium Question Zone. The problems might not look any different, but don't let that fool you. Answers that seem very easy are probably too easy to be the right answers.

Question 8 talks a lot about the integer b, but it's easier to understand what happens to the 3 in front of the variable. If there is a 3 *outside* a square root sign, what value would it be *inside*? To put it another way, 3 is the square root of what number? The answer is 9, and this shouldn't come as some big surprise.

Because you need a 9 inside the square root sign, **A** and **D** are a bust. Cross them out. From here, you have at least a one-in-three chance when guessing if the b^4 stumps you. Many students gravitate toward **C** because 16 is the square of 4. That's true for regular numbers, but we're looking at exponents here (tiny raised numbers and all), not regular numbers.

Let's go back to the 3 and use it as an example. You can write 3 as 3^1 if you want. Once we place it inside the square root sign, the 3 becomes a 9, or 3^2. In Mathspeak:

$$3 = \sqrt{9}$$
$$3^1 = \sqrt{3^2}$$

So the exponent doubles from 1 to 2 when it comes under the square root sign. You can expect the exponent of b^4 to double as well, becoming b^8 under the sign. The answer is **B**.

9.   **B**

Here's a roman numeral question, and you might want to skip these questions until the very end. The reason is simple: You have to do the work of three questions to get credit for one. It's not the best use of your time, especially because there are other medium questions still to be encountered that are not divided into three parts.

Having said that, let's jump in and solve the problem. Set S contains all positive prime integers greater than 5, which is a huge amount of numbers. The first bunch of numbers in set S is going to be 7, 11, 13, 17, 19, and 23, but it will go on and on.

Set T is a little more constrained. We could actually write out all positive odd integers less than 21:

$$\text{Set } T = \{1, 3, 5, 7, 9, 11, 13, 15, 17, 19\}$$

All this work and still no payoff. Time to review the roman numerals.

Roman numeral I is wrong. Crazy wrong because set S has an infinite number of numbers, and set T has 10. So we can go into the answer choices and cross out any choice that contains roman numeral I. This gets rid of **A**, **C**, and **E**. You have only two remaining choices, **B** "II only" and **D** "II and III only."

Think carefully about this. What roman numeral should you check next? If you said numeral III, good for you. There's nothing to be gained by checking numeral II because you still have to check numeral III to determine the right answer. However, if you try III next, you have your answer without having to check II at all. If III works, the answer is **D**. If it doesn't, the only choice left is **B**, and that's the answer.

Roman numeral III claims, "All numbers in set S are in set T." A quick glance at the numbers in sets S and T shows you this isn't true. III is wrong, so **B** must be the right answer.

10. **A**

This question is a geometric sequence, and the numbers are larger, but you can attack it the same way you handled question 4. And why not? The low-tech approach got that question right. It can do the same on this medium question.

The problem asks for n_9 and gives you the first five values of the sequence. Jotting away, you would write down:

$n1$	$n2$	$n3$	$n4$	$n5$	$n6$	$n7$	$n8$	$n9$
4	12	36	108	324				

How are the numbers changing? It's not addition this time. It's multiplication. Each value is 3 times larger than the previous one. So type 324 into your calculator, then multiply by 3 to get the next value and the next, and so on, until you reach n_9:

$n1$	$n2$	$n3$	$n4$	$n5$	$n6$	$n7$	$n8$	$n9$
4	12	36	108	324	972	2916	8748	26,244

Without a calculator, working out these numbers takes too much time. But that's a moot point because you get to use one. Use it to fill out this sequence table, and you find 26,244. Now you use your flat electronic friend to go through the answer choices. Starting with **A**, you find:

$$(2^2)(3^8) = 4 \times 6561 = 26{,}244$$

There's your answer.

11. **D**

This question requires two things:

1. You have to remember what a *remainder* is.
2. You need to realize that using real numbers is better than trying to solve this problem algebraically.

If there is some abstract way to determine the answer, it's not worth printing here. Instead, come up with a real number that leaves a remainder of 5 whenever it's divided by 6. This is question 11, and it just so happens that when 11 is divided by 6, the dividend—there's some third-grade Mathspeak coming at you—is 1, and the remainder is 5.

So $s = 11$. That means $2s = (2)(11) = 22$. Now let's divide 22 by 6 and see what we get.

$$6 \overline{)22} \quad \begin{array}{r} 3\ r4 \\ \hline -18 \\ \hline 4 \end{array}$$

You get 4 as your remainder, which is **D**. Without worrying about the abstract reasons for this, move on.

12.   **A**

The number 2 is a prime number, so the best approach to this question is to make a factor tree out of 288. If you do it correctly, you have a slew of 2's at the bottom of the tree. You can then add them up to find the greatest value.

288

2×144

$2 \times 2 \times 72$

$2 \times 2 \times 2 \times 36$

$2 \times 2 \times 2 \times 2 \times 18$

$2 \times 2 \times 2 \times 2 \times 2 \times 9$

$2^5 \times 9$

You might have taken a faster route, but the bottom of your factor tree will look the same. The greatest possible value for n is 5, **A**.

13.   **E**

This question sounds very confusing, but if you understand the terms, you have little to worry about. If a is an even integer divisible by both z and y, then a must be a number divisible by both 3 and 5 (these are the two numbers that z and y are multiples of). The safest way to find a number that's divisible by both 3 and 5 is to multiply 3 and 5 together, then search for values divisible by this new number, 15. Anything divisible by 15 is going to be a multiple of both 3 and 5.

   A, 45, seems to fit the bill because $45 = 15 \times 3$. Before you head on to the next question, though, take care to recall that a is an **even** integer, but 45 is not even. The answer is **E**, 90, because this is the only value that satisfies all the conditions for a.

14.   **E**

The difficulty of this question lies in a simple fact of math: Multiplying by negative fractions less than 1 is an exercise in weirdness. Most numbers get bigger when you multiply them by themselves but not fractions less than 1. They get smaller. Add in the negative value, and you get values flipping back and forth between positive and negative, depending on whether the exponent is even or odd.

   Let's give x an easy value to mess with. We say $x = -\frac{1}{2}$ and place this value into every x in the answer choices. Then it's just a matter of seeing what turns up.

   For no reason other than it's there, let's start with **A**:

$$x^2 < x^3 < x$$

$$\left(-\frac{1}{2}\right)^2 < \left(-\frac{1}{2}\right)^2 < -\frac{1}{2}$$

$$\frac{1}{4} < -\frac{1}{8} < -\frac{1}{2}$$

Nope. Each value is wrong.

You can continue plugging away, but we can also stare at these results and see whether there's anything we can learn. We stated earlier that the value of the x term was going to flip back and forth between positive and negative, depending on the value of the exponent. You can see this in **A**, where the largest value is $x^2 = \frac{1}{4}$, because the exponent is even.

Think about this fact before attempting **B** and **C**. Each choice has x^2 as a middle value, supposedly less than the x term to the right of it that has an odd exponent. This is wrong, and you know it's wrong because a negative fraction isn't going to be larger than a positive one, regardless of what's in the numerator or denominator. You've proven that in choice **A**.

This knocks out **B** and **C** without having to do the math. It's down to **D** or **E**. You need only try one of them. If it's right, pick it. If not, choose the other. Let's try **D**:

$$x^3 < x < x^2$$

$$\left(-\frac{1}{2}\right)^3 < -\frac{1}{2} < \left(-\frac{1}{2}\right)^2$$

$$-\frac{1}{8} < -\frac{1}{2} < \frac{1}{4}$$

That doesn't work because $-\frac{1}{8}$ is greater than $-\frac{1}{2}$: Remember, the smaller a negative value is, the closer it is to zero. **E** is the correct answer.

15. **C**

Whoa! If you don't understand how the SAT works, this question will leave you pole-axed. If there is an abstract mathematical way to solve this question, only math wizards know it.

You should just start writing stuff down. Again and again on the SAT, the students who are willing to place work on paper get rewarded. Figuring out what 8^{263} is would take a supercomputer, not a calculator. Why not start smaller? Figure out some simpler values of 8 and see what happens. Your calculator will do all the heavy lifting:

		Units Digit
$8^1 =$	8	8
$8^2 =$	64	4
$8^3 =$	512	2
$8^4 =$	4096	6
$8^5 =$	37268	8
$8^6 =$	262144	4

Look at the units digits. It goes 8, 4, 2, 6, 8, then 4. See a pattern? Multiply 262,144 by 8, and you get a units digits of 2 because the pattern seems to be 8-4-2-6, over and over again, all the way to 8^{263} and beyond.

If you divide 263 by 4, you get 65 with a remainder of 3. Your chart shows you that $8^4 = 4,096$, so you would start at the 6, then go three places to the left in the pattern.

Pattern

$$8\ 4\ 2\ 6\ 8\ 4\ 2\ 6\ 8\ 4\ 2\ 6\ 8\ 4\ 2\ 6$$
$$\underbrace{}_{1}\ \underbrace{}_{2}\ \underbrace{}_{3}$$

$$\frac{263}{4} = 65\ \text{r}3$$

The answer is **C**, 2.

16. **B**

All hard questions involve multiple steps. There's no getting around that. However, some can be answered easier than others if you don't bother with the highfalutin math and consider just the answer choices given to you. Consider this sequence problem. There's probably some wacky formula you can devise. Don't. Just take what the question gives you and run with it. Here's one way:

You have six numbers, and you know the last one. Each answer choice represents what the constant might be. All six numbers add up to 297. So write down:

$$\_\ \_\ \_\ \_\ \_\ \ 67 = 297$$

Let's start with **C**. If 14 is the constant value, then the value next to 67 will be $67 - 14 = 53$. The next value will be $53 - 14 = 39$. Use your calculator and figure out all the values. Your six numbers will look like this:

−3	11	25	39	53	67

What does this add up to? $-3 + 11 + 25 + 39 + 53 + 67 = 192$. This is not right because it has to add up to 297 to be the right answer. The problem is that 14 is too large a number to subtract each time. If you subtract 14 from each value, you end up with six numbers that are too small. Therefore, you need a number smaller than 14.

This crosses out choices **D** and **E**. You have a 50/50 shot right now because it's either **A** or **B**. You can take a guess if time is running out, or you can try one. Let's try **B**. Starting with 67 and subtracting 7 to get the other five values, you end up with:

32	39	46	53	60	67

What does this add up to? $32 + 39 + 46 + 53 + 60 + 67 = 297$. There's your answer.

The goal of the SAT is to answer questions correctly. Nothing more, nothing less.

17. **E**

The quicker you place pencil to paper and start writing stuff down, the faster you'll find the answer. To find the mode of set A, you need some more values. You have two to start with, 2 and 3. Following the somewhat convoluted directions, because 3 is odd, the next term is found by adding the two last terms together. $2 + 3 = 5$, so the third term is 5:

$$\text{Set } A = \{2, 3, 5\}$$

The number 5 is also odd, so the next term is $3 + 5 = 8$. The number 8 is even, so the next term is found by subtracting the term before it, $8 - 5 = 3$. Going on, set A shapes up like this:

$$\text{Set } A = \{2, 3, 5, 8, 3, 11, 14, 3, 17, 20, 3, 23, \ldots\}$$

Every third term is 3, and all other terms keep getting bigger and bigger. The mode is 3, **E**.

18. D

You have to be able to manipulate s^m to get the smallest number for $s - m$ that you can.

The first thing to do is make m as big as you can and s as small as possible. 64 is 8^2, but this can be reduced even more:

$$64 = 8^2$$
$$64 = (4 \times 2)^2$$
$$64 = (2 \times 2 \times 2)^2$$
$$64 = (2^3)^2$$
$$64 = 2^6$$

That's pretty good. You have a small s (2) and a large m (6), so $s - m$ would be $2 - 6 = -4$. Not bad. Not correct, either. Because you have an even exponent (6), you can have a negative value for s, such as −2:

$$2^6 = 64 = (-2)^6$$

This gives you a value for $s - m$ that is $-2 - 6 = -8$, **D**. That's the lowest value possible.

19. D

To determine what $\sqrt[3]{2}^x$ is, you need to find a value for x. That's where the equation $4^x = 64^{12}$ comes in.

Let's tackle the equation first. You could use your calculator and try to find the value of 64^{12}, but there's a better way to solve for x. You need to know how to manipulate exponents:

$$4^x = (64)^{12}$$
$$4^x = (4 \times 16)^{12}$$
$$4^x = (4 \times 4 \times 4)^{12}$$
$$4^x = (4^3)^{12}$$
$$4^x = 4^{36}$$

64 is the cube of 4. When you have an exponent taken to another exponent, you multiply the two numbers together, for example:

$$3 \times 12 = 36$$

This gives you a value for x of 36. When you take the cube root of a number with an exponent, you divide the exponent by 3. See what we mean about really knowing how to manipulate exponents?

$$(\sqrt[3]{2})^x = (\sqrt[3]{2})^{36} = 2^{\frac{36}{3}} = 2^{12} \text{, choice } \textbf{D.}$$

20. C

Like question 16, you should sidestep the math and jump into the answers. It's unlikely that a sequence where five numbers are multiplied by 4 and sum to 1023 would start with a negative value because a negative value would make the entire sum negative.

We can cross out **A** and **B**, then. Let's try **D**, 6, and see what happens. We'll create the five numbers exactly as the stem asks us. Take the first term, multiply by 4 to get the second term, then multiply the second term by 4 to find the third term, and so on:

6	24	96	384	1536

Does this sum to 1023? Not likely because the last term is 1536. Because this is too large, the first term must be smaller than 6. There's only one choice, **C**, that's smaller than 6. It's the answer. Double-check if you like.

PRACTICE SET 2: GRID-INS

1. If the prime factors of y are 2, 5, and 11, what is one possible value for y, when $y > 500$?

2. In a certain parking lot, there are 24 blue cars, 16 red cars, and the rest are white cars. If there is a total of 48 cars in the parking lot, what is the ratio of white cars to blue cars?

3. It takes $^1/_3$ lb. of sausage mixed with $^2/_3$ lb. of beans mixed with 1 lb. of rice to make jambalaya for 6 people. How many pounds of sausage are needed to make jambalaya for 27 people?

4. Integer k is a multiple of 3 and between 100 and 150. When k is divided by 7, the remainder is 4. What is one possible value of k?

5. At Ambrose Bierce's family Thanksgiving dinner, he offered his relatives both turkey and tofurkey. At dinner, 16 relatives had turkey, and 24 had tofurkey. If 12 relatives had both turkey and tofurkey, how many relatives came to Ambrose Bierce's Thanksgiving dinner?

6. Set A consists of all even integers, and set B consists of all integers equal to or less than 1. If x is the intersection of the two sets, what is one possible value of x?

7. 500% of 30% of 36 is what percent of 216?

8. What is the least of seven consecutive integers whose sum equals 168?

9. If $x^3 > x^4$, what is one possible value of x?

10. Integers 1–49 are written out to create one number (1,234,567, 891,011,121,314, . . . 4,849). The number will consist of how many digits?

11. Consecutive integers 15–30 are multiplied together to produce one product. How many factors of 3 does the product contain?

12. There are 150 students in the junior class at Joseph McCarthy High School. Of them, $^1/_3$ bike to school, and the rest take the bus. If there are 45 boys in the class and 15 of them bike, how many girls take the bus?

13. Set R consists of a geometric sequence where the first term is 17 and the constant ratio is 6. Set S consists of an arithmetic sequence where the first term is 87, and the constant term is 175. If set T consists of all positive integers less than 1,000, what is the intersection of all three sets?

14. There are 3,600 pieces of candy divided into three different colors: red, blue, and green. There are more blue pieces than red and more green pieces than blue. If there are 1,000 red pieces, what is the LARGEST amount of blue pieces possible?

15. Delilah decides to start saving money, but she wants to start slow. On the first day, she saves 1 cent, on the second day she saves 2 cents, and on the third day she saves 4 cents. Each day she continues to save double what she saved the previous day. In dollars, how much will she have saved after 8 days?

ANSWERS & EXPLANATIONS

1.   **550**

Add up the prime factors you have and see where you are: $(2)(5)(11) = 110$. This is less than 500, so you can't just stop here. What you can do is multiply 110 by 2, 5, or 11. It said these numbers were the prime factors, but it didn't say there was only one 2, one 5, and one 11. Multiplying 110 by another 5 gives you $(110)(5) = 550$. Grid this number in.

There are other values that would also work, such as $(110)(11) = 1,210$. That's one of the strange things about the grid-in questions. There is often more than one correct answer that you can use.

2.   **1/3**

To find the number of white cars, subtract the two values that you do know:

$$\text{Total cars} = \text{blue cars} + \text{red cars} + \text{white cars}$$

$$48 = 24 + 16 + \text{white cars}$$

$$48 = 40 + \text{white cars}$$

$$8 = \text{white cars}$$

The question wants the ratio of white cars to blue cars:

$$\text{White cars/blue cars} = \frac{8}{24} = \frac{1}{3} . \text{ Grid in this ratio.}$$

3.   **1.5**

This question also employs ratios, but it does so in a more subtle manner. The simplest way to find out how much sausage is needed for 27 people is to set up a ratio, then cross multiply:

$$\frac{1/3 \text{ lb sausage}}{6 \text{ people}} = \frac{s \text{ lbs sausage}}{27 \text{ people}}$$

$$\left(\frac{1}{3}\right)(27) = 6s$$

$$9 = 6s$$

$$\frac{9}{6} = s = \frac{3}{2} = 1.5$$

Remember that you can grid in either $\frac{3}{2}$ or 1.5, but you can't grid in the mixed fraction $1\frac{1}{2}$.

4.   **102**

Ah, if there were multiple-choice answers below, we could jump down to them and start trying them out. This would be preferable to what we have to do, which is to actually do the math. It's one reason why multiple-choice questions are easier to tackle than grid-in questions—you have more options for how to solve them.

Let's start with 99, which is the multiple of 3 just less than 100. The next multiple of 3 up from 99 is $99 + 3 = 102$. If we divide 102 by 7, we get $102/7 = 14$, remainder 4. Huzzah! There's one of the possible values for k that satisfies all the requirements. Grid in 102 and escape.

5.   **28**

This question raises the even bigger question, "Who would actually eat tofurkey?" Setting that aside for the moment, the problem calls for you to figure out the total number of guests. To do this, add together the ones who ate turkey (16) and the ones who ate tofurkey (24), then subtract the number of guests who had both (12). 16 + 24 − 12 = 28. Your answer is 28 total guests.

6. **0**

Set B has a large set of numbers, but because most of them are negative, you can't grid them in. The only positive values in set B are zero and 1. The number 1 is odd, but zero is an even integer. This makes zero the only intersection between sets A and B.

7. **25**

Convert the words in this problem into the following equation using the following key:

Term	Means
of	multiply
percent	divide by 100
is	equals

500% of 30% of 36 is what percent of 216?

$$\frac{500}{100} \times \frac{30}{100} \times 36 = \frac{n}{100} \times 216$$

$$5 \times \frac{3}{10} \times 36 = \frac{216n}{100}$$

$$54 = \frac{54n}{25}$$

$$\left(\frac{25}{54}\right)(54) = \frac{54n}{25}\left(\frac{25}{54}\right)$$

$$25 = n$$

The answer is 25.

8. **21**

Reluctantly and with a formal protest written into the log, we must answer a sequence problem by doing the math. If there are seven consecutive integers, they could be written this way:

$$b$$
$$b + 1$$
$$b + 2$$
$$b + 3$$
$$b + 4$$
$$b + 5$$
$$b + 6$$

They each increase by one because that's the definition of *consecutive*. Because all seven integers equal 168 when added together, you have:

$$b + (b + 1) + (b + 2) + (b + 3) + (b + 4) + (b + 5) + (b + 6) = 168$$

$$7b + 21 = 168$$

$$7b = 147$$

$$b = 21$$

The lowest integer is 21.

9. **1/3**

How good is your memory? Things you learned on question 14 of the multiple-choice set can really help you here because that is the question where you kept multiplying $-\frac{1}{2}$ by itself. On that question, you learned that most numbers get larger when you square them, unless they happen to be fractions between zero and 1 or zero and –1. For these fractions, the denominators swell when you square them, and a larger denominator makes a smaller fraction.

Let's try $^1/_3$ on this question.

$$x^3 > x^4$$

$$\left(\frac{1}{3}\right)^3 > \left(\frac{1}{3}\right)^4$$

$$\left(\frac{1}{3}\right)\left(\frac{1}{3}\right)\left(\frac{1}{3}\right) > \left(\frac{1}{3}\right)\left(\frac{1}{3}\right)\left(\frac{1}{3}\right)\left(\frac{1}{3}\right)$$

$$\frac{1}{27} > \frac{1}{81}$$

Any fraction between zero and 1 works.

10. **89**

You actually have two choices on how to solve this problem:

1. You can find the total number of numbers between 1 and 49, then add to that all the numbers that have two digits.
2. You can determine how many numbers have one digit, then how many numbers have two digits, then add the two together.

Because we care, we are showing both. With method 1, there are 49 numbers total. (You can't subtract 49 – 1 and get 48 numbers because this would forget the 1 as a number.) Numbers 10 through 49 all have two digits—a units value and a tens value—and there are 40 of them in all:

$$49 + 40 = 89 \text{ total digits}$$

That's method 1. With method 2, we count up the number of single-digit numbers first:

$$1, 2, 3, 4, 5, 6, 7, 8, 9 = 9 \text{ digits}$$

Numbers 10 through 49 have two digits, and there are 40 of them, so the number of digits in the two-digit numbers is $(2)(40) = 80$ digits.

$$80 + 9 = 89 \text{ digits}$$

Both methods, as you might expect, give you the value of 89.

11. **9**

Before you start multiplying all these numbers together, write them out first:

$$15 \times 16 \times 17 \times 18 \times 19 \times 20 \times 21 \times 22 \times \ldots \times 29 \times 30 =$$

The question asks how many factors of 3 the end product will contain. Anything else is unimportant. For this reason, we can cull any numbers in the series that do not have 3 as a factor:

$$15 \times 18 \times 21 \times 24 \times 27 \times 30 =$$

There are six numbers to worry about. Before you rush off and grid in 6, however, make sure you know how many 3s are in the numbers above:

$$15 \times 18 \times 21 \times 24 \times 27 \times 30 =$$
$$(3 \times 5) \times (3 \times 6) \times (3 \times 7) \times (3 \times 8) \times (3 \times 9) \times (3 \times 10) =$$
$$(3 \times 5) \times (3 \times 3 \times 2) \times (3 \times 7) \times (3 \times 8) \times (3 \times 3 \times 3) \times (3 \times 10)$$

You can count the 3s in the equation above, or you can rearrange it the following way:

$$3 \times 3 \times 3 \times 3 \times 3 \times 3 \times 3 \times 3 \times 3 \times 2 \times 5 \times 7 \times 8 \times 10$$
$$= 3^9 \times 2 \times 5 \times 7 \times 8 \times 10$$

There are nine 3s, so the grid-in answer is 9.

12. **70**

This question makes you work every step of the way. If there are 150 students total and 1/3 of them bike, then 2/3 take the bus. 2/3 of 150 is 100:

150 students

50 bike, 100 take the bus

There are 45 boys in the class. If 15 of them bike, then 45 − 15 = 30 take the bus. You know that 100 total students take the bus, so 100 − 30 = 70 girls ride the bus.

13. **612**

An intersection of three sets is a number that appears in every set. Set T doesn't need much explaining, so let's focus on the other two. The stem states that set R consists of a geometric sequence where the first term is 17, and the constant ratio is 6. So start with 17 and start multiplying each subsequent term by 6:

Set $R = \{17, 102, 612, 3672, \ldots\}$

You can stop here because you've gone over 1,000, set T's upper limit. Set S is an arithmetic sequence, where you start with 87and add 175 to each subsequent term:

Set $S = \{87, 262, 437, 612, 787, 962, 1137, \ldots\}$

What number do these two sets have in common? 612. This is a positive integer less than 1,000, so it fits set T's description as well. The union is 612.

14. **1,299**

Let's take the stem and convert it into Mathspeak. If there are more blue pieces than red ones, then B > R. If there are more green pieces than blue, G > B. We can combine these two terms and write:

G > B > R

Now we add 1,000 red pieces to the mix:

G > B > 1,000

If there are 3,600 pieces total, the amount of blue and green pieces must be 3,600 − 1,000 = 2,600. Half of this number is 1,300. If green has 1,301 pieces, and blue has 1,299 pieces, you have:

G > B > R

1,301 > 1,299 > 1,000

If you add any more to the blue pieces, the green pieces would no longer outnumber them. So 1,299 is the greatest number of blue pieces you can have.

15. **2.55**

There are three stages to this question, and each contains a potential trap. The first step consists of setting up a good table. Write out Days 1 through 10, then start filling things in:

Days	1	2	3	4	5	6	7	8
Money Saved	1	2	4	8	16	32	64	128

Some of you might grid in 512 or 5.12 at this point. Mistake. The problem wants to know how much Delilah saved, so you have to add everything up:

$$1 + 2 + 4 + 8 + 16 + 32 + 64 + 128 = 255$$

That was the second step. The third step is to convert this amount into dollars because the problem asks for the amount in dollars. The answer in cents is 255, but 2.55 is the answer in dollars, so that's what you must grid in.

DATA, STATISTICS, AND PROBABILITY

PROBABILITY

THESE ARE THE SAT MATH TOPICS that slipped through the cracks. Not quite Numbers and Operations, not nearly Geometry, but still something the SAT wants you to know.

STATISTICAL ANALYSIS

Statistical analysis sounds like dental surgery. Scientific and sticky and gross. But SAT statistical analysis is actually not so bad. On these questions, the SAT gives you a data set—a collection of measurements or quantities. An example of a data set is the set of math test scores for the 20 students in Ms. Mathew's fourth-grade class:

> 71, 83, 57, 66, 95, 96, 68, 71, 84, 85, 87, 90, 88, 90, 84, 90, 90, 93, 97, 99

You are then asked to find one or more of the following values:

1. Arithmetic Mean
2. Median
3. Mode
4. Range

Arithmetic Mean (a.k.a. Average)

Arithmetic mean means the same thing as average. It's also the most commonly tested concept of statistical analysis on the SAT. The basic rule of finding an average isn't complicated: It's the value of the sum of the elements contained in a data set divided by the number of elements in the set.

$$\text{Arithmetic Mean} = \frac{\text{the sum of the elements of a set}}{\text{the number of elements in the set}}$$

Take another look at the test scores of the 20 students in Ms. Mathew's class. We've sorted the scores in her class from lowest to highest:

> 57, 66, 68, 71, 71, 83, 84, 84, 85, 87, 88, 90, 90, 90, 90, 93, 95, 96, 97, 99

To find the arithmetic mean of this data set, sum the scores and then divide by 20, since there are 20 students in her class:

$$\text{mean} = \frac{57 + 66 + 68 + \cdots + 96 + 97 + 99}{20}$$
$$\text{mean} = \frac{1600}{20}$$
$$\text{mean} = 80$$

But the SAT Is Sneaky When It's Mean

But that's not the way that the SAT usually tests mean. It likes to be more complicated and conniving. For example,

> If the average of four numbers is 22, and three of the numbers are 7, 11, and 18, then what is the fourth number?

Here's the key: If you know the average of a group and also know how many numbers are in the group, you can calculate the sum of the numbers in the group. The question above tells you that the average of the numbers is 22 and that there are four numbers in the group. If the average of four numbers is 22, then the four numbers, when added together, must equal $4 \times 22 = 88$. Since you know three of the four numbers in the set, and since you now know the total value of the set, you can write:

$$7 + 11 + 18 + \text{unknown number} = 88$$

Solving for the unknown number is easy. All you have to do is subtract the sum of 7, 11, and 18 from 88: $x = 88 - (7 + 11 + 18) = 88 - 36 = 52$.

As long as you realize that you can use an average to find the sum of all the values in a set, you can solve pretty much every question about arithmetic mean on the SAT:

> The average of a set of seven numbers is 54. The average of three of those seven numbers is 38. What is the average of the other four numbers?

This question seems really tough, since it keeps splitting apart its set of seven mysterious numbers. Students often freak out when SAT questions ask them for numbers that seem impossible to determine. Chill out. You don't have to know the exact numbers in the set to answer this problem. All you have to know is how averages work.

There are seven numbers in the entire set, and the average of those numbers is 54. The sum of the seven numbers in the set is $7 \times 54 = 378$. And, as the problem states, three particular numbers from the set have an average of 38. Since the sum of three questions is equal to the average of those three numbers multiplied by three, the sum of the three numbers in the problem is $3 \times 38 = 114$. Once you've got that, you can calculate the sum of the four remaining numbers, since that value must be the total sum of the seven numbers minus the sum of the mini-set of three: $378 - 114 = 264$. Now, since you know the total sum of the four numbers, you can get the average by dividing by 4: $264 \div 4 = 66$.

And here's yet another type of question the SAT likes to ask about mean: the dreaded "changing mean" question.

> The mean age of the 14 members of a scuba diving club is 34. When a new member joins, the mean age increased to 37. How old is the new member?

Actually, you shouldn't dread "changing mean" questions at all. They're as simple as other mean questions. Watch. Here's what you know from the question: the original number of members, 14, and the original average age, 34. And you can use this information to calculate the sum of the ages of the members of the original group by multiplying $14 \times 34 = 476$. From the question, you also know the total members of the group after the new member joined, $14 + 1 = 15$, and you know the new average age of the group, 37. So, you can find the sum of the ages of the new group as well: $15 \times 37 = 525$. The age of the new member is just the sum of the age of the new group minus the sum of the age of the old group: $555 - 476 = 79$. That is one ancient scuba diver.

Median

The median is the number whose value is exactly in the middle of all the numbers in a particular set. Take the set {6, 19, 3, 11, 7}. If the numbers are arranged in order of value, you get

$$\{3, 6, 7, 11, 19\}$$

It's clear that the middle number in this group is 7, so 7 is the median.

If a set has an even number of questions, it's impossible to isolate a single number as the median. Here's the last set, but with one more number added:

$$\{3, 6, 7, 11, 19, 20\}$$

In this case, the median equals the average of the two middle numbers. The two middle numbers in this set are 7 and 11, so the median of the set is $^{(7+11)}/_2 = 9$.

Mode

The mode is the number within a set that appears most frequently. In the set {10, 11, 13, 11, 20}, the mode is 11, since it appears twice, and all the others appear once. In a set where more than one number appears at the same highest frequency, there can be more than one mode: The set {2, 2, 3, 4, 4} has modes of 2 and 4. In the set {1, 2, 3, 4, 5}, where all of the numbers appear an equal number of times, there is no mode.

Range

The range measures the spread of a data set, or the difference between the smallest element and the largest. For the set of test scores in Ms. Mathew's class, {57, 66, 68, 71, 71, 83, 84, 84, 85, 87, 88, 90, 90, 90, 90, 93, 95, 96, 97, 99}, the range is 99 − 57 = 42.

GRAPHS, CHARTS, AND TABLES

There are countless ways to organize and present data. Luckily, the SAT uses only three of them: graphs, charts, and tables. On easy graphs, charts, and tables questions, the SAT just tests to see if you can understand the data being presented. More complicated questions ask you to perform some type of operation on data found in a chart or graph, such as calculating a mean or a percent.

Simple Charts, Graphs, and Tables Questions

Reading charts and graphs questions is pretty straightforward. The SAT shows you a chart. You answer a question about the data in the chart.

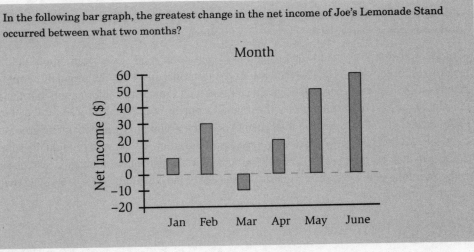

In the following bar graph, the greatest change in the net income of Joe's Lemonade Stand occurred between what two months?

Maybe you looked at this question and realized that you didn't know what the term "net income" means. Well, whether you did or didn't know the term, *it doesn't matter.* The graph tells you that the bars represent net income; you don't have to know what net income is to see between which months the net income differed most.

For this graph, a quick look makes it clear that the two biggest differences in terms of net income per month are between April and May and between February and March. The net income in April was $20, and the net income in May was $50, making the April–May difference $30. The net income in February was $30, and the net income in March was –$10, so the February–March difference was $40. The answer, therefore, is February to March. This question throws a tiny trick at you by including negative numbers as net income. If you don't realize that March is negative, then you might choose the April–May difference.

When dealing with graphs and charts, be sure to pay attention to negative and positive values. And ignore distracting information—like the meaning of net income—that makes easy questions seem complex.

Performing Operations on Data

The second type of charts and graphs question asks you to take a further step. You have to use the data in the chart or graph to perform some operation on it. For instance, you could be asked to figure out the mean of the data shown in a graph. Or, you could be asked something like this:

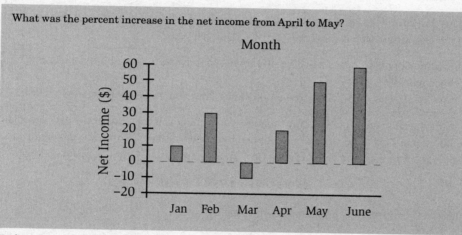

What was the percent increase in the net income from April to May?

To find the percent increase in net income from April to May, you have to find out how much the net income increased between April and May and then compare that increase to the original net income in April. The difference in net income between April and May is

$$\text{May net income (\$50)} - \text{April net income (\$20)} = \$30$$

Now, to calculate the percent increase, you have to divide the change in net income by the original income in April:

$$\frac{30}{20} = 1.5$$

But there's a final trick in the question. The answer is *not* 1.5%. Remember, to get percents, you have to multiply by 100. The answer is $1.5 \times 100 = 150\%$. The SAT will certainly include 1.5% as one of its answer choices to try to fool you.

Double Table Questions

The SAT puts special emphasis on questions that ask you to relate the data contained in two different tables.

Costs of Ice Cream

	Vanilla	Chocolate
1 scoop	$1.00	$1.25
2 scoops	$1.50	$1.75
3 scoops	$1.75	$2.00

Ice Cream Cones Eaten in a Year

	1 scoop	2 scoops	3 scoops
Tiny Tim	5	12	8
King Kong	16	10	6

If Tiny Tim only eats vanilla ice cream and King Kong only eats chocolate, how much do the two of them spend on ice cream in a year?

You need to be able to see the relationship between the data in the two tables and the question to figure out the answer. Here's what the two tables tell you:

1. How much one-scoop, two-scoop, and three-scoop cones cost for both vanilla and chocolate.
2. How many one-, two-, and three-scoop cones Tiny Tim and King Kong ate in a year.

Since the question tells you that Tiny Tim only eats vanilla and King Kong only eats chocolate, you know that Tiny Tim eats 5 one-scoop vanilla cones ($1.00), 12 two-scoop vanilla cones ($1.50), and 8 three-scoop vanilla cones ($1.75). So, in one year, Tiny Tim spent

$$(5 \times 1) + (12 \times 1.5) + (8 \times 1.75) = 5 + 18 + 14 = 37$$

dollars on ice cream. King Kong, meanwhile, spent

$$(16 \times 1.25) + (10 \times 1.75) + (6 \times 2) = 20 + 17.5 + 12 = 49.5$$

dollars. So, together, these two pigged out on $86.50 of ice cream.

Scatterplots

The SAT may also give you a special kind of graph called a scatterplot. A scatterplot lives up to its name. It's a graph with a whole lot of points scattered around:

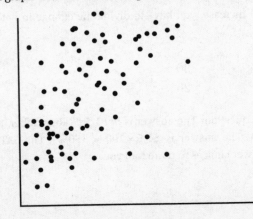

But the thing about a scatterplot is that the plots aren't scattered randomly. They have some sort of trend. And if you see the trend, you can draw a line that makes an average of the all the plots scattered around. Here's a line for the previous example:

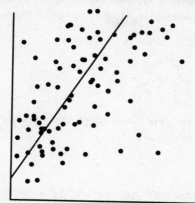

On the SAT, you won't have to do more than identify which line is the right one for a particular scatterplot and perhaps tell whether the slope of that line is negative or positive. You already know how to tell positive and negative slope, so these should be a breeze.

PROBABILITY

The probability is high that at least one question on the SAT will cover probability. The probability is even higher that the probability formula will help you on SAT probability questions. Here's the formula:

$$\text{Probability} = \frac{\text{number of times a certain event might occur}}{\text{total number of events that might occur}}$$

Let's say you go on a game show and are put in a room that contains 52 doors. Behind 13 of the doors are awesome prizes, including new cars, diamond watches, and infinity millions of dollars. Behind the rest of the doors are goats. What's the probability that you'll draw an awesome prize?

$$P = \frac{\text{awesomeness}}{\text{doors}} = \frac{13}{52} = \frac{1}{4}$$

And what's the probability that you'll end up with the goat?

$$P = \frac{\text{goats}}{\text{doors}} = \frac{(52-13)}{52} = \frac{39}{52} = \frac{3}{4}$$

Here's a more complicated example, involving the SAT's favorite probability prop: marbles! That SAT sure knows how to have a good time with marbles.

> Joe has 3 green marbles, 2 red marbles, and 5 blue marbles, and if all the marbles are dropped into a dark bag, what is the probability that Joe will pick out a green marble?

There are three ways for Joe to pick a green marble (since there are three different green marbles), but there are ten total possible outcomes (one for each marble in the bag). Therefore, the probability of picking a green marble is

$$P = \frac{3}{10}$$

When you calculate probability, always be careful to divide by the total number of chances. In the last example, you may have been tempted to leave out the three chances of picking a green marble from the total possibilities, yielding $P = {}^3/_7$. Brutal wrongness.

Backwards Probability

The SAT might also ask you a "backwards" probability question. For example, if you have a bag holding twenty marbles, and you have a $^1/_5$ chance of picking a blue marble, how many blue marbles are in the bag? All you have to do is set up the proper equation, following the model of $P = {}^m/n$:

$$\frac{1}{5} = \frac{x}{20}$$

in which x is the variable denoting the number of blue marbles. Cross-multiplying through the equation, you get $5x = 20$, which reduces to $x = 4$.

The Range of Probability

The probability, P, that any event will occur is always $0 \le P \le 1$. A probability of 0 for an event means that the event will *never* happen. A probability of 1 means the event will *always* occur. Drawing a bouquet of flowers from a standard deck of cards has a probability of 0. Becoming Lord (or Lady) of the Universe after scoring 2400 on the SAT has a probability of 1.

The Probability That an Event Will *Not* Occur

Some SAT questions ask you to determine the probability that an event will *not* occur. In that case, just figure out the probability of the event occurring, and subtract that number from 1.

Probability an event will not occur $= 1 -$ probability of the event occurring

Probability and Multiple Unrelated Events

More difficult SAT probability questions deal with multiple unrelated events. For these questions, the probability of both events occurring is the product of the outcomes of each event: $P_A \times P_B$, where P_A is the probability of the first event, and P_B is the probability of the second event.

A perfect example of two unrelated events is this: Drawing a spade from a full deck of cards *and* rolling a one with a six-sided die is the product of the probability of each event. Neither outcome will affect the outcome of the other. The probability of both events occuring is

$$P = \frac{13}{52} \times \frac{1}{6}$$
$$= \frac{1}{4} \times \frac{1}{6}$$
$$= \frac{1}{24}$$

The same principle can be applied to finding the probability of a series of events. Take a look at the following problem:

> A teacher keeps a jar full of different flavored jelly beans on her desk and hands them out randomly to her class. But one greedy student likes only the licorice-flavored ones. One day after school, the student sneaks into the dark classroom and steals three jelly beans. If the jar has 50 beans in all—15 licorice, 10 cherry, 20 watermelon, and 5 blueberry—what is the probability that the student got at least one licorice-flavored bean?

In order to find the probability of three consecutive events, first find the probability of each event separately. The first jelly bean has a $^{15}/_{50}$ chance of being licorice-flavored. The second jellybean, however, is a different story. There are now only 49 jelly beans left in the jar, so the probability of getting another licorice-flavored one is $^{14}/_{49}$. The probability of getting a third licorice-flavored jelly bean is $^{13}/_{48}$. The odds of all three happening are

$$P = \frac{15}{50} \times \frac{14}{49} \times \frac{13}{48}$$

$$= \frac{3}{10} \times \frac{2}{7} \times \frac{13}{48}$$

$$= \frac{1}{10} \times \frac{1}{7} \times \frac{13}{8}$$

$$= \frac{13}{560}$$

The moral of this sad tale of larceny and candy is that crime pays only $^{13}/_{560}$ of the time.

Geometric Probability

The SAT occasionally asks questions to which it has given the exciting name "geometric probability." The SAT could have saved itself some time by just saying that it's going to ask you questions about playing darts.

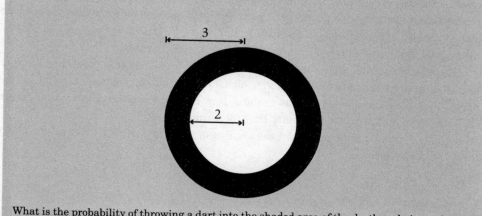

What is the probability of throwing a dart into the shaded area of the dartboard pictured above?

Here you have to find the area of some shaded (or unshaded) region and divide that by the total area of the figure. In this question, the dartboard is a circle of radius 3. The shaded region is the area of the circle minus a circle of radius 2.

$$P = \frac{(\pi 3^2) - (\pi 2^2)}{\pi 3^2} = \frac{9\pi - 4\pi}{9\pi} = \frac{5\pi}{9\pi} \approx \frac{5(3.14)}{9(3.14)} \approx 0.56$$

and 0.56 equals 56%.

PERMUTATIONS AND COMBINATIONS

If the SAT is a haunted forest, permutation and combination problems are the deepest, darkest, rarest trees. No, they are the mysterious fluorescent fungus growing on those trees. Permutation and combination problems are almost always hard, and most students skip them because they take so long. But if you're going for a Math score above 700, you should know how to deal with them. And to deal with permutations and combinations, you first have to know about factorials. If you're rushed for study time, though, and you're not trying to score a 700 on the Math section, this would be a good section to skip.

Factorials!

The factorial of a number, represented by $n!$, is the product of the natural numbers up to and including n:

$$n! = n \times (n-1) \times (n-2) \times \cdots \times 3 \times 2 \times 1$$

The factorial of n is the number of ways that the n elements of a group can be ordered. So, if you become a wedding planner, and you're asked how many different ways six people can sit at a table with six chairs, the answer is $6! = 6 \times 5 \times 4 \times 3 \times 2 \times 1 = 720$.

Permutations

Mutations are genetic defects that result in three-headed fish. A permutation, however, is an ordering of elements. For example, say you're running for office in California, and there are six different offices to be filled—governor, lieutenant governor, secretary, treasurer, spirit coordinator, and head cheerleader. If there are six candidates running, and the candidates are celebrities who don't care which office they're elected to, how many different ways can the California government be composed? Except that California politics are funny, this question is no different from the question about the ordering of six people in six chairs around the table. The answer is $6! = 720$ because there are six candidates running for office, and there are six job openings.

But, what if a terrible statewide budget crisis caused three California government jobs to be cut? Now only the offices of governor, lieutenant governor, and spirit coordinator can be filled. The same six candidates are still running. How many different combinations of the six candidates could fill the three positions? Time for permutations.

In general, the permutation, nP_r, is the number of subgroups of size r that can be taken from a set with n elements:

$$_nP_r = \frac{n!}{(n-r)!}$$

For the California election example, you need to find $_6P_3$:

$$_6P_3 = \frac{6!}{6-3!} = \frac{6!}{3!} = \frac{6 \times 5 \times 4 \times 3 \times 2 \times 1}{3 \times 2 \times 1} = \frac{720}{6} = 120$$

Notice that on permutations questions, calculations become much faster if you cancel out. Instead of multiplying everything out, you could have canceled out the $3 \times 2 \times 1$ in both numerator and denominator, and just multiplied $6 \times 5 \times 4 = 120$.

Permutations and Calculators

Graphing calculators and most scientific calculators have a permutation function, labeled nP_r. Though calculators do differ, in most cases, you must enter n, then press the button for permutation, and then enter r. This will calculate a permutation for you, but if n is a large number, the calculator often cannot calculate $n!$. If this happens to you, don't give up! Remember, the SAT never deals with huge numbers: Look for ways to cancel out.

Combinations

A combination is an unordered grouping of a set. An example of a combination scenario in which order doesn't matter is a hand of cards: A king, an ace, and a five is the same as an ace, a five, and a king.

Combinations are represented as nC_r, where unordered subgroups of size r are selected from a set of size n. Because the order of the elements in a given subgroup doesn't matter, this means that $\binom{n}{r}$ will be less than $_nP_r$. Any one combination can be turned into more than one permutation. $\binom{n}{r}$ is calculated as follows:

$$\binom{n}{r} = \frac{_nP_r}{r!} = \frac{n!}{(n-r)!r!}$$

Here's an example:

Suppose six people are running for three leadership positions, each of which has the same duties and title. How many ways can this be done?

In this example, the order in which the leaders are assigned to positions doesn't matter—the leaders aren't distinguished from one another in any way, unlike in the California government example. This distinction means that the question can be answered with a combination rather than a permutation. So, to figure out how many different groups of three can be taken from a group of six, do this:

$$_6C_3 = \frac{6!}{(6-3)!3!} = \frac{6 \times 5 \times 4 \times 3 \times 2 \times 1}{(3 \times 2 \times 1)(3 \times 2 \times 1)} = \frac{120}{6} = 20$$

There are only 20 different ways to elect three leaders, as opposed to 120 ways when the leadership jobs were differentiated.

Combinations and Calculators

As with permutations, there should be a combination function on your graphing or scientific calculator labeled nC_r. Use it the same way you use the permutation key.

That's it, everything, the whole SAT Data, Statistics, and Probability banana. Now, for some practice.

PRACTICE SET 1.
MULTIPLE CHOICE

Questions 1 and 2 refer to the following graph.

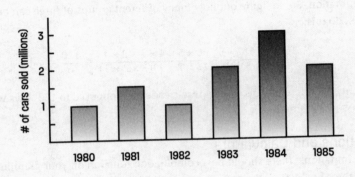

1. According to the information in the graph, what year saw a decrease in the number of cars sold?

    (A) 1980
    (B) 1981
    (C) 1982
    (D) 1983
    (E) 1984

2. According to the information in the graph, in what two years were the number of cars sold closest to equal?

    (A) 1980 and 1981
    (B) 1981 and 1982
    (C) 1981 and 1983
    (D) 1983 and 1985
    (E) 1984 and 1985

Question 3 refers to the following set.

   Set A {6, 8, 3, 2, 3, 5, 9, 5, 12, 3, 9, 1, 1, 6, 7}

3. The numbers in set A represent the amount of money in dollars that 15 students brought to school. Which of the following is the median amount of money the students brought to school?

    (A) 3
    (B) 5
    (C) 6
    (D) 7
    (E) 8

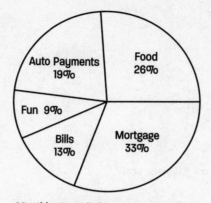

Monthly Household Income = $2,400

The pie chart above represents the monthly distribution of family *X*'s income.

4. According to the graph, how much is family *X*'s mortgage in dollars?

    (A) 216
    (B) 312
    (C) 456
    (D) 624
    (E) 792

5. If family *X* completed all its car payments and transferred all the auto money into the "Fun" budget, then family *X* would most nearly spend the same amount on fun as they spend on

    (A) food
    (B) mortgage
    (C) bills
    (D) food and bills
    (E) food and mortgage

Set *D* {9, 11, 6, *x*, *x*}

6. In set *D* above, what is the value of *x* if the average of the five numbers is 8?

    (A) 4
    (B) 7
    (C) 8
    (D) 10
    (E) 14

Set *G* {5, 8, 13, *x*, *y*}

7. If *x* and *y* are distinct positive integers and the average of set *G* is 6.8, then which of the following <u>could be</u> the mode of set *G*?

    (A) 13
    (B) 11
    (C) 9
    (D) 8
    (E) 5

8. A certain deck of cards consists only of 10's, Jacks, Queens, and Kings, and is divided up evenly in a 52-card deck. What is the probability of not drawing a Jack?

(A) $\frac{1}{4}$

(B) $\frac{1}{3}$

(C) $\frac{1}{2}$

(D) $\frac{2}{3}$

(E) $\frac{3}{4}$

Questions 9 and 10 refer to the following graph.

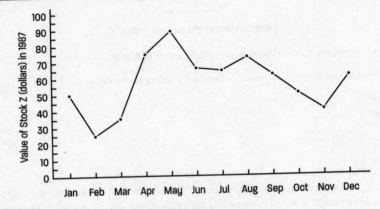

The graph shows the values of Stock Z for the year 1987.

9. The greatest increase for Stock Z, compared to the month before, occurred during which month?

(A) April
(B) May
(C) December
(D) March
(E) August

10. For the overall year, 1987, what was the percent increase of Stock Z?

(A) 250%
(B) 100%
(C) 50%
(D) 20%
(E) 0%

Question 11 refers to the following graph.

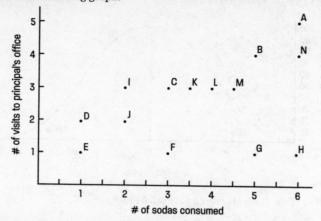

# of sodas consumed

Of all the students sent to the principal's office on one school day, each was asked his/her soda consumption for that day. The graph above represents each child's answer.

11. If you were to draw a line showing the average ratio of principal's office visits to sodas consumed, this line would most likely pass through point

(A) K
(B) I
(C) H
(D) G
(E) F

12. The average income of Ironville, Pennsylvania, is $24,000 a year. A new mill has brought in six new incomes that increase the average to $32,000. If there were initially eight incomes in Ironville, what is the average income of the six new families?

(A) $42,666.67
(B) $74,666.67
(C) $106,666.67
(D) $192,000.00
(E) $256,000.00

13. In a certain bag of candy-coated chocolates with peanut centers, seven are yellow, three are red, five are blue, five are brown, and eight are green. If two candies are chosen at random, what is the probability that the first is green and the second is red?

(A) $\frac{3}{98}$

(B) $\frac{2}{63}$

(C) $\frac{1}{30}$

(D) $\frac{1}{10}$

(E) $\frac{11}{28}$

Questions 14 and 15 refer to the following graph.

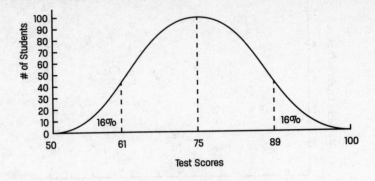

14. What percent of the students scored between 61 and 89?

   (A) 2%
   (B) 14%
   (C) 50%
   (D) 68%
   (E) 74%

15. What are the mean, median, and mode, respectively, of the test scores?

   (A) 89, 80, 75
   (B) 75, 75, 75
   (C) 61, 75, 89
   (D) 89, 75, 61
   (E) 75, 61, 89

16. Iron Chef is preparing an eclectic six-course meal to consist of shrimp cocktail, mango salad, miso soup, stir-fried eggplant, turducken (chicken stuffed into a duck stuffed into a turkey), and a chocolate éclair. Disregarding all formality to the traditional order of the courses, in how many different orders can the courses be presented?

   (A) 240
   (B) 440
   (C) 720
   (D) 1,440
   (E) 1,640

Questions 17 and 18 refer to the following graph.

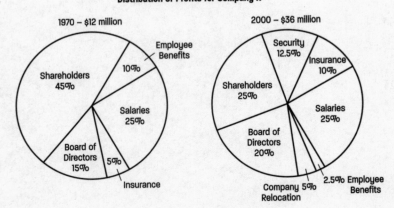

17. In 2000, Company X had to add security costs and company relocation to its profit distribution. These expenses were taken out of employee benefits. What was the approximate percent decrease in employee benefits from 1970 to 2000?

(A) 7.5%
(B) 17.5%
(C) 25%
(D) 33.3%
(E) 35%

18. If the Board of Directors consists of the same eight people for both 1970 and 2000, then between 1970 and 2000, each board member, on average, saw his or her portion of profits increase by how much?

(A) $225,000
(B) $675,000
(C) $900,000
(D) $1,200,000
(E) $1,800,000

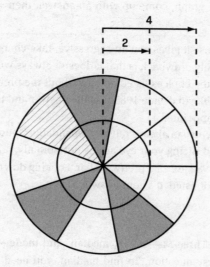

Note: all 9 arc sectors
are of equal area.

19. If one dart is thrown at the figure above, what is the probability of it hitting the white regions of the inner circle?

(A) $\frac{1}{9}$

(B) $\frac{2}{9}$

(C) $\frac{1}{3}$

(D) $\frac{4}{9}$

(E) $\frac{5}{9}$

20. The student committee to investigate the missing prom funds is to be made up of four members of the student council. If there are seven members in the student council, then how many different committees are possible?

(A) 840
(B) 210
(C) 120
(D) 35
(E) 24

ANSWERS & EXPLANATIONS

1. C

The first question is the easiest on a section, and this one is no exception. The only trick is that you have to look at the year *before* the year in the answer choice to tell whether there was a decrease. Consider **A**, 1980. You would have to know how many cars were sold in 1979 to say whether 1980 was a better or worse year. For that reason, **A** is incorrect. The only two years that see decreases are 1982 and 1985, but since 1985 isn't an answer choice, the answer must be **C**, 1982.

2. D

Here's another straight "Can you use your eyes?" kind of problem. There are two ways to approach this one:

1. You can start with the answer choices and check them all out, making notes about how close you think the car sales were in two years.
2. You can start with the graph, come up with an answer, then scan the answer choices to see if it's there.

Option 2 is good because it gives you an aggressive, take-charge attitude that is beneficial when taking a test. The only drawback is that it doesn't always work because the answer you find might not be one of the choices listed. (Think about the previous question and imagine what it would have been like to decide 1985 was the answer and then hit the answer choices. You would have been disappointed.)

Still, if Option 2 fails, you can always rely on dependable Option 1, so let's try it first. Gazing at the vertical bars and slicing your eye across horizontally, it appears that 1983 and 1985 are very close. 1980 and 1982 are also pretty similar. Looking down at the choices, **D** is '83 and '85, and '80 and '82 are not listed. **D**'s your answer.

3. B

So long as you keep the Three Ms—mean, median, and mode—straight in your head, you won't stumble on this easy question. To find median, you need to rearrange set A in order from least to greatest.

Current set A: {6, 8, 3, 2, 3, 5, 9, 5, 12, 3, 9, 1, 1, 6, 7}

Set A after housecleaning: {1, 1, 2, 3, 3, 3, 5, 5, 6, 6, 7, 8, 9, 9, 12}

As you rearrange, you might want to cross out the numbers in the original Set A, to keep track of which ones you've rearranged and which ones you haven't.

There is an odd number (15) of numbers in set A, so the median, or middle, value will be the eighth number. This turns out to be 5, **B**.

4. E

Because pie charts often show percentages—like this one—they are often accompanied by a real number, such as "Monthly Household Income = \$2,400." This allows the test-makers to fashion questions like this one, where you have to find the right percentage, then convert this to an actual dollar amount.

The conversion is fairly straightforward. If the mortgage is 33% of the total monthly income, and this income is \$2,400, then:

$$(33\%)(\$2,400) = (0.33)(\$2,400) = \$792$$

That's **E**.

5.   A

Here you get your first taste of fiddling with a chart. *Auto Payment* and *Fun* are right next to each other—imagine erasing the line between the two. You would now have a new pie piece. To paraphrase the problem, your goal is to find an old pie piece that is the same size as this new "Auto Payments plus Fun" piece. The answer is literally right next to the new piece because *Food*, **A**, is roughly the same size as the new piece. This shouldn't be surprising because food consists of 26% of the budget, and the new piece combines auto (19%) and fun (9%). Together they combine to make 19% + 9% = 28%.

6.   B

There are two ways to crack this question. You can set up the equation for averages, or you can go into the answer choices and start trying out different numbers to see which one satisfies the stem. Because this is only question 6, setting up the equation won't be too hard, but keep in mind that as the questions get harder, you're better off solving them using unexpected methods. In other words, this problem is designed to trip up people who set up an equation. Avoiding this route will help you avoid potential distractors.

Let's take **C**, 8, and see what average we get:

$$\text{Average} = \frac{\text{sum of elements}}{\text{number of elements}}$$

$$\text{Average} = \frac{9 + 11 + 6 + x + x}{5}$$

$$\text{Average} = \frac{9 + 11 + 6 + 8 + 8}{5}$$

$$\text{Average} = \frac{42}{5}$$

$$\text{Average} = 8.4$$

If $x = 8$ (**C**), then we get an average of 8.4. This is not correct, though, because the problem asks for an average of 8. If **C** is too large, you can eliminate **D** and **E** as well, because they are also going to be too large. This leaves only **A** or **B** as the possible answer.

8.4 is only slightly more than 8, so we need an answer choice that is slightly less than **C**. **B**, 7, fits the bill perfectly, whereas **A** is much smaller. **B** is your answer. You can double-check this answer if you want, but once you gain enough experience in the way the SAT works, you'll know that this step isn't necessary.

7.   E

Just knowing the definition of *mode* will help you cross out some answer choices. The mode of the set is the number that appears the most. The actual numbers are 5, 8, and 13, with x and y as two distinct unknowns. The term *distinct* means that x and y are not the same number. The mode, then, of this set would be any of the real numbers that appears twice as either x or y. You can cross out **B** and **C** because they are not numbers of the set.

You now have a one-in-three shot. The answer has to be 5, 8, or 13. You could set up an equation at this point, but again, don't glibly do things that the question wants you to do.

Look at the numbers 5, 8, and 13. The stem states that the average of set G is 6.8. Two of the known numbers (8 and 13) are larger than 6.8. It makes sense that the unknown number would have to be smaller than 6.8 in order to balance out the 8 and 13. That's what averages are all about, isn't it?

You have only one answer choice, 5, that's smaller than 6.8. Pick it.

Yes, you could go through all the math exactly the way the questions wants you to, but you'll just end up with **E**. It's better to get in the habit of approaching questions from an unexpected flank.

8. **E**

A probability question rears its ugly head, a clear sign that we have left the Land of the Easy Questions and entered the Realm of Medium Difficulty. The deck of cards is divided up evenly between *four* kinds of cards: 10s, Jacks, Queens, and Kings. There's your UNDER number right there: It's 4, the total number of kinds of cards. The stem asks for the probability of NOT drawing a Jack. Only one kind of card is a Jack. The other three are not. Three is your OVER number, then. The probability is 3/4, **E**. On this question, the total number of cards didn't come into play, but it was not the toughest probability you'll ever see.

9. **D**

Eye and Brain time! This problem is very similar to question 1, only this time you have a line graph instead of a bar graph. Using your eyes, you can see that there are two big upward spikes in the graph. March–April is a big one, and so is November–December. But writing the spikes as "March–April" and "November–December" is not exactly accurate, and it confuses things by mentioning two months. The more accurate description is that the two big spikes occur during "March 1st–March 31st" and "November 1st–November 30th." This is what the line graph is really describing. There is no November answer choice, so **D** must be the correct answer.

10. **D**

Finding the starting stock price is simple because the line starts at 50 immediately above January 1st. The endpoint of the line is farther away from the vertical axis denoting dollars, but you can eyeball it and tell that the ending price is above 50 but below 75.

Your eye has done its part. Now it's your brain's turn. Because there was a stock increase, **E** is incorrect, so you can cross it out. If the stock had increased by $75, the increase would have been $75 − $50 = $25. Twenty-five dollars is half of $50, so that increase would have been 50%, **C**. But you know that the line *doesn't* reach 75, so 50%, **C**, is too big. If **C** is too big and **E** is not enough, there's only one answer it can be: **D**, 20%.

11. **A**

This scatterplot graph doesn't feature an overwhelming number of points, which is nice. Primarily, this question hopes to blow your mind with its strangeness. Remember that with a scatterplot, the whole point—get it, *point*—is to find the average trend. The line through all the different points shows this average trend.

For this scatterplot graph, the line would go through that dense mass of points in the middle and should look something like this:

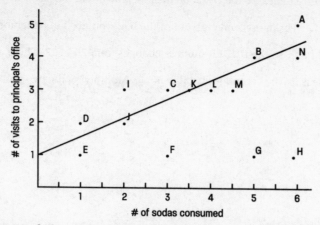

Three of your answer choices—points *F*, *G*, and *H*—are way too low, while point *I* is a little high. Point *K* is right in the thick of things, and that's a good place to be when dealing with scatterplots. **A** is the answer.

12. **A**

As always, you can do the math, or you can try the unconventional road. Taking the unconventional method will get you there safer, but we'll show you how to do the math this time to illustrate all the different ways to get the correct answer.

With the addition of the six new families, there are 14 families total (the new six plus the old eight). The average for this group is $32,000. If the old group of eight averaged $24,000, then the total amount of money they make could be found by multiplying 24,000 by 8. If you make the new average income n, you can say:

$$\text{Average} = \frac{\text{sum of elements}}{\text{number of elements}}$$

$$32,200 = \frac{8(24,000) + 6n}{14}$$

$$448,000 = 8(24,000) + 6n$$

$$448,000 = 192,000 + 6n$$

$$256,000 = 6n$$

$$42,666.67 \approx n$$

That's **A**. The unconventional way would have you look over the answer choices and understand how averages work. If six families come in and raise the average income by 1/3 ($24,000 to $32,000), then the new income has to be a bit higher than the current number. Scanning the answer choices, **C**, **D**, and **E** are all very big. This makes them highly unlikely to be correct. **A** and **B** are the only real possibilities, and **B** is a long shot. **A**'s the answer.

13. **B**

To find the UNDER value, total up the number of candies.

$$\text{Yellow} = 7$$

$$\text{Red} = 3$$

$$\text{Blue} = 5$$

$$\text{Brown} = 5$$

$$\text{Green} = 8$$

$$\text{Total at the start} = 7 + 3 + 5 + 5 + 8 = 28$$

There are 8 green candies, so the OVER on the first grab out of the bag is 8. This gives the first probability of $\frac{8}{28}$. For the second grab out of the bag, you need to remember that one candy has been pulled out, so the UNDER number changes from 28 to 27. There are still 3 reds, so the OVER value is 3. The second probability is $\frac{3}{27}$. Multiplying the two probabilities together will give you:

$$\frac{8}{28} \times \frac{3}{27} = \frac{2}{7} \times \frac{1}{9} = \frac{2}{63}$$

That's **B**.

14. **D**

The whole point of most graph questions is to freak you out visually. Once you get over the freakiness, the answer is often not too hard to find. On this question, those two cute 16% values hiding in the lower parts of the bell curve are the key to this question. The first 16% shows the percentage of students who scored lower than 61. The second 16% at the far end shows the number of students who scored better than 89. Everyone else scored between a 61 and 89, and you can find this percentage by starting with a 100% and subtracting the two 16% values:

$$100\% - 16\% - 16\% = 68\%$$

There's **D**.

15. **B**

You need to use the multiple-choice format to your benefit on this question. Use your eyes and look at the line that shows the hill at its highest. The score there is 75. This means 75 is the mode because more students scored a 75 than anything else.

Now look at your answer choices. Only **A** and **B** have 75 as the mode. You can cross out **C**, **D**, and **E**, leaving you with a 50/50 shot. Speaking of 50/50, you can also see that the line up from 75 evenly divides the curve into two equal parts. This makes 75 the median of the set of scores. This gets rid of **A** as an answer, so the correct answer must be **B**.

Mean doesn't even matter. You found the right answer, so move on.

16. **C**

The last five problems are hard for a reason. They have strangely worded questions with multiple steps needed to unlock them. That's just the way it is.

Once you wade through the problem, you should find that it's a basic factorial question. You start out with six possible first courses, followed by five possible second courses (one less because you have a first course), followed by four possible third courses, and so on. Mathematically, this looks like:

$$6 \times 5 \times 4 \times 3 \times 2 \times 1$$

Now use your trusty calculator and multiply everything together. The product should be 720. This means there are 720 possible combinations, which is **C**.

17. C

The answer is not 7.5%. Anyone who approaches question 17 and thinks the answer can be found by subtracting the 2000 employee benefits percentage (2.5%) from the 1970 employee benefits percentage of 10% needs to go over the Order of Difficulty thing. Hard questions are hard for a reason. If they seem very easy, it's because you're falling for a trap. That's how it works, pure and simple.

To tackle this question correctly, you need to find actual cash values for employee benefits in 1970 and 2000. You can't just add or subtract percentages because the amount of money made by the company changed from $12 million to $36 million.

1970 Employee Benefits:

$$(10\%)(\$12,000,000) = (0.10)(12,000,000) = \$1,200,000.$$

2000 Employee Benefits:

$$(2.5\%)(\$36,000,000) = (0.025)(36,000,000) = \$900,000.$$

Those are the actual amounts. The decrease is employee benefits, in dollars, was $1,200,000 – $900,000 = $300,000. This is a percentage decrease of 25% because $300,000 is 1/4 of $1,200,000. The answer is **C**.

18. B

Again, you have to find actual number values. You can't go adding and subtracting percentages willy-nilly. First, you have to find out how much each board member made in 1970.

Amount made in 1970:

$$(\text{percentage made by Board})(\text{total profits}) =$$

$$(15\%)(12 \text{ million}) = (0.15)(\$12,000,000) = \$1,800,000.$$

This is the amount made by all eight board members. Each member made about 1/8 of this, or $225,000.

Amount made in 2000:

$$(\text{percentage made by Board})(\text{total profits}) =$$

$$(20\%)(36 \text{ million}) = (0.20)(\$36,000,000) = \$7,200,000.$$

Again, this is the amount made by all of the Board of Directors. Dividing by 8 gives us the average earnings of one board member equals $900,000.

One more computation to go. To find the increase in pay, we must subtract the 1970 value from the 2000 value:

$$\$900,000 - \$225,000 = \$675,000.$$

This is **B**.

19. A

If you clutch to the OVER/UNDER method for probability, you have a chance on this one. The goal is to think in terms of area. The UNDER portion is the area of the whole circular dartboard with a radius of 4.

$$\text{Area of circle} = \pi r^2 = \pi 4^2 = 16\pi$$

Doesn't look too promising, does it? Before you abandon all hope, let's look at the inner circle. The odds of hitting the inner circle alone would be computed the same way—by finding the area of the inner circle. But only 4 out of 9 inner circle pie sectors are white, so this number for inner circle area would then have to be multiplied by $\frac{4}{9}$. As ugly as it seems, this is the way to find the OVER value:

$$(\text{area of inner circle})\left(\frac{4}{9}\right) = \text{OVER value}$$

$$(\pi r^2)\left(\frac{4}{9}\right) = (\pi 2^2)\left(\frac{4}{9}\right) = \frac{16\pi}{9}$$

Never let it be said that the SAT doesn't award hard work. When we place the OVER value on top of the UNDER value, we get:

$$\frac{\text{OVER}}{\text{UNDER}} = \frac{\frac{16\pi}{9}}{16\pi} = \left(\frac{16\pi}{9}\right)\left(\frac{1}{16\pi}\right) = \frac{1}{9}$$

When you're dividing with fractions, you have to flip the value in the denominator over and then multiply. This makes 16π become $\frac{1}{16\pi}$, and then the 16πs cancel each other out. The answer is **A**.

20. **D**

If this question is harder than the last one, you know it's going to be a doozy. This is actually a combination of a factorial, and if you're one of the few people walking around with the formula $_nC_r = \frac{n!}{(n-r)!r!}$ in your head, then you're in luck. It's what you need to solve this problem.

The number n is the total members of the student council, and r is the number of members in the smaller investigation committee. The stem gives us values of $n = 7$ and $r = 4$. Put those into the formula, and you get:

$$_nC_r = \frac{n!}{(n-r)!r!}$$

$$_nC_r = \frac{7!}{(7-4)!4!}$$

$$_nC_r = \frac{7 \times 6 \times 5 \times 4 \times 3 \times 2 \times 1}{(3 \times 2 \times 1)(4 \times 3 \times 2 \times 1)}$$

$$_nC_r = \frac{7 \times 6 \times 5}{3 \times 2 \times 1}$$

$$_nC_r = \frac{210}{6}$$

$$_nC_r = 35$$

That's **D**. This last question is indicative of how the SAT will pull out an obscure idea (combinations) in order to make a question very hard to solve.

PRACTICE SET 2: GRID-INS

Questions 1–4 refer to the following set.

Set Q {x, 6, 8, 12, –4, x, 8, 3, x}

1. In set Q, if $x = 7$, what is the average of set Q?

2. What is one possible integer value for x so that the median of set Q is 3?

3. In set Q, if the value of x is 2 greater than the largest numerical value present, what is the range of the set?

4. If the average of set Q is 5, what is the mode of set Q?

Questions 5 and 6 refer to the following graph.

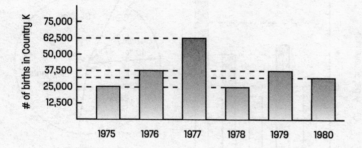

The graph above illustrates the number of births in Country K over a six-year period.

5. In Country K, the greatest percent change—either increase or decrease—for any two consecutive years is equal to what?

6. What is the LEAST percentage change for any two years?

7. Two six-sided dice, numbered 1–6 on each, are thrown simultaneously. What is the probability that the sum of the two sides is greater than 9?

Questions 8 and 9 refer to the following graph.

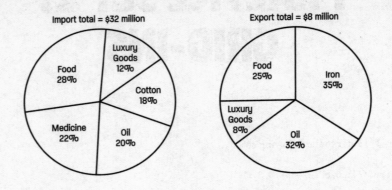

8. The amount imported in food is how much greater, in millions of dollars, than the entire amount of goods exported?

9. What is the change in dollars between the amount of medicine imported and the amount of iron exported? Grid your answer in millions of dollars.

10. The average of five positive integers is 6. No more than two numbers are the same. All numbers are greater than 3 and less than 10. What is one possible value of the mode?

Questions 11, 12, and 13 refer to the following graph.

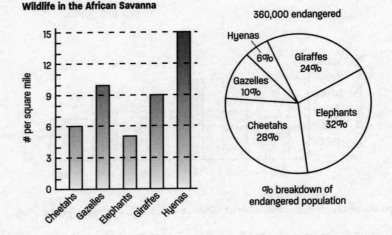

11. According to the graph, what fraction of the entire population for one square mile is composed of giraffes?

12. If there is a total of 180,000 gazelles in the savanna, then how many per square mile are endangered?

13. If 6 hyenas per square mile are endangered, then how many hyenas, in thousands, are there in the savanna?

14. Fonzy is sitting down to a meal of macaroni and cheese. He has four different condiments to choose from: ketchup, picante sauce, Tabasco sauce, and ranch dressing. If he is going to use at least one and no more than four, then how many different combinations of condiments does he have to choose from?

15. Ben decides to get an ice cream cone. He is going to choose two toppings out of an available six. Ben also has a choice between a plain cone and a waffle cone. If Ben chooses vanilla ice cream, how many different combinations of toppings and cones does Ben have to choose from?

ANSWERS & EXPLANATIONS

1. 6

There would be many different ways to attack this question if it were in the multiple-choice section. With grid-ins, you're forced to approach the problem by doing the math. Sigh. Grid-ins are no fun.

After you place everything into the equation for mean average, all you have to do is solve the question by manipulating the equation correctly. The missing piece is the average:

$$\text{Average} = \frac{x + 6 + 8 + 12 + (-4) + x + 8 + 3 + x}{9}$$

$$\text{Average} = \frac{7 + 6 + 8 + 12 + (-4) + 7 + 8 + 3 + 7}{9}$$

$$\text{Average} = \frac{54}{9} = 6$$

2. 3

When dealing with median, it always helps to line things up. Here's set Q without the three xs:

$$-4, 3, 6, 8, 8, 12$$

As you can see, the 3 is way to the left of the list, and for it to be the median, it needs to be in the middle. To get 3 into the middle, you would need a value for x less than 3. Any integer less than 3 would work, but on grid-in questions, there's no way to grid in negative numbers, so this constrains things a bit. Your best answers are 0, 1, and 2. If you picked $x = 1$, for instance, your set would look like:

$$-4, 1, 1, 1, 3, 6, 8, 8, 12$$

That puts 3 in the middle. You can even have $x = 3$, which would make 3 not only the median but the mode as well.

3. 18

The range of a set is the difference between the largest numerical value and the smallest. In set Q, 12 is the largest number visible, but the stem states that x is 2 greater than this value, so $x = 14$. The smallest value is -4, so the range would be

$$14 - (-4) = 18$$

Grid that in.

4. 4

This question will look a lot like the first question, only here the missing piece is not the average but the value of x.

$$\text{Average} = \frac{x + 6 + 8 + 12 + (-4) + x + 8 + 3 + x}{9}$$

$$5 = \frac{33 + 3x}{9}$$

$$9(5) = \frac{33 + 3x}{9}(9)$$

$$45 = 33 + 3x$$

$$12 = 3x$$

$$\frac{12}{3} = 4$$

Because there are three xs in the equation, this value of x is the mode for the set—no other number appears as often.

5. 66.67

The drop from 1977 to 1978 sure looks the steepest, but it might not be the steepest in terms of percentage. The difference in numbers between the two years is $62,500 - 25,000 = 37,500$. What percent of 62,500 is 37,500? The answer is

$$\frac{n}{100}(62,500) = 37,500$$
$$625n = 37,500$$
$$n = 60$$

Sixty percent is a steep drop. However, we should check the percentage increase from 1976 to 1977 before moving on. Even though the actual number of births is less, the percentage change may be greater.

To understand why this is, consider a room with only one person in it. If another person enters, the occupancy of the room increases by 100%. Now imagine a room with 100 people in it. If 10 people enter, the occupancy increases by 10%. Even though more people actually entered, the percentage change was less because there were more people to begin with.

The difference in births between 1976 and 1977 is $62,500 - 37,500 = 25,000$. What percent of 37,500 is 25,000? The answer is

$$\frac{n}{100}(37,500) = 25,000$$
$$375n = 25,000$$
$$n \approx 66.67$$

There's the real answer. The big drop-off between 1977 and 1978 is like a cliff. If you weren't looking for a percentage change, you would have fallen right over it.

6. 0

Here's a question meant to trick your eye again. Between 1979 and 1980, there's an ever-so-slight drop of 2,500 births. Your eye would see this slight drop and say, "That's the smallest drop." This is true, but it is only true for consecutive years. The problem says "any two years." The nonconsecutive years 1976 and 1979 had the same amount of births. The percentage between these two years is, therefore, zero. This is the smallest change, smaller even than whatever slight decrease occurred between 1979 and 1980. The answer is 0.

7. 1/6

Determining the UNDER portion of the probability is easier, so let's start there. If there are two dice with six sides, then the total number of probabilities is $(6)(6) = 36$. That's the bottom part; now on to the top. Throwing a number that will be greater than 9 isn't easy. In fact, here are the only ways that could happen:

Ways to Throw Higher Than a 9	
First Throw	Second Throw
4	6
5	5
5	6
6	4

Ways to Throw Higher Than a 9	
6	5
6	6

Count up the number of different ways. There are six different ways, so that's your OVER number. The probability is $\frac{6}{36}$, which simplifies to $\frac{1}{6}$.

8.   0.96

The entire amount exported appears above the second pie chart as $8 million. To figure out the amount of food imported, multiply the percent spent on food by the total of $32 million:

$$(28\% \text{ imported food})(\$32 \text{ million import total}) =$$

$$(0.28)(\$32,000,000) = \$8,960,000$$

The amount imported in food is greater than total exports by:

$$\$8,960,000 - \$8,000,000 = \$960,000$$

Don't try to grid this huge number in, however. Recall that the stem asks for the answer in millions of dollars. In millions of dollars, $960,000 = 0.96.

9.   4.24

We hope you are getting the hang of these percent questions and would never, ever consider simply adding or subtracting percentages. You need to find the real numbers.

Amount of medicine imported:

$$(22\% \text{ of total})(\text{import total}) =$$

$$(0.22)(\$32 \text{ million}) = \$7.04 \text{ million}$$

Amount of iron exported:

$$(35\% \text{ of total})(\text{export total}) =$$

$$(0.35)(\$8 \text{ million}) = \$2.8 \text{ million}$$

Now you need to subtract the two real values. Because the answer is in millions of dollars, there's no need to write out 7.04 million as 7,040,000. In fact, that would only cause trouble.

$$\$7.04 - \$2.8 = \$4.24 \text{ million.}$$

Grid in the number 4.24.

10.   5

This question seems tough, but the word *possible* makes things a bit easier. You don't have to figure out a single solution. If you try something and it works, then that's a possible answer.

Why not try a number next to 6, such as 5? If 5 were the mode, it would appear twice, and no other number could appear more than once. This will help once we look at the formula for averages and determine what our missing piece is

$$\text{Average} = \frac{\text{sum of elements}}{\text{total number of elements}}$$

$$6 = \frac{\text{sum of elements}}{5}$$

$$30 = \text{sum of the elements}$$

If two of the elements are 5, then the other three elements have to equal 20 because $30 - 2(5)$ $= 30 - 10 = 20$. The question now becomes, "Can you think of three distinct integers greater than 3 but less than 10 that sum to 20?" If you can, you've found a possible answer.

This will take some scratch work. You might get frustrated. If so, try a different number as the mode that appears twice. If you stick with it, though, you should come up with:

$$7 + 9 + 4 = 20$$

If the set of numbers was 4, 5, 5, 7, and 9, the mode would be 5, and the average would be 6. So 5 is one possible answer.

11. **1/5**

The danger on this question is using the wrong graph. You might have a great urge to look at the pie chart and pluck that 24% giraffe number out. Don't. The problem talks about the population per square mile, so the bar graph must be used. To find out what fraction of the population per square mile is giraffes, you need to determine the total number of animals per square mile. From the bar graph, this would be

Cheetahs $= 6$

Gazelles $= 10$

Elephants $= 5$

Giraffes $= 9$

Hyenas $= 15$

Total number of animals $= 45$

Man, that place is crawling with hyenas. But don't worry about that for now. Take the total number of animals and place the number of giraffes per square miles on top of it. This will give you the right fraction:

$$\frac{9 \text{ giraffes per square mile}}{45 \text{ total animals per square mile}} = \frac{9}{45} = \frac{1}{5}$$

12. **2**

Both graphs come into play on this one, signaling that we're in Hard Grid-In Territory. First, use the pie chart to determine the number of endangered gazelles. If there are 360,000 total endangered animals, and 10% of these are gazelles, then the actual number of endangered gazelles is

$$(10\%)(360,000) = (0.10)(360,000) = 36,000.$$

The problem states that the total population of gazelles is 180,000, so obviously not all gazelles are in trouble. In fact, only $\frac{36,000}{180,000} = 0.2 = 20\%$ of them are in trouble. If 20% of all gazelles are endangered, and there are 10 gazelles per square mile (from the bar chart), then 20% of these 10 gazelles are endangered. 20% of 10 is 2, your grid-in answer.

13. **54**

This question is like the last one in reverse. There are 15 hyenas per square mile, and 6 of the hyenas are endangered. That means $\frac{6}{15} = 0.4 = 40\%$ of all hyenas are in trouble. Going over to the pie chart, you find the actual number of endangered hyenas is

$$(6\%)(360{,}000 \text{ endangered animals}) = (0.06)(360{,}000) = 21{,}600.$$

Now you have the number and percentage of endangered hyenas. You must now ask yourself, "21,600 is 40% of what number?" In Mathspeak, this is

$$21{,}600 = (40\%)(n)$$
$$21{,}600 = 0.4n$$
$$54{,}000 = n$$

There are 54,000 hyenas on the savanna. In thousands, you would grid in 54.

14. **15**

You can whip out that freaky-deaky permutation of a factorial formula, but even that won't get you through this question cleanly. The best way might be to go low-tech: list out the different combinations. There aren't as many as you might think:

Using all four condiments: 1 possibility

Using only one condiment: 4 possibilities
because there are four condiments

Using three condiments: 4 possibilities (all three minus one of them)

Using two condiments: 6 possibilities (K-P, K-T, K-R, P-T, P-R, R-T)

Adding up all the possibilities gives you 15 possible combinations. There's your answer.

15. **60**

Here's where that funky permutation formula comes in. Because Ben is going to choose two toppings out of six, you have:

$$_nP_r = \frac{n!}{(n-r)!}$$
$$_nP_r = \frac{6!}{(6-2)!}$$
$$_nP_r = \frac{6!}{4!}$$
$$_nP_r = \frac{6 \times 5 \times 4 \times 3 \times 2 \times 1}{4 \times 3 \times 2 \times 1}$$
$$_nP_r = 6 \times 5$$
$$_nP_r = 30$$

But that covers only the toppings. There are two kinds of cones, so you must multiply 30 by 2 to show that all those different combinations could be placed on either a plain cone or a waffle cone. The correct answer is 60.

GEOMETRY

A BASIC REVIEW OF THE BASICS

Here's a quick review of the fundamental concepts and ideas of geometry. SAT questions assume you know these topics and will throw around basic geometry jargon, so you need to have the fundamentals down pat.

Points

A point is a way to describe a specific location in space. Below, the point B is pictured. Isn't it lovely?

$B_{\bullet}$

A point has no length or width. Though in the picture, point B is a black dot, in real life points take up no space. Points are useful for identifying specific locations but are not objects in themselves. They only appear as objects when drawn on a page.

Lines

A line is an infinite set of points assembled in a straight formation. A line has no thickness but is infinitely long in both directions. To form a line, take any two points, A and B, and draw a straight line through them. The resulting line is called line AB.

A line can be drawn through any two points.

Line Segments

A line segment is the portion of a line that lies between two points on that line—in this example, the portion between points A and B makes up a line segment. Whereas a line has infinite length, a line segment has a finite length. A line segment is named by the two points it lies between

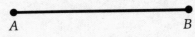

A line segment can be drawn between any two points.

Rays

Imagine a line and a line segment mating. The result is a ray, a cross between a line and a line segment. It extends infinitely in one direction but not in the other.

A ray is named by its endpoint and another point that it passes through.

Okay. Painless basic geometric knowledge: acquired. That was quick. Now on to the real meat and potatoes of the geometry that the SAT tests.

A NOTE ON NOTATION

The SAT uses standard geometric notation to indicate lines, line segments, rays, length, and congruence. Why is this a big deal? Because it makes interpreting questions and drawing figures more difficult. It's possible that if you don't know the notation, you won't know what the question is asking you to do. So here's a list of the correct notation. Memorize it.

What	Notation
Line AB	$\overleftrightarrow{AB}$
Line segment AB	$\overline{AB}$
Ray AB	$\overrightarrow{AB}$
Length of $\overline{AB}$	AB

Finally, you need to know the term *congruent*, which means "exactly the same" or "equal." The SAT may also test to see if you know the symbol that indicates congruence. To say that angle A is congruent to angle B, you'd write: $A \cong B$.

ANGLES AND LINES

An angle is a geometric figure consisting of two lines, rays, or line segments that share a common endpoint called a *vertex*:

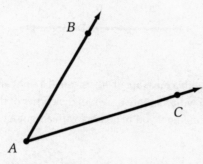

In the angle above, the vertex is point A. The angle can be called either angle CAB or angle BAC. The only rule for naming an angle is that the vertex must be the middle "initial" of the angle. The SAT may also refer to angles using symbols: $\angle A$.

Degrees

Angles are measured in degrees, which have nothing to do with Nelly or temperature. Geometric degrees are sometimes denoted by this little guy: °. There are 360° in a complete rotation around a point (that's why a circle has 360°).

Two Lines Meet in a Bar . . .

When two lines meet, they produce angles. And when two lines meet, they form four angles! That must be exhausting.

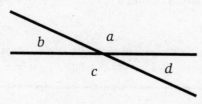

These aren't just any old four angles, either. Together, the angles encompass one full revolution around the point of intersection of the two lines. So, the four angles produced by two intersection lines total 360°: angle $a + b + c + d = 360°$.

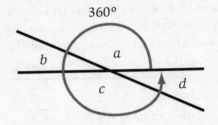

If you know the value of three of the four angles formed by intersecting lines, you can always find the value of the fourth.

Types of Angles

The different types of angles are named and categorized according to their number of degrees.

Zero Angles

A zero angle has, you guessed it, 0°. To visualize a zero angle, first picture two lines that form some angle greater than 0°. Then imagine one of the lines rotating toward the other until they both fall on the same line. The angle they create has shrunk from its original measure to 0°, forming a zero angle:

Right Angles

For some reason, an angle with a measure of 90° is called a right angle. For some other reason, right angles are symbolized with a square drawn in the corner of the angle. Whenever you see that reliable little square, you know you're dealing with a right angle.

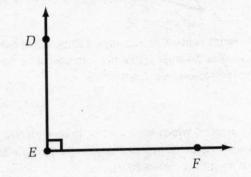

Right angles are extremely important on the SAT. They appear in math questions all the time. Knowing their special properties will help you solve right angle questions. We give you a detailed look at those properties a little later in this chapter. For now, just remember: *Always* be on the lookout for right angles on the SAT.

Straight Angles

An angle with a measure of 180° is called a straight angle. It looks just like a line. Don't confuse straight angles with zero angles, which look like a single ray.

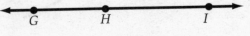

Acute and Obtuse Angles

An angle can also be classified according to whether its measure is greater or less than 90°. If an angle measures less than 90°, it's called an acute angle. If it measures more than 90°, it's called an obtuse angle. Right angles are neither acute nor obtuse. They're just right. In the picture below, $\angle ABC$ is acute, while $\angle DEF$ is obtuse.

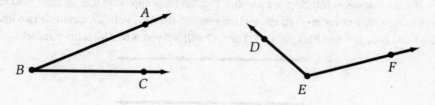

Complementary and Supplementary Angles

Special names are given to pairs of angles whose sums equal either 90° or 180°. Angles whose sum is 90° are called complementary angles, while angles whose sum is 180° are called supplementary angles.

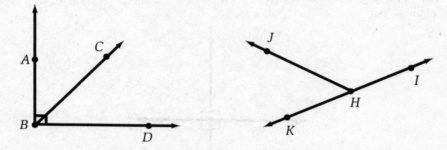

In the picture above, $\angle ABC$ and $\angle CBD$ are complementary, since together they make up a right angle. Angles $\angle JHK$ and $\angle JHI$ are supplementary, since they make up a straight line.

On the SAT, you'll have to use the rules of complementary and supplementary angles to figure out the degree measure of an angle.

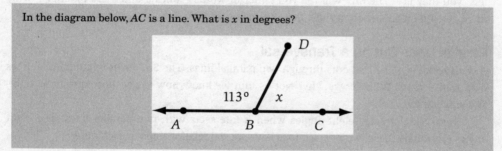

In the diagram below, AC is a line. What is x in degrees?

The picture tells you that $\angle ABD$ is 113°, but how many degrees is $\angle DBC$? Well, since you know that AC is a line, $\angle ABC$ must be a straight angle (meaning it equals 180°). So $\angle ABD$ and $\angle DBC$ are supplementary angles that add up to 180°. To find out the value of $\angle DBC$, you can simply take 180° and subtract 113°. $\angle DBC = 67°$.

Vertical Angles

When two lines (or line segments) intersect, the angles that lie opposite each other, called vertical angles, are *always* equal.

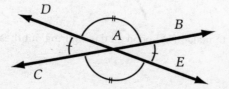

Angles ∠DAC and ∠BAE are vertical angles and are therefore equal. Angles ∠DAB and ∠CAE are also vertical (and equal) angles. We promise that the SAT will ask you at least one question involving vertical angles. Promise.

Parallel and Perpendicular Lines

Pairs of lines that never intersect are parallel. Parallel lines appear to line up right next to each other because they never meet in space. However, on the SAT, you can't assume two lines are parallel just because they look parallel. The SAT will tell you if two lines are parallel.

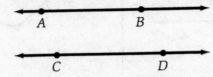

Lines (or segments) are perpendicular if their intersection forms a right angle. And if one of the angles formed by the intersection of two lines or segments is a right angle, then all four angles created will also be right angles. By the way, this also shows that the degree measurement of four angles formed by two intersecting lines will add up to 360°, since 90° + 90° + 90° + 90° = 360°.

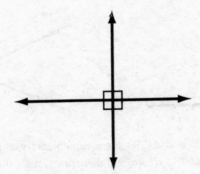

As with parallel lines, don't assume that lines on the SAT are perpendicular unless the SAT tells you they are. The SAT will tell you either in words ("lines a and b are parallel") or by using the little reliable box to show that the angles are 90°.

Parallel Lines Cut by a Transversal

A transversal is a line that cuts through two parallel lines. The SAT loves to cut parallel lines with transversals. Who knows why? Not us. But we know how to get those questions right, and you will too.

A transversal creates eight angles when it intersects with two parallel lines. The eight angles created by these two intersections have special relationships to each other.

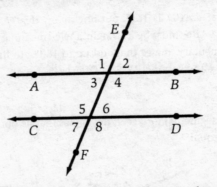

You now have a choice to make: (1) Spend all day figuring out these relationships, or (2) use our list.

Good choice:

- Angles 1, 4, 5, and 8 are equal to each other because they're vertical angles.
- Angles 2, 3, 6, and 7 are equal to each other because they're vertical angles.
- The sum of any two adjacent angles, such as 1 and 2 or 7 and 8, equals 180° because these are supplementary angles.

By using these three rules, you can figure out the degrees of angles that may seem unrelated. For example, since angles 1 and 2 sum to 180°, and since angles 2 and 7 are equal, the sum of angles 1 and 7 also equals 180°. The SAT will almost definitely include a question that asks you to solve for an angle whose measurement at first glance seems impossible to determine.

TRIANGLES

Triangles pop up all over the Math section. There are questions specifically about triangles, questions that ask about triangles inscribed in polygons and circles, and questions about triangles in coordinate geometry.

Three Sides, Four Fundamental Properties

Every triangle, no matter how special, follows four main rules.

1. Sum of the Interior Angles

If you were trapped on a deserted island with tons of SAT questions about triangles, this is the one rule you'd need to know:

The sum of the interior angles of a triangle is 180°.

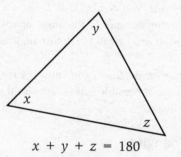

$$x + y + z = 180$$

If you know the measures of two of a triangle's angles, you'll always be able to find the third by subtracting the sum of the first two from 180.

2. Measure of an Exterior Angle

The exterior angle of a triangle is always supplementary to the interior angle with which it shares a vertex and equal to the sum of the measures of the remote interior angles. An exterior angle of a triangle is the angle formed by extending one of the sides of the triangle past a vertex. In the image below, d is the exterior angle.

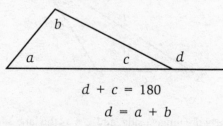

$$d + c = 180$$
$$d = a + b$$

Since d and c together form a straight angle, they are supplementary: $d + c = 180°$. According to the first rule of triangles, the three angles of a triangle always add up to $180°$, so $a + b + c = 180°$. Since $d + c = 180°$ and $a + b + c = 180°$, d must equal $a + b$.

3. Triangle Inequality Rule

If triangles got together to write a declaration of independence, they'd have a tough time, since one of their defining rules would be this:

The length of any side of a triangle will always be less than the sum of the lengths of the other two sides and greater than the difference of the lengths of the other two sides.

There you have it: Triangles are unequal by definition.

Take a look at the figure below:

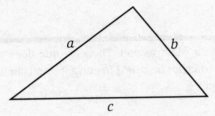

The triangle inequality rule says that $c - b < a < c + b$. The exact length of side a depends on the measure of the angle created by sides b and c. Witness this triangle:

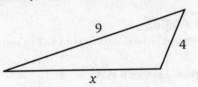

Using the triangle inequality rule, you can tell that $9 - 4 < x < 9 + 4$, or $5 < x < 13$. The exact value of x depends on the measure of the angle opposite side x. If this angle is large (close to $180°$) then x will be large (close to 13). If this angle is small (close to $0°$), then x will be small (close to 5).

The triangle inequality rule means that if you know the length of two sides of any triangle, you will always know the range of possible side lengths for the third side. On some SAT triangle questions, that's all you'll need.

4. Proportionality of Triangles

Here's the final fundamental triangle property. This one explains the relationships between the angles of a triangle and the lengths of the triangle's sides.

In every triangle, the longest side is opposite the largest angle and the shortest side is opposite the smallest angle.

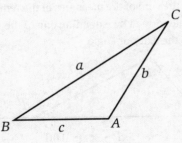

In this figure, side a is clearly the longest side, and $\angle A$ is the largest angle. Meanwhile, side c is the shortest side, and $\angle C$ is the smallest angle. So $c < b < a$ and $C < B < A$. This proportionality of side lengths and angle measures holds true for all triangles.

See if you can use this rule to solve the question below:

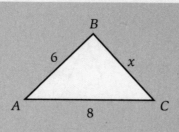

What is one possible value of x if angle $C < A < B$?

(A)   1
(B)   6
(C)   7
(D)   10
(E)   15

According to the proportionality of triangles rule, the longest side of a triangle is opposite the largest angle. Likewise, the shortest side of a triangle is opposite the smallest angle. The largest angle in triangle ABC is $\angle B$, which is opposite the side of length 8. The smallest angle in triangle ABC is $\angle C$, which is opposite the side of length 6. This means that the third side, of length x, measures between 6 and 8 units in length. The only choice that fits the criteria is 7. **C** is the correct answer.

Special Triangles

Special triangles are "special" not because they get to follow fewer rules than other triangles but because they get to follow more. Each type of special triangle has its own special name: *isosceles*, *equilateral*, and *right*. Knowing the properties of each will help you tremendously, humongously, a lot, on the SAT.

But first we have to take a second to explain the markings we use to describe the properties of special triangles. The little arcs and ticks drawn in the figure below show that this triangle has two sides of equal length and three equal angle pairs. The sides that each have one tick through them are equal, as are the sides that each have two ticks through them. The angles with one little arc are equal to each other, the angles with two little arcs are equal to each other, and the angles with three little arcs are all equal to each other.

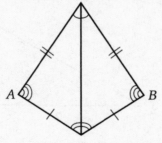

Isosceles Triangles

In ancient Greece, Isosceles was the god of triangles. His legs were of perfectly equal length and formed two opposing congruent angles when he stood up straight. Isosceles triangles share many of the same properties, naturally. An isosceles triangle has two sides of equal length, and those two sides are opposite congruent angles. These equal angles are usually called base angles. In the isosceles triangle below, side $a = b$ and $\angle A = \angle B$:

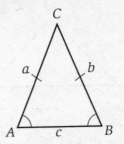

If you know the value of one of the base angles in an isosceles triangle, you can figure out all the angles. Let's say you've got an isosceles triangle with a base angle of 35°. Since you know isosceles triangles have two congruent base angles by definition, you know that the other base angle is also 35°. All three angles in a triangle must always add up to 180°, right? Correct. That means you can also figure out the value of the third angle: 180° – 35° – 35° = 110°.

Equilateral Triangles

An equilateral triangle has three equal sides and three congruent 60° angles.

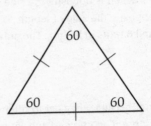

Based on the proportionality rule, if a triangle has three equal sides, that triangle must also have three equal angles. Similarly, if you know that a triangle has three equal angles, then you know it also has three equal sides.

Right Triangles

A triangle that contains a right angle is called a right triangle. The side opposite the right angle is called the hypotenuse. The other two sides are called legs. The angles opposite the legs of a right triangle are complementary (they add up to 90°).

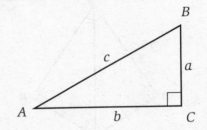

In the figure above, $\angle C$ is the right angle (as indicated by the box drawn in the angle), side c is the hypotenuse, and sides a and b are the legs.

If triangles are an SAT favorite, then right triangles are SAT darlings. In other words, know these rules. And know the Pythagorean theorem.

The Pythagorean Theorem

The Greeks spent a lot of time reading, eating grapes, and riding around on donkeys. They also enjoyed the occasional mathematical epiphany. One day, Pythagoras discovered that the sum of the squares of the two legs of a right triangle is equal to the square of the hypotenuse. "Eureka!" he said, and the SAT had a new topic to test.

Here's the Pythagorean theorem: In a right triangle, $a^2 + b^2 = c^2$:

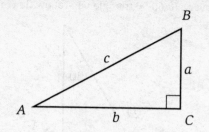

where c is the length of the hypotenuse, and a and b are the lengths of the two legs.

The Pythagorean theorem means that if you know the measures of two sides of a right triangle, you can *always* find the third. "Eureka!" you say.

Pythagorean Triples

Because right triangles obey the Pythagorean theorem, only a specific few have side lengths that are all integers. For example, a right triangle with legs of length 3 and 5 has a hypotenuse of length $\sqrt{3^2 + 5^2} = \sqrt{9 + 25} = \sqrt{34} = 5.83$.

The few sets of three integers that do obey the Pythagorean theorem and can therefore be the lengths of the sides of a right triangle are called Pythagorean triples. Here are some common ones:

$$\{3, 4, 5\}$$

$$\{5, 12, 13\}$$

$$\{7, 24, 25\}$$

$$\{8, 15, 17\}$$

In addition to these Pythagorean triples, you should also watch out for their multiples. For example, $\{6, 8, 10\}$ is a Pythagorean triple, since it is a multiple of $\{3, 4, 5\}$.

The SAT is full of right triangles whose side lengths are Pythagorean triples. Study the ones above and their multiples. Identifying Pythagorean triples will help you cut the amount of time you spend doing calculations. In fact, you may not have to do any calculations if you get these down cold.

Extra-Special Right Triangles

Right triangles are pretty special in their own right. But there are two *extra*-special right triangles. They are 30-60-90 triangles and 45-45-90 triangles, and they appear all the time on the SAT.

In fact, knowing the rules of these two special triangles will open up all sorts of time-saving possibilities for you on the test. Very, very often, instead of having to work out the Pythagorean theorem, you'll be able to apply the standard side ratios of either of these two types of triangles, cutting out all the time you need to spend calculating.

30-60-90 Triangles

The guy who named 30-60-90 triangles didn't have much of an imagination. These triangles have angles of 30° , 60° , and 90° . What's so special about that? This: The side lengths of 30-60-90 triangles always follow a specific pattern. Suppose the short leg, opposite the 30° angle, has length x. Then the hypotenuse has length $2x$, and the long leg, opposite the 60° angle, has length $x\sqrt{3}$. The sides of every 30-60-90 triangle will follow this ratio of $1: \sqrt{3}: 2$.

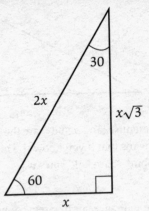

This constant ratio means that if you know the length of *just one* side in the triangle, you'll immediately be able to calculate the lengths of all the sides. If, for example, you know that the side opposite the 30° angle is 2 meters long, then by using the $1: \sqrt{3}: 2$ ratio, you can work out that the hypotenuse is 4 meters long, and the leg opposite the 60° angle is $2\sqrt{3}$ meters.

And there's another amazing thing about 30-60-90 triangles. Two of these triangles joined at the side opposite the 60° angle will form an equilateral triangle.

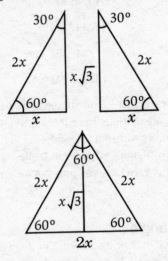

Here's why you need to pay attention to this extra-special feature of 30-60-90 triangles. If you know the side length of an equilateral triangle, you can figure out the triangle's height: Divide the side length by two and multiply it by $\sqrt{3}$. Similarly, if you drop a "perpendicular bisector" (this is the term the SAT uses) from any vertex of an equilateral triangle to the base on the far side, you'll have cut that triangle into two 30-60-90 triangles.

Knowing how equilateral and 30-60-90 triangles relate is incredibly helpful on triangle, polygon, and even solids questions on the SAT. Quite often, you'll be able to break down these large shapes into a number of special triangles, and then you can use the side ratios to figure out whatever you need to know.

45-45-90 Triangles

A 45-45-90 triangle is a triangle with two angles of 45° and one right angle. It's sometimes called an isosceles right triangle, since it's both isosceles and right. Like the 30-60-90 triangle, the lengths of the sides of a 45-45-90 triangle also follow a specific pattern. If the legs are of length x (the legs will always be equal), then the hypotenuse has length $x\sqrt{2}$:

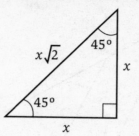

Know this $1:1:\sqrt{2}$ ratio for 45-45-90 triangles. It will save you time and may even save your butt.

Also, just as two 30-60-90 triangles form an equilateral triangles, two 45-45-90 triangles form a square. We explain the colossal importance of this fact when we cover polygons a little later in this chapter.

Similar Triangles

Similar triangles have the same shape but not necessarily the same size. Or, if you prefer more math-geek jargon, two triangles are "similar" if the ratio of the lengths of their corresponding sides is constant (which you now know means that their corresponding angles must be congruent). Take a look at a few similar triangles:

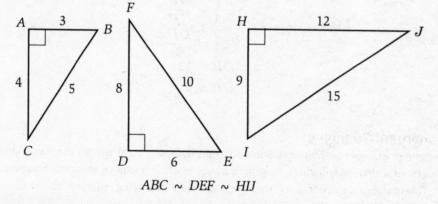

$$ABC \sim DEF \sim HIJ$$

As you may have assumed from the figure above, the symbol for "is similar to" is $\sim$. So, if triangle ABC is similar to triangle DEF, we write $ABC \sim DEF$.

There are two crucial facts about similar triangles.

- Corresponding angles of similar triangles are identical.
- Corresponding sides of similar triangles are proportional.

For $ABC \sim DEF$, the corresponding angles are $\angle A = \angle D$, $\angle B = \angle E$, $\angle C = \angle F$. The corresponding sides are $^{AB}/_{DE} = {}^{BC}/_{EF} = {}^{CA}/_{FD}$.

The SAT usually tests similarity by presenting you with a single triangle that contains a line segment parallel to one base. This line segment creates a second, smaller, similar triangle. In the figure below, for example, line segment *DE* is parallel to *CB*, and triangle *ABC* is similar to triangle *AE*.

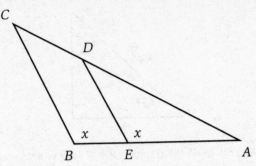

After presenting you with a diagram like the one above, the SAT will ask a question like this:

If $CB = 6$ and $AD = \frac{2}{3}AC$, what is DE?

Notice that this question doesn't tell you outright that *DE* and *CB* are parallel. But it does tell you that both lines form the same angle, $x°$, when they intersect with *BA*, so you should be able to figure out that they're parallel. And once you see that they're parallel, you should immediately recognize that $ABC \sim AED$ and that the corresponding sides of the two triangles are in constant proportion. The question tells you what this proportion is when it tells you that $AD = {}^2/_3AC$. To solve for *DE*, plug it into the proportion along with *CB*:

$$\frac{2}{3} = \frac{DE}{CB}$$
$$\frac{2}{3} = \frac{DE}{6}$$
$$3 \times DE = 12$$
$$DE = 4$$

Congruent Triangles

Congruent triangles are identical. Some SAT questions may state directly that two triangles are congruent. Others may include congruent triangles without explicit mention, however.

Two triangles are congruent if they meet any of the following criteria:

1. All the corresponding sides of the two triangles are equal. This is known as the Side-Side-Side (SSS) method of determining congruency.

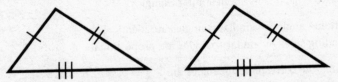

2. The corresponding sides of each triangle are equal, and the mutual angles between those corresponding sides are also equal. This is known as the Side-Angle-Side (SAS) method of determining congruency.

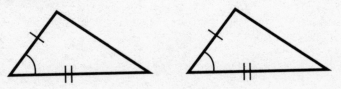

3. The two triangles share two equal corresponding angles and also share any pair of corresponding sides. This is known as the Angle-Side-Angle (ASA) method of determining congruency

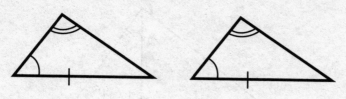

Perimeter of a Triangle

The perimeter of a triangle is equal to the sum of the lengths of the triangle's three sides. If a triangle has sides of lengths 4, 6, and 9, then its perimeter is $4 + 6 + 9 = 19$. Easy. Done and done.

Area of a Triangle

The formula for the area of a triangle is

$$A = \frac{1}{2}bh$$

where b is the length of a base of the triangle, and h is height (also called the altitude). The heights of a few triangles are pictured below with their altitudes drawn in as dotted lines.

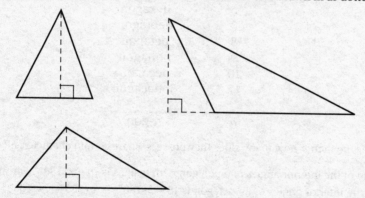

We said "a base" above instead of "the base" because you can actually use any of the three sides of the triangle as the base; a triangle has no particular side that has to be the base. You get to choose.

The SAT may test the area of a triangle in a few ways. It might just tell you the altitude and the length of the base, in which case you could just plug the numbers into the formula. But you probably won't get such an easy question. It's more likely that you'll have to find the altitude, using other tools and techniques from plane geometry. For example, try to find the area of the triangle below:

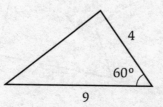

To find the area of this triangle, draw in the altitude from the base (of length 9) to the opposite vertex. Notice that now you have two triangles, and one of them (the smaller one on the right) is a 30-60-90 triangle.

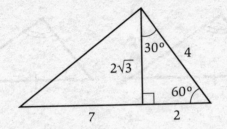

The hypotenuse of this 30-60-90 triangle is 4, so according to the ratio $1 : \sqrt{3} : 2$, the short side must be 2, and the medium side, which is also the altitude of the original triangle, is $2\sqrt{3}$. *Now* you can plug the base and altitude into the formula to find the area of the original triangle: $^{1}/_{2}bh = {}^{1}/_{2}(9)(2\sqrt{3}) = 9\sqrt{3}$.

POLYGONS

A polygon is a two-dimensional figure with three or more straight sides. (So triangles are actually a type of polygon.) Polygons are named according to the number of sides they have.

Number of Sides	Name
3	triangle
4	quadrilateral
5	pentagon
6	hexagon
7	heptagon
8	octagon
9	nonagon
10	decagon
12	dodecagon
n	n-gon

All polygons, no matter how many sides they possess, share certain characteristics:

- The sum of the interior angles of a polygon with n sides is $(n-2)\,180°$. For instance, the sum of the interior angles of an octagon is $(8-2)\,180° = 6(180°) = 1080°$.
- The sum of the exterior angles of any polygon is $360°$.
- The perimeter of a polygon is the sum of the lengths of its sides. The perimeter of the hexagon below is $5 + 4 + 3 + 8 + 6 + 9 = 35$.

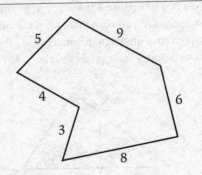

Regular Polygons

The polygon whose perimeter you just calculated was an irregular polygon. But most of the polygons on the SAT are regular: Their sides are of equal length and their angles congruent. Neither of these conditions can exist without the other. If the sides are all equal, the angles will all be congruent, and vice versa. In the diagram below, you'll see, from left to right, a regular pentagon, a regular octagon, and a square (also known as a regular quadrilateral):

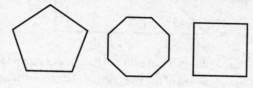

Quadrilaterals

Good news: Most polygons on the SAT have just four sides. You won't have to tangle with any dodecahedrons on the SAT you take. But this silver cloud actually has a dark lining: There are *five* different types of quadrilaterals that pop up on the test. These five quadrilaterals are trapezoids, parallelograms, rectangles, rhombuses, and squares.

Trapezoids

A trapezoid may sound like a new *Star Wars* character. Certainly, it would be less annoying than Jar Jar Binks. But it's actually the name of a quadrilateral with one pair of parallel sides and one pair of nonparallel sides.

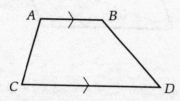

In this trapezoid, *AB* is parallel to *CD* (shown by the arrow marks), whereas *AC* and *BD* are not parallel.

The formula for the area of a trapezoid is

$$A = \frac{s_1 + s_2}{2} h$$

where s_1 and s_2 are the lengths of the parallel sides (also called the bases of the trapezoid), and h is the height. In a trapezoid, the height is the perpendicular distance from one base to the other.

To find the area of a trapezoid on the SAT, you'll often have to use your knowledge of triangles. Try to find the area of the trapezoid pictured below:

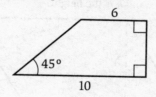

The question tells you the length of the bases of this trapezoid, 6 and 10. But to find the area, you first need to find the height. To do that, split the trapezoid into a rectangle and a 45-45-90 triangle by drawing in the height.

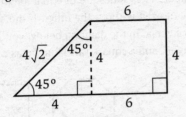

Once, you've drawn in the height, you can split the base that's equal to 10 into two parts: The base of the rectangle is 6, and the leg of the triangle is 4. Since the triangle is 45-45-90, the two legs must be equal. This leg, though, is also the height of the trapezoid. So the height of the trapezoid is 4. Now you can plug the numbers into the formula:

$$A = \frac{6+10}{2}(4) = 8(4) = 32$$

Parallelogram

A parallelogram is a quadrilateral whose opposite sides are parallel.

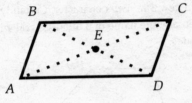

In a parallelogram,

- Opposite sides are equal in length: $BC = AD$ and $AB = DC$.
- Opposite angles are equal: $\angle ABC = \angle ADC$ and $\angle BAD = \angle BCD$.
- Adjacent angles are supplementary: $\angle ABC + \angle BCD = 180°$.
- The diagonals bisect (split) each other: $BE = ED$ and $AE = EC$.
- One diagonal splits a parallelogram into two congruent triangles: $\triangle ABD = \triangle BCD$.
- Two diagonals split a parallelogram into two pairs of congruent triangles:
  $\triangle AEB = \triangle DEC$ and $\triangle BEC = \triangle AED$.

The area of a parallelogram is given by the formula

$$\text{Area} = bh$$

where b is the length of the base, and h is the height.

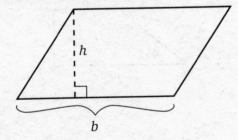

Rectangles

A rectangle is a quadrilateral in which the opposite sides are parallel, and the interior angles are all right angles. Another way to look at rectangles is as parallelograms in which the angles are all right angles. As with parallelograms, the opposite sides of a rectangle are equal.

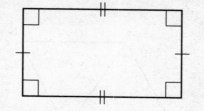

The formula for the area of a rectangle is

$$A = bh$$

where b is the length of the base, and h is the height.

The diagonals of a rectangle are always equal to each other. And one diagonal through the rectangle cuts the rectangle into two equal right triangles. In the figure below, the diagonal BD cuts rectangle $ABCD$ into congruent right triangles ABD and BCD.

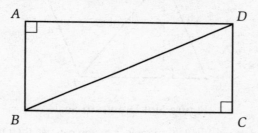

Since the diagonal of the rectangle forms right triangles that include the diagonal and two sides of the rectangle, if you know two of these values, you can always calculate the third with the Pythagorean theorem. If you know the side lengths of the rectangle, you can calculate the diagonal. If you know the diagonal and one side length, you can calculate the other side. Also, keep in mind that the diagonal might cut the rectangle into a 30-60-90 triangle. That would make your calculating job even easier.

Rhombus

A rhombus is a specialized parallelogram in which all four sides are of equal length.

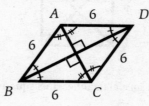

In a rhombus,

- All four sides are equal: $AD = DC = CB = BA$.
- The diagonals bisect each other and form perpendicular lines (but note that the diagonals are not equal in length).
- The diagonals bisect the vertex angles ($\angle ADB = \angle CDB$, $\angle DCA = \angle BCA$).

The formula for the area of a rhombus is

$$A = bh$$

where b is the length of the base and h is the height.

To find the area of a rhombus on the SAT (you guessed it), you'll probably have to split it into triangles:

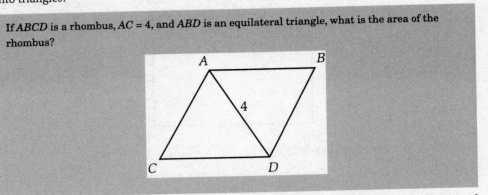

If $ABCD$ is a rhombus, $AC = 4$, and ABD is an equilateral triangle, what is the area of the rhombus?

Since ABD is an equilateral triangle, the length of each side of the rhombus must be 4, and angles ADB and ABD are 60°. All you have to do is find the height of the rhombus. Draw an altitude from A to DC to create a 30-60-90 triangle.

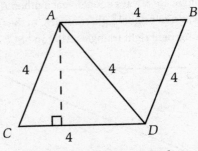

Figure Not Drawn to Scale

Since the hypotenuse of the 30-60-90 triangle is 4, you can use the ratio $1 : \sqrt{3} : 2$ to calculate that the length of this altitude is $2\sqrt{3}$. The area formula for a rhombus is bh, so the area of this rhombus is $4 \times 2\sqrt{3} = 8\sqrt{3}$.

Square
A square combines the special features of the rectangle and rhombus: All its angles are 90°, and all four of its sides are equal in length.

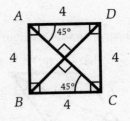

The square has two more crucial special qualities. In a square,

- Diagonals bisect each other at right angles and are equal in length.
- Diagonals bisect the vertex angles to create 45° angles. (This means that one diagonal will cut the square into two 45-45-90 triangles, while *two* diagonals break the square into *four* 45-45-90 triangles.)

The formula for the area of a square is

$$A = s^2$$

where s is the length of a side of the square.

Because a diagonal drawn into the square forms two congruent 45-45-90 triangles, if you know the length of one side of the square, you can always calculate the length of the diagonal:

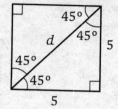

Since d is the hypotenuse of the 45-45-90 triangle that has legs of length 5, according to the ratio $1:1:\sqrt{2}$, you know that $d = s\sqrt{2}$.

Similarly, if you know the length of the diagonal, you can calculate the length of the sides of the square.

CIRCLES

A circle is the collection of points equidistant from a given point, called the *center*. A circle is named after its center point. The distance from the center to any point on the circle is called the radius, (r), the most important measurement in a circle. If you know a circle's radius, you can figure out all its other characteristics. The diameter (d) of a circle is twice as long as the radius $(d = 2r)$ and stretches between endpoints on the circle, passing through the center. A chord also extends from endpoint to endpoint on the circle, but it does not necessarily pass through the center. In the figure below, point C is the center of the circle, r is the radius, and AB is a chord.

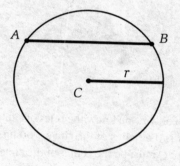

Tangent Lines

Tangents are lines that intersect a circle at only one point. You can bet that the SAT will make sure to cram at least one tangent question into every test.

Just like everything else in geometry, tangent lines are defined by certain fixed rules. Know these rules, and you'll be able to handle anything the SAT throws at you. Here's the first: A radius whose endpoint is the intersection point of the tangent line and the circle is always perpendicular to the tangent line. See?

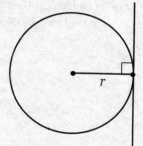

And the second rule: Every point in space outside the circle can extend exactly two tangent lines to the circle. The distance from the origin of the two tangents to the points of tangency are always equal. In the figure below, $XY = XZ$.

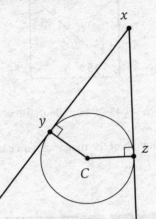

Tangents and Triangles

Tangent lines are most likely to appear in conjunction with triangles.

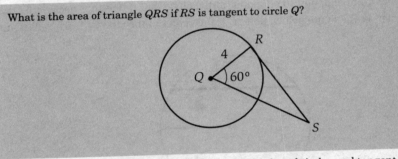

What is the area of triangle QRS if RS is tangent to circle Q?

You can answer this question only if you know the rules of circles and tangent lines. The question doesn't tell you that QR is the radius of the circle; you just have to know it. Because the circle is named circle Q, point Q must be the center of the circle, and any line drawn from the center to the edge of the circle is the radius. The question also doesn't tell you that QR is perpendicular to RS. You have to know that they're perpendicular because QR is a radius, RS is a tangent, and they meet at the same point.

If you know how to deduce those key facts about this circle, then the actual math in the question is simple. Since QR and RS are perpendicular, and angle RQS is 60°, triangle QRS is a 30-60-90 triangle. The image tells you that side QR, the side opposite the 30° angle equals 4. Side QR is the height of the triangle. To calculate the area, you just have to figure out which of the other two sides is the base. Since the height and base of the triangle must be perpendicular to each other, side RS must be the base. To find RS, use the $1 : \sqrt{3} : 2$ ratio. RS is the side opposite 60°, so it's the $\sqrt{3}$ side: $RS = 4\sqrt{3}$. The area of triangle QRS is $^{1}/_{2}(4)(4\sqrt{3}) = 8\sqrt{3}$.

Central Angles and Inscribed Angles

An angle whose vertex is the center of the circle is called a *central angle*.

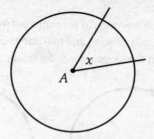

The degree of the circle (the slice of pie) cut by a central angle is equal to the measure of the angle. If a central angle is 25°, then it cuts a 25° arc in the circle.

An inscribed angle is an angle formed by two chords originating from a single point.

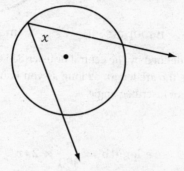

An inscribed angle will always cut out an arc in the circle that is *twice* the size of the degree of the inscribed angle. If an inscribed angle has a degree of 40, it will cut an arc of 80° in the circle.

If an inscribed angle and a central angle cut out the same arc in a circle, the central angle will be twice as large as the inscribed angle.

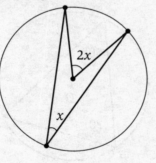

Circumference of a Circle

The circumference is the perimeter of the circle. The formula for circumference of a circle is

$$C = 2\pi r$$

where r is the radius. The formula can also be written $C = \pi d$, where d is the diameter. Try to find the circumference of the circle below:

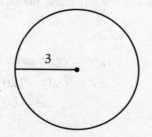

Plugging the radius into the formula, $C = 2\pi r = 2\pi\,(3) = 6\pi$.

Arc Length

An arc is a *part* of a circle's circumference. An arc contains two endpoints and all the points on the circle between the endpoints. By picking any two points on a circle, two arcs are created: a major arc, which is by definition the longer arc, and a minor arc, the shorter one.

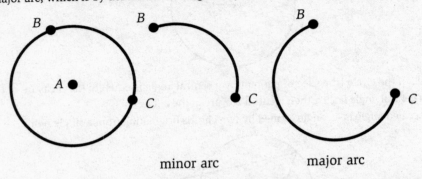

minor arc   major arc

Since the degree of an arc is defined by the central or inscribed angle that intercepts the arc's endpoints, you can calculate the arc length as long as you know the circle's radius and the measure of either the central or inscribed angle.

The arc length formula is

$$\text{arc length} = \frac{n}{360} \times 2\pi r$$

where n is the measure of the degree of the arc, and r is the radius.

Here's the sort of question the SAT might ask:

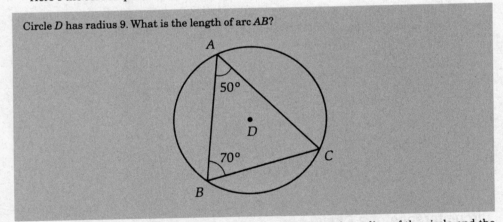

Circle D has radius 9. What is the length of arc AB?

In order to figure out the length of arc AB, you need to know the radius of the circle and the measure of $\angle C$, the inscribed angle that intercepts the endpoints of AB. The question tells you the radius of the circle, but it throws you a little curveball by not providing you with the measure of $\angle C$. Instead, the question puts $\angle C$ in a triangle and tells you the measures of the other two angles in the triangle. Like we said, only a little curveball: You can easily figure out the measure of $\angle C$ because, as you (better) know, the three angles of a triangle add up to 180°.

$$\angle c = 180° - (50° + 70°)$$
$$\angle c = 180° - 120°$$
$$\angle c = 60°$$

Since angle c is an inscribed angle, arc AB must be 120°. Now you can plug these values into the formula for arc length:

$$AB = \frac{120}{360} \times 2\pi9$$
$$AB = \frac{1}{3} \times 18\pi$$
$$AB = 6\pi$$

Area of a Circle

If you know the radius of a circle, you can figure out its area. The formula for area is

$$\text{Area} = \pi r^2$$

where r is the radius. So when you need to find the area of a circle, your real goal is to figure out the radius.

Area of a Sector

A sector of a circle is the area enclosed by a central angle and the circle itself. It's shaped like a slice of pizza. The shaded region in the figure below is a sector:

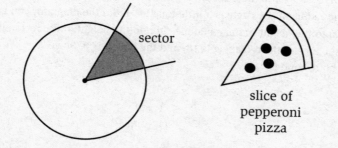

sector

slice of
pepperoni
pizza

There are no analogies on the SAT anymore, but here's one anyway: The area of a sector is related to the area of a circle just as the length of an arc is related to the circumference. To find the area of a sector, find what fraction of 360° the sector makes up and multiply this fraction by the area of the circle.

$$\text{Area of Sector} = \frac{n}{360} \times \pi r^2$$

where n is the measure of the central angle that forms the boundary of the sector, and r is the radius.

Try to find the area of the sector in the figure below:

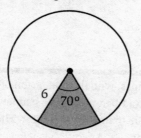

The sector is bounded by a 70° central angle in a circle whose radius is 6. Using the formula, the area of the sector is

$$A = \frac{70}{360} \times \pi(6)^2 = \frac{7}{36} \times 36\pi = 7\pi$$

Polygons and Circles

We've talked already about triangles in circle problems. But all kinds of polygons have also been known to make cameos on SAT circle questions. Here's an example:

What is the length of minor arc *BE* if the area of rectangle *ABCD* is 18?

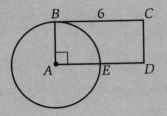

To find the length of minor arc *BE*, you have to know two things: the radius of the circle and the measure of the central angle that intersects the circle at points *B* and *E*. Because *ABCD* is a rectangle, and rectangles only have right angles, figuring out the measure of the central angle is simple. ∠*BAD* is 90°, so the measure of the central angle is 90°.

Finding the radius of the circle is a little tougher. From the diagram, you can see that the radius is equal to the height of the rectangle. To find the height of the rectangle, you can use the fact that the area of the rectangle is 18, and the length is 6. Since A = *bh*, and you know the values of both *a* and *b*,

$$h = A \div b$$
$$= 18 \div 6$$
$$= 3$$

Now that you've got the radius and measure of the angle, plug them into the arc length formula to find the length of minor arc *BE*.

$$BE = \frac{90}{360} \times 2\pi(3)$$
$$BE = \frac{1}{4} \times 6\pi$$
$$BE = \frac{6\pi}{4}$$
$$BE = \frac{3\pi}{2}$$

SOLID AS A ROCK

Solids are three-dimensional shapes, with the dimension of depth added to length and height. With solids, there's good news and bad news. The bad news is that solids can be difficult to visualize. But the good news more than makes up for it: The only solids on the SAT are cubes, rectangular solids, and right cylinders. Learn to visualize these three shapes now, before the test, and you'll be fine.

Rectangular Solids

A rectangular solid is a prism with a rectangular base and edges that are perpendicular to its base. It looks a lot like a cardboard box.

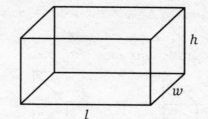

A rectangular solid has three important dimensions: length (l), width (w), and height (h). If you know these three measurements, you can find the solid's volume, surface area, and diagonal length.

Volume of a Rectangular Solid

The formula for the volume of a rectangular solid takes the formula for area of a rectangle and adds another dimension. The area of a rectangle is $A = lh$ (area equals length times height). The formula for the volume of a rectangular solid adds on width:

$$\text{Volume} = lwh$$

Here's a good old-fashioned example:

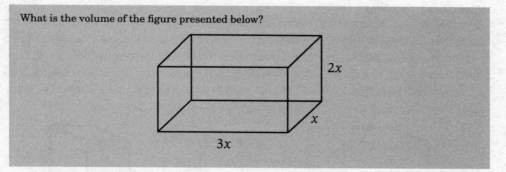

What is the volume of the figure presented below?

Just plug the values into the volume formula and you're good to go: $V = (3x)(2x)(x) = 6x^3$.

Surface Area of a Rectangular Solid

The surface area of a solid is the area of its outermost skin. In the case of rectangular solids, imagine a cardboard box all closed up. The surface of that closed box is made of six rectangles: The sum of the areas of the six rectangles is the surface area of the box. To make things even easier, the six rectangles come in three congruent pairs. We've marked the congruent pairs by shades of gray in the image below: One pair is clear, one pair is light gray, and one pair is dark gray.

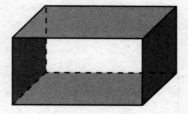

Two faces have areas of $l \times w$, two faces have areas of $l \times h$, and two faces have areas of $w \times h$. The surface area of the entire solid is the sum of the areas of the congruent pairs:

$$\text{Surface Area} = 2lw + 2lh + 2wh$$

Wanna practice? Alright. What's the surface area of this guy?

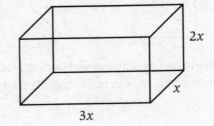

Plug in. Plug in. Plug in.

$$
\begin{aligned}
\text{Surface Area} &= 2lw + 2lh + 2wh \\
&= 2(3x)(x) + 2(3x)(2x) + 2(x)(2x) \\
&= 6x^2 + 12x^2 + 4x^2 \\
&= 22x^2
\end{aligned}
$$

Meat Cleaver Problems

The SAT won't just hand you surface area questions on a silver platter. It'll make you work for them. One of the ways the SAT likes to make you work goes like this. A question will describe a solid, give you all of its measurements, and then tell you that the box has been cut in half. You'll then have to find the combined surface area of the two new boxes. For example, pictured below is a rectangular solid that has a length of 8, a depth of 4, and a height of 4. Then, out of the blue, a giant cleaver comes down and cuts the solid into two cubes.

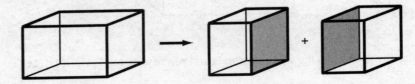

As you can see from the diagram, when the rectangle was cut in two, two new surfaces suddenly appeared (these are the darkened surfaces). But notice that the total volume of the two cubes has remained the same. So here's a rule: *Whenever a solid is cut into smaller pieces, its surface area increases, but its volume is unchanged.* The SAT loves to test this little factoid.

Diagonal Length of a Rectangular Solid

The diagonal of a rectangular solid, d, is the line segment whose endpoints are opposite corners of the solid. Every rectangular solid has four diagonals, each with the same length, that connect each pair of opposite vertices. Here's one diagonal drawn in:

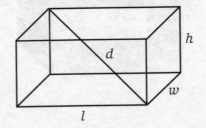

It's possible that an SAT question will test to see if you can find the length of a diagonal. Now you can:

$$d = \sqrt{l^2 + w^2 + h^2}$$

where l is the length, w is the width, and h is the height. The formula is like a pumped up Vin Diesel version of the Pythagorean theorem. Check it out in action:

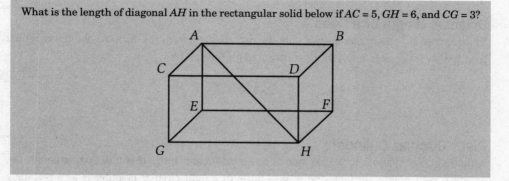

What is the length of diagonal AH in the rectangular solid below if $AC = 5$, $GH = 6$, and $CG = 3$?

The question gives the length, width, and height of the rectangular solid, so you can just plug those numbers into the formula:

$$AH = \sqrt{5^2 + 6^2 + 3^2} = \sqrt{25 + 36 + 9} = \sqrt{70}$$

Cubes

A cube is a square brought into 3-D. The length, width, and height of a cube are equal, and each of its six faces is a square.

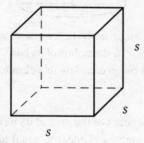

Volume of a Cube

The formula for finding the volume of a cube is essentially the same as the formula for the volume of a rectangular volume. However, since a cube's length, width, and height are all equal, the formula for the volume of a cube is

$$\text{Volume of a Cube} = s^3$$

where s is the length of one edge of the cube.

Surface Area of a Cube

Since a cube is just a rectangular solid whose sides are all equal, the formula for finding the surface area of a cube is the same as the formula for finding the surface area of a rectangular solid, except with s substituted in for l, w, and h:

$$\text{Surface Area of a Cube} = 6s^2$$

Diagonal Length of a Cube

The formula for the diagonal of a cube is also adapted from the formula for the diagonal length of a rectangular solid, with s substituted for l, w, and h.

$$\sqrt{3s^2} = s\sqrt{3}$$

Right Circular Cylinders

A right circular cylinder looks like one of those cardboard things that toilet paper comes on, except it isn't hollow. In fact, one way to think of a right circular cylinder is as a rectangle curved around so that its ends meet.

A right circular cylinder has two connected congruent circular bases and looks like this:

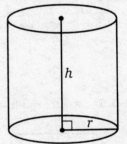

The height of a cylinder, h, is the length of the line segment whose endpoints are the centers of the bases. The radius of a cylinder, r, is the radius of its base. For the SAT, all you need to know about a right circular cylinder is how to calculate its volume.

Volume of a Cylinder

The volume of a cylinder is the product of the area of its base and its height. Because a cylinder has a circular base, the volume of a cylinder is equal to the area of the circle that is the base times the height:

$$\text{Volume of a Cylinder} = \pi r^2 h$$

Try to find the volume of the cylinder below:

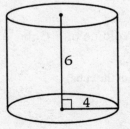

This cylinder has a radius of 4 and a height of 6. Using the volume formula,

$$\text{Volume} = \pi(4)^2(6) = 96\pi$$

Sketchy Word Problems

The SAT has been known to ask word problems about solids. Because solids are so difficult to visualize, these problems can seem brutally difficult. So here's the rule: *Always sketch out what the question is describing.* Once you see what the question's talking about, you seldom have to do much more than plug the right numbers into the right equation.

GEOMETRIC VISUALIZATIONS

Geometric-visualization questions give you an image on paper and ask you to twist or flip it in your mind.

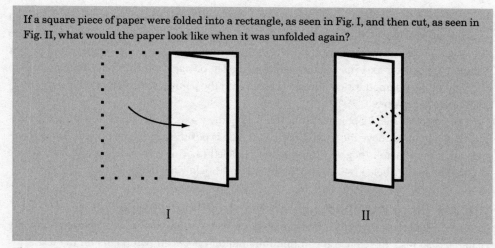

If a square piece of paper were folded into a rectangle, as seen in Fig. I, and then cut, as seen in Fig. II, what would the paper look like when it was unfolded again?

I   II

There are no formulas on these types of questions, no surefire method of attack. All we're really doing is warning you that they're lurking out there, and telling you to draw a sketch *before* looking at the answer choices. The answer, incidentally, is

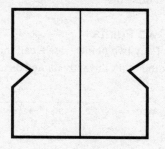

COORDINATE GEOMETRY

Coordinate geometry is the study of geometric shapes on the coordinate plane. If you think the coordinate plane is a ferocious type of new jet fighter, don't worry. We're about to clear this all up for you.

The Coordinate Plane

The coordinate plane is where all the magic happens. It's the space in which coordinate geometry exists. Pretty snazzy.

Every point on a coordinate plane can be mapped by using two perpendicular number lines. The x-axis defines the space from left to right. The y-axis defines the space up and down. And the two meet at a point called the origin.

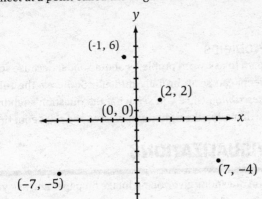

Every point on the plane has two coordinates. Because it's the center of the plane, the origin gets the coordinates (0, 0). The coordinates of all other points indicate how far they are from the origin. These coordinates are written in the form (x, y). The x-coordinate is the point's location along the x-axis (its distance either to the left or right of the origin). If the point is to the right of the origin, the x-coordinate is positive. If the point is to the left of the y-axis, the x-coordinate is negative.

The y-coordinate of a point is its location along the y-axis (either up or down from the origin). If the point is above the x-axis, its y-coordinate is positive, and if the point is below the x-axis, its y-coordinate is negative. So the point labeled (2, 2) is 2 to the right and 2 above the origin. The point labeled (–7, –5) is 7 to the left and 5 below the origin.

Are We There Yet? Distance on the Coordinate Plane

The SAT tests to see if you can find the distance between any two points on the coordinate plane. It also tests to see if you can find the midpoint between two points on the test. This news should make you happy. Why? Because these are easy questions that you can answer easily as long as you know the two necessary formulas. Now we're going to make sure you know those two formulas. Memorize them.

The Distance Between Two Points

If you know the coordinates of any two points—we'll call them (x_1, y_1) and (x_2, y_2)—you can find their distance from each other with the aptly named distance formula:

$$\text{Distance} = \sqrt{(x_2 - x_1)^2 + (y_2 - y_1)^2}$$

Let's say you were suddenly overcome by the desire to calculate the distance between the points (4,–3) and (–3,8). Just plug the coordinates into the formula:

$$\text{Distance} = \sqrt{(-3 - 4)^2 + (8 - (-3))^2}$$
$$= \sqrt{49 + 121}$$
$$= \sqrt{170}$$

Finding Midpoints

As for the midpoint between the two points (x_1, y_1) and (x_2, y_2), the formula to use is

$$\text{Midpoint} = (\frac{x_1 + x_2}{2}, \frac{y_1 + y_2}{2})$$

In other words, the x- and y-coordinates of the midpoint are the averages of the x- and y-coordinates of the endpoints. To find the midpoint of the points (6,0) and (3,7),

$$\text{Midpoint} = (\frac{6 + 3}{2}, \frac{0 + 7}{2})$$
$$= (\frac{9}{2}, \frac{7}{2})$$
$$= (4.5, 3.5)$$

Lines in the Coordinate Plane

You already know that a line is just an infinite set of points arrayed in a straight formation. But once you stick one of those "infinite set of points" into a coordinate plane, it has all sorts of properties you can analyze. And the SAT will make sure you know how to analyze 'em.

The Slope of a Line

A line's slope is a measurement of how steeply that line climbs or falls as it moves from left to right. If you want the technical jargon, slope is a line's vertical change divided by its horizontal change. Or, if you prefer the poetic version,

Slope is "the rise over run."

If you've got two points on a line, once again (x_1, y_1) and (x_2, y_2), the slope of that line can be calculated using the following formula:

$$\text{Slope} = \frac{y_2 - y_1}{x_2 - x_1}$$

The variable most often used to represent slope is m.

So, for example, the slope of a line that contains the points (−2, −4) and (6, 1) is

$$m = \frac{1 - (-4)}{6 - (-2)} = \frac{1 + 4}{6 + 2} = \frac{5}{8}$$

Positive and Negative Slopes

The slopes of some lines are positive; the slopes of others are negative. Whether a line has a positive or negative slope is easy to tell just by looking at a graph of the line. If the line slopes uphill as you trace it from left to right, the slope is positive. If a line slopes downhill as you trace it from left to right, the slope is negative. Uphill = positive. Downhill = negative.

You can get a sense of the magnitude of the slope of a line by looking at the line's steepness. The steeper the line, the greater the slope; the flatter the line, the smaller the slope. Note that an extremely positive slope is *larger* then a moderately positive slope, while an extremely negative slope is *smaller* than a moderately negative slope.

Check out the lines below and try to determine whether the slope of each line is negative or positive and which has the greatest slope:

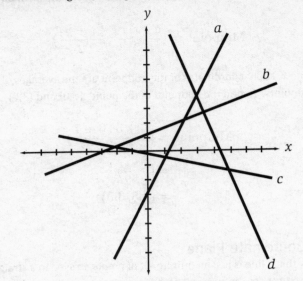

Lines a and b have positive slopes, and lines c and d have negative slopes. In terms of slope magnitude, line $a > b > c > d$.

Slopes You Should Know by Sight

There are certain easy-to-recognize slopes that it pays to recognize by sight. Knowing how to pick them out instantly will save you precious time.

- A horizontal line has a slope of zero. Since there is no "rise," $y_2 - y_1 = 0$, $m = (y_2 - y_1)/(x_2 - x_1) = 0/(x_2 - x_1) = 0$.
- A vertical line has an undefined slope. In this case, there is no "run," and $x_2 - x_1 = 0$. So, $m = (y_2 - y_1)/(x_2 - x_1) = (y_2 - y_1)/0$, and any fraction with zero in its denominator is, by definition, undefined.
- A line that makes a 45° angle with a horizontal line has a slope of either 1 or –1, depending on whether it's going up or down from left to right. In this case, the rise equals the run: $y_2 - y_1 = x_2 - x_1$, or $y_2 - y_1 = -(x_2 - x_1)$.

Of the four lines pictured below, which has a slope of 0, which has a slope of 1, which has a slope of –1, which has an undefined slope?

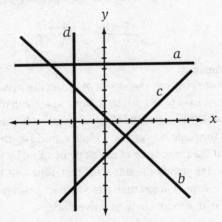

Line a has slope 0 because it's horizontal. Line b has slope –1 because it slopes downward at 45° as you move from left to right. Line c has slope 1 because it slopes upward at 45° as you move from left to right. Line d has undefined slope because it is vertical.

The Slopes of Parallel and Perpendicular Lines

They always have the same relationships.

- The slopes of parallel lines are always the same. If one line has a slope of m, any line parallel to it will also have a slope of m.
- The slopes of perpendicular lines are always the opposite reciprocals of each other. A line with slope m is perpendicular to a line with a slope of $-1/m$.

In the figure below, lines q and r both have a slope of 2, so they are parallel. Line s is perpendicular to both lines q and r, so it has a slope of $-1/2$.

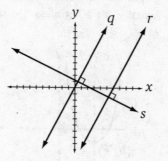

Equation of a Line

Coordinate geometry is actually where algebra and geometry meet. Coordinate geometry allows you to "graph" algebraic equations. For the SAT, you need to know the equation of a line and how to graph that equation. The equation of a line is

$$y = mx + b$$

where m is the slope of the line, and b is the y-intercept of the line (the y-coordinate of the point where the line intersects the y-axis). As long as you know the slope of the line and the y-intercept, you can write the equation of the line.

To sketch a line whose equation you know, first plot the y-intercept, and then use the slope of the line to plot another point. Connect the two points to form your line. The figure below graphs the line $y = -2x + 3$.

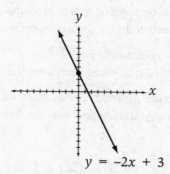

$$y = -2x + 3$$

Since the y-intercept is at 3, the line crosses the y-axis at $(0, 3)$. And since the slope is equal to -2, the line descends two units for every one unit it moves in the positive x direction. In other words, from $(0,3)$, the line moves one unit to the right and two units down, to point $(1,1)$. You could graph the line using those two points.

Finding the *x*- and *y*-Intercepts of a Line

The x-intercept of a line is the x-coordinate of the point where the line intersects the x-axis. The y-intercept of a line is the y-coordinate of the point where the line intersects the y-axis. You can find either the x- or y-intercept of a line by using the slope-intercept form of the line equation.

Finding the intercepts is very straightforward. To solve for the x-intercept, set $y = 0$ and solve for x. To find the y-intercept, set $x = 0$ and solve for y. For example, if you've got the line equation $y = -3x + 2$, the y-intercept equals 2, since $y = -3(0) + 2 = 2$. To find the x-intercept, set $y = 0$ and solve:

$$0 = -3x + 2$$
$$3x = 2$$
$$x = \frac{2}{3}$$

Parabolas Attack! Quadratic Equations Invade the Coordinate Plane

When a quadratic equation is graphed on the coordinate plane, the result is a parabola, which is a giant man-eating insect. Actually, it's a harmless, U-shaped curve that can open either upward or downward.

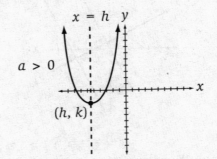

If the SAT covers parabolas at all, it'll most likely do one of these things:

1. Give you an equation and ask you to choose which graph matches the equation.
2. Give you a graph and ask you to choose which equation matches the graph.

You can answer either of these questions as long as you can read the quadratic equation to identify the location of a parabola's vertex and determine whether the parabola opens upward or downward. Here's how to do it.

The equation for a parabola looks like this:

$$y = ax^2 + bx + c$$

where a, b, and c are constants. By plugging a, b, or c into the correct formulas, you can figure out where the vertex is and whether the parabola opens upward or downward:

1. The vertex of the parabola is located at point $(-{}^{b}/_{2a}, c - {}^{b2}/_{4a})$.
2. The parabola opens upward if $a > 0$ and downward if $a < 0$.

So, if you're given the quadratic equation $y = 2x^2 - 3x + 4$, you know that the parabola opens upward, since $a > 0$. And you could figure out the vertex by plugging in. The x-coordinate would be

$$-\frac{b}{2a} = -\left(\frac{-3}{4}\right) = \frac{3}{4}$$

And the y-coordinate would be

$$c - \frac{b^2}{4a} = 4 - \frac{(-3)^2}{4(2)} = 4 - \frac{9}{8} = 2\frac{7}{8}$$

Put it all together, and you've got a parabola that looks something like this:

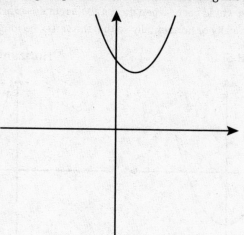

Of course, if you had a graphing calculator, you wouldn't have to go through any of this calculation at all. This is one of the many reasons we steadfastly demand that you have a graphing calculator and know how to use it for the SAT.

Transformations

There's just one more bit of coordinate geometry you have to know for the SAT: how slight changes to a function change the way that the graph of that function looks in the coordinate plane. There are two different kinds of transformations you have to know how to deal with: shifts and stretches.

Shifts

Imagine a graph. No, better yet, look at this graph:

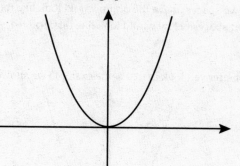

It's a pretty simple graph: a parabola that has a vertex at the origin. To put it into math, $f(x) = x^2$. A shift of this graph would occur when the parabola remains exactly the same shape but is shifted over either vertically or horizontally so that the vertex no longer rests on the origin.

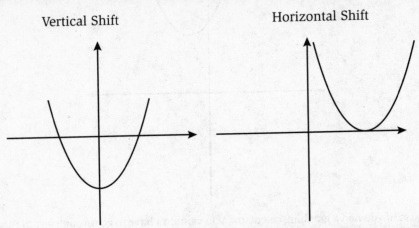

Vertical Shift   Horizontal Shift

To get a vertical or horizontal shift, you have to do slightly different things, but each type of shift has one thing in common: addition or subtraction.

Horizontal Shifts

To get a horizontal shift, in which the graph moves either to the left or right, you use addition. But this time, you need to add within the parentheses. So, if you want to move the graph of the function $f(x)$ two spaces to the right, you make the function $f(x - 2)$. If you want to move it four spaces to the left, you make the function $f(x + 4)$.

Vertical Shifts

Vertical shifts are extremely easy. If you want the image to shift up two spots, just add the number 2 to it. If you want it to shift down four spots, subtract the number 4. So an equation of a parabola that is two spaces above the origin would look like this: $f(x) + 2 = x^2 + 2$. And an equation that's four spaces below would look like this: $f(x) - 4 = x^2 - 4$.

Stretches

Imagine a graph. No better yet, look at that same example we showed you before:

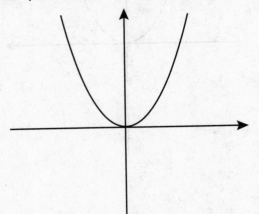

Stretching a graph makes it either fat or thin:

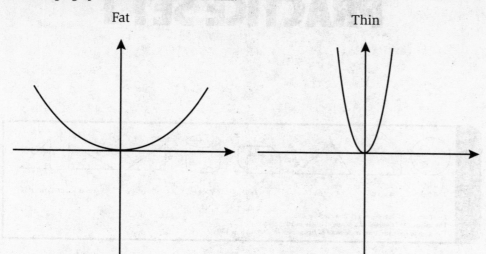

Fat   Thin

A graph stretches when a function is multiplied, whether that multiplication is $3f(x)$ or $f(3x)$. If a function is multiplied by a number greater than 1, it gets taller and thinner, while if it is multiplied by a number less than 1, it gets stubbier and wider.

That's all the SAT covers on geometry. Once again, here are a few practice sets.

PRACTICE SET 1

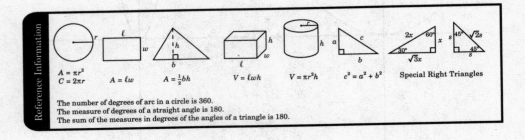

$A = \pi r^2$
$C = 2\pi r$ $A = \ell w$ $A = \frac{1}{2}bh$ $V = \ell wh$ $V = \pi r^2 h$ $c^2 = a^2 + b^2$ Special Right Triangles

The number of degrees of arc in a circle is 360.
The measure of degrees of a straight angle is 180.
The sum of the measures in degrees of the angles of a triangle is 180.

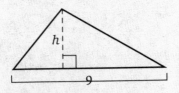

1.   If the triangle above has an area of 27, then $h =$

(A) 3
(B) 5
(C) 6
(D) 8
(E) 10

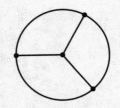

2.   The circle above has been divided into three congruent segments. If the circumference of the circle is 12π, what is the area of one segment?

(A) 4π
(B) 6π
(C) 12π
(D) 24π
(E) 36π

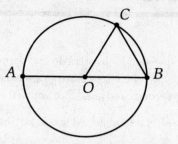

3. If O is the center of the circle above and $\overline{AO} \cong \overline{CB}$, what is the degree measure of angle $\angle AOC$?

(A) 120
(B) 115
(C) 90
(D) 60
(E) 45

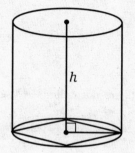

Note: Figure not drawn to scale.

4. A square is inscribed in the base of a right circular cylinder of height 3. If the area of the square is 4, then what is the volume of the cylinder?

(A) 6π
(B) $6\pi\sqrt{2}$
(C) 12π
(D) $12\pi\sqrt{2}$
(E) 36π

5. At noon a large marble statue casts a 50-foot shadow. If the angle from the tip of the shadow to the top of the statue is 60°, approximately what is the height of the statue?

The following information may be used to help you find the answer:

$\tan 60° \approx 1.73$
$\sin 60° \approx 0.866$
$\cos 60° \approx 0.5$

(A) 25 ft
(B) 43.3 ft
(C) 50 ft
(D) 75 ft
(E) 86.6 ft

SAT
Math
Workbook

ANSWERS & EXPLANATIONS

1. C

All you need to answer the question is the triangle area formula, which you can find in the Math test-reference section. Now, you might make a careless error if you don't write out your work, so spend the extra ten seconds and guarantee yourself a right answer.

Area of a triangle $= (1/2)(base)(height)$

$$A = \frac{1}{2}bh$$
$$27 = \frac{1}{2}(9)h$$
$$27 = 4.5h$$
$$\frac{27}{4.5} = \frac{4.5h}{4.5}$$
$$6 = h$$

The correct answer is **C**.

2. C

Here is the path you must follow:

Given the circumference $\rightarrow$ figure out radius $\rightarrow$ use radius to determine entire area $\rightarrow$ divide by 3

The circumference is given as 12π, so you can place that into the proper formula to figure out the radius.

$$C = 2\pi r$$
$$12\pi = 2\pi r$$
$$\frac{12\pi}{2\pi} = \frac{2\pi r}{2\pi}$$
$$6 = r$$

Once you have the radius, it's off to the races. In this case, *races* means the "formula for the area of a circle."

$$A = \pi r^2$$
$$A = \pi 6^2$$
$$A = 36\pi$$

Of course, 36π is an answer choice just waiting for those in too much of a hurry to complete the final step. That's the area for the entire circle, but you want the area for one of the three congruent segments. This would be one-third of 36π, or 12π. That's **C**.

3. A

The key clue here is that $\overline{AO} \cong \overline{CB}$. AO is a radius, and so are OC and OB, two legs of the inscribed triangle. All radii are of the same length, and since $\overline{AO} \cong \overline{CB}$, this means that the following four line segments are all equal: AO, OC, CB, and OB. The last three segments form the triangle, and since they are all equal, this means triangle OCB is an equilateral triangle. All angles in an equilateral triangle are 60°, so angle COB = 60°. Angle COB and AOC form a line, so together they equal 180°.

$$\angle COB + \angle AOC = 180$$
$$60 + \angle AOC = 180$$
$$\angle AOC = 120$$

That's **A**. If you had no idea how to approach this question, you could have used your eyes. Angle *AOC* is definitely greater than 90°, and that eliminates **C**, **D**, and **E**. At this point, you would have a fifty-fifty chance.

4. **A**

The problem mentions cylinders and squares, but once again it's the unsung triangle that brings home the bacon. The volume formula for the cylinder—one of the useful formulas provided to you at the beginning of the section—is $V = \pi r^2 h$. The height is given to you outright, and by now you are enough of a sleuth to realize that you have to take what's given (the area of the inscribed square) and manipulate this information to get the radius, since that is what is needed for the volume formula.

Your journey is aided by the triangle within the inscribed square. Viewing the cylinder from above, it would look like this:

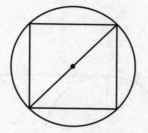

If the area is 4, then the side of the square is 2. Remember that two sides of a square and a diagonal form a 45-45-90 right triangle, which means that the hypotenuse will be the length of a side times $\sqrt{2}$. This makes the diagonal here equal to $2\sqrt{2}$. This diagonal is also a diameter. Since you only need a radius for the volume formula, you must cut it in two to get the radius value of $\sqrt{2}$. Place $\sqrt{2}$ into the volume formula and you get:

$$V = \pi r^2 h$$
$$V = \pi(\sqrt{2})^2 3$$
$$V = \pi(2)3$$
$$V = 6\pi$$

It's **A**.

5. **E**

At last, trigonometry rears its ugly head, but it's only there to scare the uninformed test-taker. Rev up your third eye and get ready to draw because this problem needs to be visualized:

60°

50 ft.

Once drawn, you will see your friend the 30-60-90 right triangle makes an appearance. For these triangles, the side opposite the 60° angle is $\sqrt{3}$ times as large as the side opposite of the 30° angle (the 50-foot shadow, in this instance). Time to use your calculator and determine: $50(\sqrt{3}) \approx 50(1.73) = 86.6$, **E**. But wait! We didn't use any trigonometry. Yeah, that was the whole point.

PRACTICE SET 2

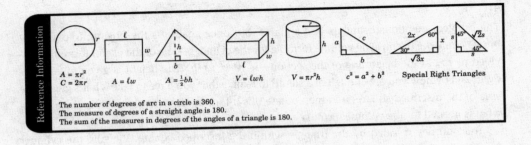

Reference Information

$A = \pi r^2$
$C = 2\pi r$

$A = \ell w$

$A = \frac{1}{2}bh$

$V = \ell w h$

$V = \pi r^2 h$

$c^2 = a^2 + b^2$

Special Right Triangles

The number of degrees of arc in a circle is 360.
The measure of degrees of a straight angle is 180.
The sum of the measures in degrees of the angles of a triangle is 180.

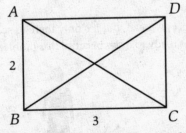

1. If square *ABCD* has an area of 16, what is the circumference of the circle with center *O*?

    (A) 2π
    (B) 4π
    (C) 8π
    (D) 16π
    (E) It cannot be determined from the information given.

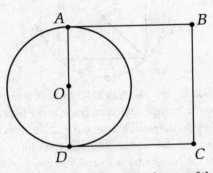

2. If rectangle *ABCD* above has a length of 3 and a height of 2, what is the product of the lengths of the diagonals $\overline{AC}$ and $\overline{BD}$?

    (A) 4
    (B) 6
    (C) 9
    (D) 12
    (E) 13

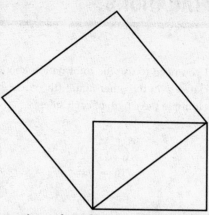

3. One side of the large square is equal to a diagonal of the small square. What is the ratio of the area of the small square to the area of the large square?

    (A) $\frac{1}{4}$

    (B) $\frac{1}{3}$

    (C) $\frac{\sqrt{2}}{3}$

    (D) $\frac{1}{2}$

    (E) $\frac{\sqrt{2}}{2}$

4. Point A is at $(-3, 2)$ and point B is at $(3, 10)$. If point D at $(3, 2)$ is the midpoint of line segment AC, what is the perimeter of triangle ABC?

    (A) 36
    (B) 32
    (C) 18
    (D) 16
    (E) 8

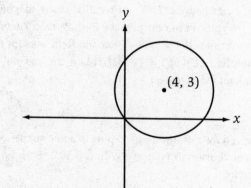

5. The circle above has its center at point $(4, 3)$ and passes through point $(0, 0)$. Which of the following points also lies on the circle?

    (A) $(-1, 1)$
    (B) $(5, -2)$
    (C) $(-2, 4)$
    (D) $(6, -2)$
    (E) $(8, 6)$

1. B

You have two figures, and you need to use the information about one figure (the square) to determine a number associated with the other figure (the circle). Since you have the area of the square, you can first determine the length of each side.

$$A = s^2$$
$$16 = s^2$$
$$\sqrt{16} = \sqrt{s^2}$$
$$4 = s$$

Each side of the square is length 4, and one side of the square is the diameter of the circle. This means the diameter of the circle is also 4. Since the circumference of a circle is given by the formula $C = \pi d$, the circumference is $C = \pi d = 4\pi$, **B**.

There it is. You've successfully made the jump from information about one figure to another. That was the whole purpose of this problem, and you can expect to perform this procedure more than once. Although some questions will be more complex, the basic challenge—using the diagram and the information given to hopscotch from one figure to another—stays the same.

2. E

The problem mentions a rectangle, but don't be fooled. This is a triangle problem dressed up as a rectangle problem. The diagonals are both hypotenuses of right triangles, so the Pythagorean Theorem can be strutted out to determine the length of each diagonal.

$$a^2 + b^2 = c^2$$
$$2^2 + 3^2 = AC^2$$
$$4 + 9 = AC^2$$
$$13 = AC^2$$
$$\sqrt{13} = AC$$

At this point, two things can happen. You can recall that the diagonals of a rectangle are always the same length, or you can run through the Pythagorean Theorem again to figure the length of BD. Either way you get $BD = \sqrt{13}$. Since the stem asks for the product of the two diagonals, you now multiply: $(AC)(BC) = (\sqrt{13})(\sqrt{13}) = 13$ and end up with **E**.

Always be on the lookout for triangles!

3. D

There are no numbers given for this question, so plug in some simple ones. You could solve it algebraically, but you could also jab your eye with a pencil: Both are *possible*, but neither comes highly recommended.

Make the side of the small square length 2. The area of the small square is 2 times 2, or 4. To find the side of the large square, you can:

1. Unholster the old Pythagorean Theorem, or
2. Realize that two sides of a square and a diagonal form a 45-45-90 right triangle, which means that the hypotenuse will be the length of a side times $\sqrt{2}$.

Whichever path you take, the side of the large square is $2\sqrt{2}$. This makes the area of the large square $(2\sqrt{2})(2\sqrt{2}) = 8$. The ratio of the small square over the large square is $\frac{4}{8}$, which reduces to answer $\frac{1}{2}$, **D**.

4.   B

The minute you realized there was no picture with this question, you should have started sketching one yourself. Trying to solve this one mentally could pop your skull. Messy.

Once you place all the points in their proper place, you should get:

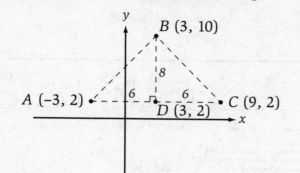

It's a little tough to figure out where *C* is. If *D* is the midpoint of *AC*, and it's six spaces away from *A*, then it must be six spaces away from *C* also. That puts *C* at (9, 2).

You can now determine that *AC* is equal to 12. Draw a line from *B* to *D* and count up. Line segment *BD* is equal to 8. You now know the value of two sides of a right triangle. You could "Pythagorize" to find *AB* or *BC*, or you could eyeball it and realize that you have two 6:8:10 right triangles, which is just a 3:4:5 right triangle enlarged by a factor of two. Either way both *AB* and *BC* are of length 10. The entire perimeter is 32, **B**.

5.   E

You can try to eyeball it and figure out which point lies on the circle, but this technique doesn't always work on a hard question. All the points are pretty close, so you could take a guess if you had to, but the odds aren't great for this question.

Determining the radius of the circle may help, so try doing that. Can you guess what hidden figure needs to be drawn? If you said, "Triangle," you're starting to think like a good test-taker. First draw a line from (4, 3) to (4, 0). Now draw the circle's radius. If you draw a radius from (4, 3) to the origin (0, 0), you will have made the hypotenuse of a 3:4:5 right triangle. This means the radius is 5.

Put another way, you can now start at (4, 3) and then go 4 out and 3 up. Each time you do this on the graph, you'll make a radius of 5 and have another point on your circle. If you go 4 out from (4, 3), you'll be at (8, 3). If you go 3 up from there, you'll be at (8, 6), **E**.

PRACTICE SET 3

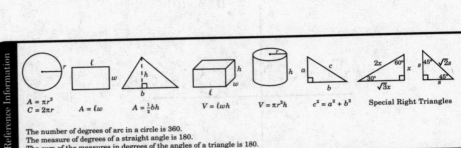

Reference Information

$A = \pi r^2$
$C = 2\pi r$

$A = \ell w$

$A = \frac{1}{2}bh$

$V = \ell wh$

$V = \pi r^2 h$

$c^2 = a^2 + b^2$

Special Right Triangles

The number of degrees of arc in a circle is 360.
The measure of degrees of a straight angle is 180.
The sum of the measures in degrees of the angles of a triangle is 180.

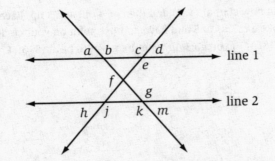

ℓ is a line

1.   Using the figure above, which of the following is equal to $2x$?

   (A) 90
   (B) 135
   (C) 180
   (D) 270
   (E) 360

2.   In the diagram above, lines 1 and 2 are parallel. Which of the following statements are true?

   I.   Angles a and h are equal.
   II.   Angles c and g are equal.
   III.   Angles k and b are equal.

   (A) I only
   (B) II only
   (C) III only
   (D) I and II
   (E) I and III

3. Let f(x) be defined as f(x) = –2x +4. What is the coordinate of a point that can be found below this function?

    (A) (0, 4)
    (B) (–1, 3)
    (C) (2, 0)
    (D) (2, 4)
    (E) (–1, 5)

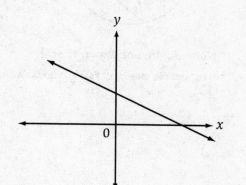

4. If the figure above is a graph of the function $f(x) = -\frac{1}{2}x + 3$, which of the following shows the transformation of $f(x)$ into $f(x-4)$?

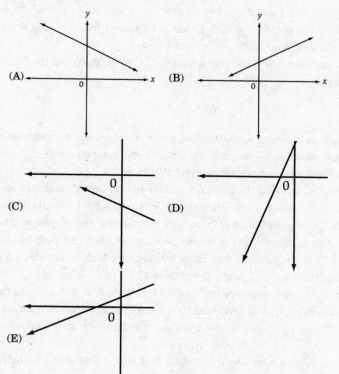

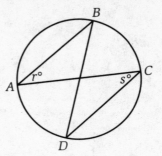

Note: Figure not drawn to scale.

5. The measure of arc AB is 110° and the measure of arc CD is 60°. What is $r° + s°$?

(A) 85°
(B) 95°
(C) 125°
(D) 170°
(E) 190°

ANSWERS & EXPLANATIONS

1. **D**

You can eyeball this diagram. The angle x is definitely over 90° in size but less than 180, since that would make it a line. If this is the case, then $2x$ has to be greater than 180° but less than 360°. Selecting from the answer choices, the answer must be **D**.

    This question was easy, since it was the first question of the set. Applying the "eyeball" strategy makes it even easier.

2. **C**

Roman Numeral (RN) questions are three questions for the price of one, since you have to slog through each portion of the question just to get credit for answering one question correctly. To use a highly technical phrase from cost-benefit analysis: that blows.

    When you do get around to working the question, always answer one RN and then look to see if any answer choices can be crossed out. For example, let's look at RN I, which claims that angles a and h are equal. There are a bunch of rules regarding similar angles created when a transversal (in other words, a line) crosses two parallel lines, but angles a and h are created by two *different* transversals. You can't just eyeball them and say they look equal; they do look equal, but that could mean that one is 43° while the other is 42°. So RN I is wrong.

    Now you can cross out any answer choice that has RN I: choices **A**, **D**, and **E** all fall to our mighty process-of-elimination ax. The answer must be either **B** or **C**. RN II has two angles that are again created with different transversals, so it's not going to be true either. That leaves **C**, the answer.

    There's a mathematical reason why RN III is correct, but why worry about it now? The point is to answer questions correctly, which you did by picking **C**. Move on!

3.   **B**

The first thing you should do is sketch out the function. The slope is –2, and the *y*-intercept is 4, so the line will look like:

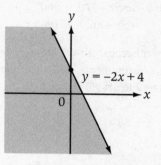

$$y = -2x + 4$$

Pretty much any point you pick that is below this line will work, but you have to choose from the five answer choices provided. **A** (the *y*-intercept) and **C** (the *x*-intercept) are classic tricks because they are values that are easy to spot when you draw out the function. If you're in a hurry, you might select one. Instead, take the time to plot the five answer choices on your graph. You'll quickly see that **B** is the correct answer.

4.   **A**

This is the kind of difficult-looking question that gives many people the willies. If you keep your cool, you'll find the question is not too difficult.

All you need to do is follow the instructions. You're given an initial equation $f(x) = -\frac{1}{2}x + 3$, and then asked how it will be different once you transform it to $f(x-4)$. Ignore the funky $f(x)$'s and just replace the *x* in the first equation with $(x-4)$. This gives you:

$$f(x) = -\frac{1}{2}x + 3$$
$$f(x) = -\frac{1}{2}(x-4) + 3$$
$$f(x) = -\frac{1}{2}x + 2 + 3$$
$$f(x) = -\frac{1}{2}x + 5$$

That's the new line you're looking for. As you can see, the slope, $-\frac{1}{2}$, has not changed, so you can eliminate **B**, **D**, and **E** since they all feature new slopes. **A** has a *y*-intercept at 5, so it's the right answer.

5.   **B**

The sum of two variables is needed here, which may create problems for some students who incorrectly believe they have to find exact values for the variables. This isn't true! This question requires remembering this obscure formula:

An arc defined by an inscribed angle is always equal to twice the measure of that angle.

If you can pull this lovely piece of geometrical knowledge out of your hat, you're in business. An entire circle measures 360°, and you are given two arc measures: Arc *AB* is 110°, and arc *CD* is 60°. These are *not* the arcs opposite *r* and *s*, so a little subtraction will give you the measure of the arcs opposite your two mystery variables.

$$\text{Whole Circle} = 360°$$
$$\text{arc } s + \text{arc } r + \text{arc } AB + \text{arc } CD = 360°$$
$$\text{arc } s + \text{arc } r + 110 + 60 = 360°$$
$$\text{arc } s + \text{arc } r + 170 = 360°$$
$$\text{arc } s + \text{arc } r = 190°$$

The numeral 190 is a trick answer because it's the arc measure for the two variables. However, the question wants the angle measurements, and since the arc measure is twice the angle measure, you must divide 190 by 2 to get 95, choice **B**.

RACTICE SET 4

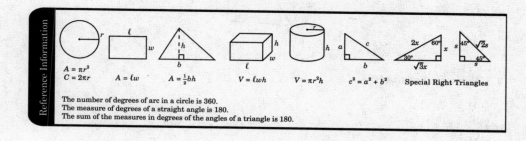

Reference Information

$A = \pi r^2$
$C = 2\pi r$

$A = \ell w$

$A = \frac{1}{2}bh$

$V = \ell wh$

$V = \pi r^2 h$

$c^2 = a^2 + b^2$

Special Right Triangles

The number of degrees of arc in a circle is 360.
The measure of degrees of a straight angle is 180.
The sum of the measures in degrees of the angles of a triangle is 180.

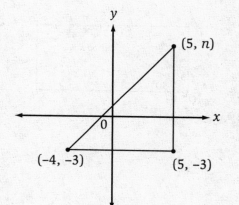

1. The points labeled in the above figure are the vertices of a triangle with an area of 45. What is n?

(A) 5
(B) 6
(C) 7
(D) 9
(E) 10

SAT
Math
Workbook

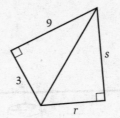

Note: Figure not drawn to scale.

2. What is the value of $r^2 + s^2$?

    (A) 27
    (B) $3\sqrt{10}$
    (C) 90
    (D) 243
    (E) 729

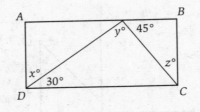

3. If $ABCD$ is a rectangle, what is $x + y + z$?

    (A) 75
    (B) 160
    (C) 175
    (D) 180
    (E) 210

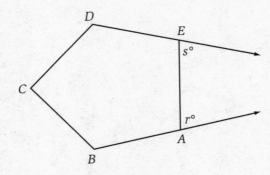

Note: Figure not drawn to scale.

4. If $\angle ABC + \angle BCD + \angle CDE = 330°$, then $r + s =$

    (A) 150°
    (B) 165°
    (C) 180°
    (D) 195°
    (E) 210°

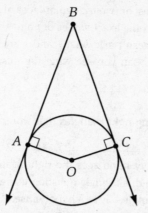

5. Rays $\overrightarrow{BA}$ and $\overrightarrow{BC}$ are each tangent to the circle with center O. If the radius of the circle is 1 and the measure of angle $\angle ABC$ is 60°, what is the area of quadrilateral $OABC$?

(A) $\frac{\sqrt{3}}{4}$

(B) $\frac{1}{2}$

(C) $\frac{\sqrt{3}}{2}$

(D) $\sqrt{3}$

(E) $2\sqrt{3}$

ANSWERS & EXPLANATIONS

1.   **C**

This question is a little harder than the standard "find the area of a triangle" question for the following reasons:

- The introduction of a grid
- No lengths
- The appearance of the variable n as part of an (x, y) point

Sure, it's a little different, but you aren't about to let that throw you.

You have the area of the triangle, 45, and you know the base is the distance between $(-4, -3)$ and $(5, -3)$. This is a length of 9, since $|-4 - 5| = 9$. Put these values into the area formula:

$$A = \frac{1}{2}bh$$
$$45 = \frac{1}{2}(9)h$$
$$45 = 4.5h$$
$$\frac{45}{4.5} = \frac{4.5h}{4.5}$$
$$10 = h$$

So the height is 10. Therefore, point $(5, n)$ is 10 spaces above point $(5, -3)$, making $n = 7$ since $|7 - -3| = 10$. That's **C**.

Those straight-line bars denote absolute value. There is a long-winded definition of absolute value, but for our purposes all you need to know is that the absolute value of a number is always positive. That's why $|-4 - 5|$ in the example above is equal to 9 instead of -9.

2. C

The diagram shows two triangles, or two triangular faces of a pyramid. Just looking at the picture, it seems impossible to find the exact values of r and s since there's not enough information given. Yet the question doesn't ask what r and s are. It asks for $r^2 + s^2$. Look at that expression and think triangles. Can you see what the missing link is? We'll give you some more hints if you can't:

- Think "right triangles."
- Think of a theorem regarding right triangles that would use the expression $r^2 + s^2$.
- It starts with *Pyth* . . .

We hope that your SAT-savvy mind sees the right triangles, the expression $r^2 + s^2$, and makes the leap to, "I can solve this triangle question using the Pythagorean Theorem." And you can, since the two right triangles share a hypotenuse.

$$r^2 + s^2 = (\text{hypotenuse})^2 = 3^2 + 9^2$$
$$(\text{hypotenuse})^2 = 9 + 81$$
$$(\text{hypotenuse})^2 = 90$$
$$r^2 + s^2 = 90$$

C is correct.

3. E

Triangles ahoy! Unpack the rule that states the sum of all three interior angles equals $180°$, and go to town with it on this question. To start the festivities, you can look at the bottom left corner and realize that angle x and $30°$ combine to form a $90°$ right angle. That means $x = 60°$. Now to solve for y. If $x = 60°$, and the angle up by A is equal to $90°$, then the third angle in that triangle is equal to $30°$. The $30°$ angle along with angle y and the $45°$ angle on the other side of y make up a line. Now do some basic math:

$$30 + y + 45 = 180$$
$$75 + y = 180$$
$$y = 105$$

Beautiful. Now we need to solve for angle z, which is part of another right triangle. We already have two angles in that triangle, the $45°$ angle given to us in the diagram and the $90°$ angle up by B. Surprise, surprise! We have a 45-45-90 right triangle. Angle $z = 45°$.

Once you have values for the three variables, it's easy enough to sum them up and get:

$: + y + z = 60 + 105 + 45 = 210$, **E**.

4. A

The question only tells you that three of the interior angles equal $330°$. Since the figure is not drawn to scale, you have to pull out the formula for the sum of the interior angles of a polygon. This formula is $(n - 2)180°$, where n is the number of sides. For our pentagon, the interior angles must equal $(5 - 2)180° = (3)(180°) = 540°$.

So this means:

$$\angle ABC + \angle BCD + \angle CDE + \angle DEA + \angle EAB = 540$$
$$330 + \angle DEA + \angle EAB = 540$$
$$\angle DEA + \angle EAB = 210$$

How do these two angles relate to r and s? One of them forms a line with r, and the other forms a line with s. A line is $180°$, so you can write:

$$\angle EAB + r = 180 \text{ and } \angle DEA + s = 180, \text{ so}$$
$$\angle EAB + r + \angle DEA + s = 180 + 180$$
$$\angle EAB + \angle DEA + r + s = 360$$
$$210 + r + s = 360$$
$$r + s = 150$$

There's your answer, **A**. The question makes you work for it, but that's why it comes later in the set.

5.   **D**

Draw the line *OB*. It gives you two triangles. Since tangential lines are perpendicular to a circle, you have two right triangles, *OAB* and *OCB*. The next step shows why this question is the hardest in the set. You have to realize that *OB* bisected angle *ABC*, creating two equal 30° angles.

You now have two identical 30-60-90 right triangles with quadrilateral *OABC*. The length of the shortest side in each triangle is 1, since this side is also the radius of the circle.

Go to town! Start crunching numbers! Because we're dealing with a 30-60-90 right triangle, we know that *BC* is $\sqrt{3}$ (remember the ratio between sides in these special right triangles). *BC* is also the height of our triangle, so the area of the triangle is

$$A = \frac{1}{2}bh$$
$$A = \frac{1}{2}(\sqrt{3})1$$
$$A = \frac{\sqrt{3}}{2}$$

Now multiply this by 2 to find the area of quadrilateral *OABC*:

$$2\left(\frac{\sqrt{3}}{2}\right) = \sqrt{3}$$

That's **D**.

PRACTICE SET 5

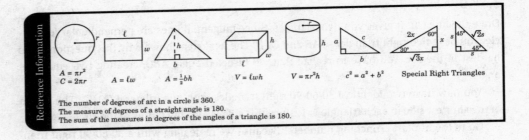

Reference Information

$A = \pi r^2$
$C = 2\pi r$

$A = \ell w$

$A = \frac{1}{2}bh$

$V = \ell wh$

$V = \pi r^2 h$

$c^2 = a^2 + b^2$

Special Right Triangles

The number of degrees of arc in a circle is 360.
The measure of degrees of a straight angle is 180.
The sum of the measures in degrees of the angles of a triangle is 180.

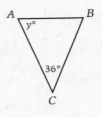

$p \parallel q$

1. If $t = 2s + 15$, what is t?

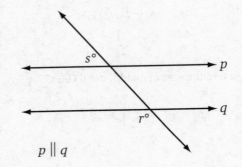

2. If $AC = BC$, then $y = ?$

3. The sum of the interior angles of a regular polygon equals 1260°. How many sides does the polygon have?

4. Two lines pass through point (2, 4). Line 1 also passes through (−2, 1), while line 2 passes through (4, 0). What is the slope of one of these lines?

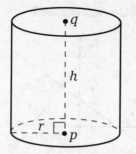

5. The volume of the right circular cylinder pictured above is 81π. If the height of the cylinder is three times the radius, what is the diameter of circle P?

ANSWERS & EXPLANATIONS

1. **125**

Since lines p and q are parallel, angles s and t are supplementary angles. This means they are equal to 180.

$$s + t = 180$$
$$s + 2s + 15 = 180$$
$$3s + 15 = 180$$
$$3s = 165$$
$$s = 55$$

Keep in mind the question asks for the value of t, not s. Placing this value of s into $t = 2s + 15$ gives you:

$$t = 2s + 15$$
$$t = 2(55) + 15$$
$$t = 125$$

2. **72**

If $AC = BC$, then triangle ABC is an isosceles triangle. The angles opposite the equal sides are also equal, so $\angle ABC = \angle BAC$. $\angle BAC$ is just another name for angle y. Since the sum of the interior angles of a triangle is 180, set up the equation like this:

$$y + \angle ABC + 36 = 180$$
$$y + y + 36 = 180$$
$$2y = 144$$
$$y = 72$$

3. **9**

The key to this question lies in remembering that the formula for the interior angles of a regular polygon is $(n - 2)180$, where n is the number of sides for that polygon.

$$(n - 2)180 = 1260$$
$$\frac{(n - 2)180}{180} = \frac{1260}{180}$$
$$n - 2 = 7$$
$$n = 9$$

It's a nine-sided polygon.

SAT
Math
Workbook

4. **3/4**

Since there's no diagram, you should draw one.

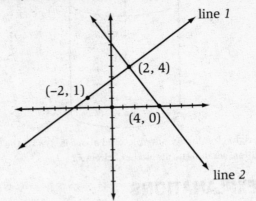

A quick sketch will help you see that line 2 has a negative slope. Since you can't grid in negative values, you have to find the slope of line 1. This line passes through points (2, 4) and (−2, 1), so placing these two points into the slope formula gives you:

$$m = \frac{y_1 + y_2}{x_1 - x_2} = \frac{4 - 1}{2 - -2} = \frac{3}{4}$$

5. **6**

You're given the volume of the cylinder, and since that's the only number you have to work with, it's the best place to start. The formula for the volume of a right circular cylinder is

$$V = \pi r^2 h$$
$$81\pi = \pi r^2 h$$
$$81 = r^2 h$$

This might seem like the end of the road, but the question gives you one more fact: The height of the cylinder is three times the radius. A light might flash in your head at this point, but if not, just create an equation that shows this relationship:

$$h = 3r$$

Now place this into the formula above:

$$81 = r^2 h$$
$$81 = r^2(3r)$$
$$81 = 3r^3$$
$$27 = r^3$$
$$3 = r$$

At this point, you might breathe a sigh of relief and then glibly place the number 3 in the grid. Don't! The question asks for the *diameter*, so the correct answer is twice the radius, 6.

ALGEBRA

THE SAT COVERS A LOT OF ALGEBRA. THERE IS SOME SILVER LINING to this dark cloud. First, the topics covered aren't that advanced: If you've taken three years of high school math, you should be familiar with them. Second, reading this chapter will prepare you for any algebra the SAT throws at you.

TO ALGEBRA OR NOT TO ALGEBRA?

When faced with an algebra question on the SAT, you could, as you might expect, try to solve it by using standard algebra—setting up and working out the equation. But there are often alternative ways to attack. You might be able to plug the answer choices back into the question until one of them works out. You could pick numbers to substitute into the various expressions given as answer choices.

For problems you know how to solve, using algebra is probably the quickest method. In contrast, a problem that's giving you trouble may suddenly become much easier if you start plugging in numbers.

We're not telling you to pick just one method and always use it. Far from it. Flexibility is the key. Some methods work for some problems, and others work better with others. When you study your practice tests and look over the algebra questions you got wrong, think about more than just what the right answer was. Ask yourself if you approached the question correctly. Did you plug in answers when you should have used algebra? Did you use algebra when plugging in answers would have simplified the problem?

Here's an example of an algebra question. We solve it using each of the different problem-solving methods, explaining what you need to know about each one in the process.

> A man flipped a coin 162 times. The coin landed with heads side up 62 more times than it landed with tails up. How many times did the coin land on heads?
>
> (A)   100
> (B)   104
> (C)   108
> (D)   112
> (E)   116

Solving by Algebra

To answer this problem with algebra, you first have to translate it into algebra. You have to set up an equation. If you assign the variable x to stand for the number of times the coin landed on heads, then tails are represented by $x - 62$, since the coin landed on heads 62 times more times than it landed on tails. And since the coin was thrown 162 total times,

$$x + (x - 62) = 162$$
$$2x - 62 = 162$$
$$2x = 224$$
$$x = 112$$

As you can see, setting up the question takes a little bit of time and knowledge, but once you've set it up, the math is quick and easy.

Using algebra will only take you longer than plugging in if you have trouble coming up with the equation $x + (x - 62) = 162$. So here's a quick rule of thumb to help you decide whether to use algebra or to plug in: If you can quickly come up with the equation, then use algebra to solve algebra problems. If you have the sense that it will take you a while to figure out the equation, then plug in.

Solving by Plugging In

There are two ways to plug in: intelligently and maniacally. Don't be a maniac. How can you avoid this? Simple. The answer choices on the SAT that contain numbers (rather than variables) always appear in either ascending or descending order. The first answer choice will be the lowest, and the last will be the largest, or vice versa.

Let's say the answer choices are in ascending order. If you start by plugging in the middle number, answer choice **C**, then even if that choice doesn't work, you can use the outcome to determine whether you need to plug in a smaller or larger number. If you need a smaller number, move to answer choice **B**. If you need a larger number, try **D**. If you follow this method, instead of having to check all five answer choices, you shouldn't ever have to check more than three. That'll save you time. $(5 - 3) / 5 \times 100 = 40\%$ of your time, to be exact.

To answer the coin-flip problem by plugging in, pick **C**, 108, as the first number to try. So, if the coin came up heads 108 times, then how many times did it land on tails? It landed on tails $162 - 108 = 54$. Are 108 heads 62 more than 54 tails? No: $108 - 54 = 54$. In order for the problem to work out you need more heads. You can eliminate **A** and **B** as possibilities. Choose **D**, 112, as your next plug-in number: $162 - 112 = 50$. Does $112 - 50 = 62$? Yes.

Picking Numbers

Picking numbers is a variation of plugging in. It should *only be used* when the answer choices contain variables. A modified version of our original sample question shows what kind of problem lends itself to picking numbers.

> A man flipped a coin z times. The coin landed on heads y more times than it landed on tails. If the number of times the coin landed heads is h, then, in terms of h and y, how many times was the coin flipped?
>
> (A) $z = h + y$
>
> (B) $z = h - y$
>
> (C) $z = \dfrac{h}{y}$
>
> (D) $z = 2h - y$
>
> (E) $z = \dfrac{2h}{y}$

Instead of testing your ability to set up and solve an equation, this question asks you only to set up an equation based on a word problem. While using algebra to set up the equation would be the faster tactic, for some people, thinking in terms of variables can be confusing. Picking numbers allows you to transform variables into concrete numbers.

To use the picking numbers method, select numbers and plug them into the answer choices. It doesn't matter what specific numbers you pick for each variable as long as you always plug the same number in for each variable and follow all guidelines given by the problem.

In the coin-flip problem, you are given three variables, z, y, and h. The question asks you to find z in terms of h and y. We'll pick some numbers. Let's say the coin landed on heads (h) 5 times, and that it landed on heads on 2 more flips (y) than it landed on tails. That would mean that the coin landed on tails 3 times, since $5 - 2 = 3$. Since the coin landed on heads on 5 flips, and on tails on 3 flips, the coin must have been flipped a total of $5 + 3 = 8$ times. Now plug 5 for h and 2 for y into all the equations and see which one comes out to 8: only **D**, which is the right answer.

In addition to giving you a method for solving tricky problems, picking numbers is also a good way to check your math for careless calculations.

Solving by Being an Amazing Genius

It's quite possible that you just looked at this problem and said to yourself, "Other than the 62 more heads, all the other flips were equally heads and tails. So: If I take the 62 out of the total of 162, then I know that the other 100 flips were 50 heads and 50 tails. Now I can just add 62 + 50 = 112. Man, I am an amazing genius!"

Yes, you are. No one knows how to teach other people how to be an amazing genius, though, and you can rest assured that almost no one taking the test will be an amazing genius on every question.

The moral of the story: Know that amazing-genius shortcuts exist, and keep a lookout for them, but don't stress over them. Only a fool would waste time looking for shortcuts. And you're no fool.

Algebra: The Bottom Line

There isn't any "right way" to answer an SAT algebra question. Some methods work best for some types of questions, and others for others. The best way to learn which methods work best for you is to take and study practice tests.

A VERY SHORT ALGEBRA GLOSSARY

There are six basic algebra terms you need to know for the SAT. You also need to know these terms to understand what we're talking about in this section of the book.

Constant. A quantity that does not change. A number.

Variable. An unknown quantity written as a letter. A variable can be represented by any letter in the English alphabet, most often x or y. Variables may be associated with specific things, like x number of apples or y dollars. Other times, variables have no specific association, but you'll need to manipulate them to show that you understand certain algebraic principles.

Coefficient. A coefficient is a number that appears next to a variable and tells how many of the variable there are. In the term $4x$, 4 is the coefficient.

Equation. Two expressions linked by an equal sign. Most of the algebra on the SAT consists of solving equations.

Term. The product of a constant and a variable. Or, a quantity separated from other quantities by addition or subtraction. For example, in the equation

$$3x^3 + 2x^2 - 7x + 4 = x - 1$$

the side to the left of the equal sign contains four terms $\{3x^3, 2x^2, -7x, 4\}$, while the right side contains two terms $\{x, -1\}$. (The constants, 4 and –1, are considered terms because they are coefficients of variables raised to the zero power: $4 = 4x^0$.) So every term, including constants, is the product of a constant and a variable raised to some power.

Expression. Any combination of terms. An expression can be as simple as a single constant term, like 5, or as complicated as the sum or difference of many terms, each of which is a combination of constants and variables, such as $\{(x^2 + 2)^3 - 6x\} / 7x^5$. Expressions don't include an equal sign—this is what differentiates expressions from equations. Expressions cannot be solved; they can only be simplified.

SUBSTITUTION QUESTIONS

We like substitution questions. Not because they have great personalities and a really good sense of humor. We love 'em because they're easy. They almost aren't algebra at all. Substitutions give you an algebraic equation and then tell you the value of the variable. Just plug in that variable and work out the answer.

If $2y + 8x = 11$, what is the value of $3(2y + 8x)$?

You might see this equation bubbling over with variables and panic. Don't. It's simple. Since the question states that $2y + 8x = 11$, and you're looking for the value of $3(2y + 8x)$, all you have to do is substitute 11 for $2y + 8x$ in the expression, and you get $3(11) = 33$.

Not many substitution questions on the SAT are this simple, though. For more complicated substitution questions, you'll have to do some extra math either before or after the substitution.

Math Before Substitution

If $3x - 7 = 8$, then $23 - 3x = ?$

In this problem, you have to find what $3x$ equals before you can substitute that value into the expression $23 - 3x$. To find $3x$, take that first equation,

$$3x - 7 = 8$$

and add 7 to both sides, giving

$$3x = 15$$

Now substitute that 15 into $23 - 3x$:

$$23 - 15 = 8$$

Math After Substitution

If $a + b = 7$ and $b = 3$, then $4a = ?$

In this question, you have to plug the value for b into $a + b = 7$ in order to find a:

$$a + b = 7$$
$$a + 3 = 7$$
$$a = 4$$

Once you know that $a = 4$, just substitute into $4a$:

$$4 \times 4 = 16$$

For substitution questions in which you have to plug in values in more than one stage, make sure you work out that last substitution. When you're taking the SAT under real time pressure, you may be so consumed with getting to the next question that, for instance, you solve for $a = 4$ but then forget to substitute that value into $4a$. SAT traps are waiting for you to do just that. Recognize that 4 is an imposter answer and defeat it.

Multiple Substitutions

There's another type of substitution problem on the SAT that you'll probably have to deal with: multiple substitutions. On these questions, you have to do more than one substitution. For instance,

If $z = \dfrac{4y}{x^2}$, $y = 3x$, and $x = 2$, then what is the value of z?

To approach this problem, you just have to substitute 2 for x to find y and then substitute those values into the equation for z. Substituting 2 for x into $y = 3x$ gives $y = 3(2) = 6$. Substituting for y and x in the equation for z, gives:

$$z = \frac{4y}{x^2} = \frac{4(6)}{2^2} = \frac{24}{4} = 6$$

SOLVING EQUATIONS

To solve an equation, you have to isolate the variable you're solving for. You have to "manipulate" the equation until you get the variable alone on one side of the equal sign. By definition, the variable is then equal to everything on the other side of the equal sign. You've just solved for the variable. Congratulations.

The Fine Art of Manipulation

You can't manipulate an equation the way you manipulate your little brother or sister. When manipulating equations, there are rules. Here's the first and most fundamental (it's so important we're going to bold it):

Whatever you do to one side of an equation, you must do to the other side.

If you divide one side of an equation by 3, divide the other side by 3. If you take the square root of one side of an equation, take the square root of the other. If you fall in love with one side of the equation, fall in love with the other. Neither side will think you're a two-timer. They'll think you're a highly skilled mathematician.

By treating the two sides of the equation in the same way, you don't change what the equation means. You change the *form* of the equation—that's the point of manipulating it—but the equation remains true since both sides stay equal.

Take, for instance, the equation $3x + 2 = 5$. You can do anything you want to it, anything at all, and as long as you do that thing to both sides of the equation, x will always equal 1. For example, if you subtract 2 from both sides:

$$3x + 2 - 2 = 5 - 2$$
$$3x = 3$$
$$x = 1$$

And if you multiply both sides by 2:

$$2(3x + 2) = 2(5)$$
$$6x + 4 = 10$$
$$6x = 6$$
$$x = 1$$

In addition to the "do the same things to both sides of the equation" rule that you must follow, there are other rules of manipulation that you *should* follow. Nothing will go horribly wrong if you don't follow them, but it will take you longer to solve the question. Here are the rules:

1. Combine like terms to make the equation simpler.
2. Manipulate the equation in the reverse order of operations.

The second rule means that you should first subtract or add any extra terms on the same side as the variable. Then divide and multiply anything on the same side as the variable. Next, raise both sides of the equation to a power or take their roots according to any exponent attached to the variable. Finally, work out anything inside parentheses. Do the order of operations backward: SADMEP! The idea is to "undo" everything that has been done to the variable so that it will be isolated in the end. Example time:

$$2 + \frac{3(2\sqrt{x} + 3)}{2} = 17$$

In this equation, poor little x is being square rooted, multiplied by 2, added to 3, and encased in parentheses. You've got to get him out of there! Undo all of these operations in order to liberate x. First, subtract 2 from both sides of the equation:

$$\frac{3(2\sqrt{x} + 3)}{2} = 15$$

Then multiply both sides by 2 to get rid of the fraction:

$$3(2\sqrt{x} + 3) = 30$$

Now divide both sides by 3 (later, parentheses):

$$2\sqrt{x} + 3 = 10$$

Subtract 3 from each side:

$$2\sqrt{x} = 7$$

Divide both sides by 2:

$$\sqrt{x} = \frac{7}{2}$$

And, finally, square each side to get rid of the square root:

$$x = \frac{49}{4}$$

Success! You've freed x from all of those bullying operations.

Location. Location. Location.

Isolating for x is all about where x is located. A variable in the numerator of a fraction is actually a pretty easy location to isolate. But if x is in the denominator of a fraction, things get more complicated.

$$\frac{1}{x+2} + 3 = 7$$

Following SADMEP, start by subtracting the 3:

$$\frac{1}{x+2} = 4$$

But now you have to get the x out of the denominator, and the only way to do that is to multiply both sides of the equation by that denominator, $x + 2$:

$$1 = 4(x+2)$$

Divide both sides by 4:

$$\frac{1}{4} = x + 2$$

Subtract 2 from each side:

$$-\frac{7}{4} = x$$

Simplification Tools

By now you know the rule: When solving an equation, never do something to one side of an equation that you don't do to the other. If you add 4 to one side, you have to add 4 to the other. But what if there were some simplification tools that didn't change the value of an expression? What if you could simplify one side of an equation without changing its value? That would rock. Why? Because it would allow you to make solving equations much simpler and save you time on the SAT.

Distributing

The first step to adding ferocious simplification tools to your arsenal is the rule of distribution, which states a can be any kind of term, meaning it could be a variable, a constant, or a combination of the two.

$$a(b+c) = (a \times b) + (a \times c)$$

When you distribute a factor into an expression within parentheses, multiply each term inside the parentheses by the factor outside the parentheses. For example, in the previous problem, when you had $1 = 4(x + 2)$, you didn't actually have to divide both sides by 4. You could have distributed the 4 and pushed off all those messy fractions until the end: $1 = 4x + 8$; $4x = -7$; $x = {}^{-7}/_4$. So, if you have the expression $3y(y^2 - 6)$:

$$3y(y^2 - 6) = 3y^3 - 18y$$

Seems logical enough. But the true value of distributing becomes clear when you see a distributable expression in an equation: $3y(y^2 + 6) = 3y^3 + 36$ looks like it'd be hard to solve, since there aren't any equal terms to add or subtract away. But wait a sec . . . what if you distribute that $3y$?

$$3y^3 + 18y = 3y^3 + 36$$

Shocking revelation! It's suddenly clear that you can subtract $3y^3$ from both sides:

$$18y = 36$$
$$y = 2$$

Factoring

Factoring an expression is the opposite of distributing. $4x^3 - 8x^2$ is one mean-looking expression. Or so it seems, until you realize that all the terms share the greatest common factor $4x^2$, which you can factor out:

$$4x^3 - 8x^2 = 4x^2(x-2)$$

With distributing and factoring, you can group or ungroup quantities in an equation to make your calculations simpler. Here are a few more examples:

$$3(x + y + 4) = 3x + 3y + 12 \quad \text{3 is distributed.}$$
$$2x + 4x + 6x + 8x = 2x(1 + 2 + 3 + 4) \quad \text{$2x$ is factored out.}$$
$$x^2(x - 1) = x^3 - x^2 \quad \text{x^2 is distributed.}$$
$$xy^2(xy^2 + x^2y) = x^2y^4 + x^3y^3 \quad \text{xy^2 is distributed.}$$
$$14xy^2 - 4xy + 22y = 2y(7xy - 2x + 11) \quad \text{$2y$ is factored out.}$$

Combining Like Terms

After factoring and distributing, you can take additional steps to simplify expressions or equations. Combining like terms is one of the simplest techniques you can use. It involves adding or subtracting the coefficients of variables that are raised to the same power. For example, by combining like terms, the expression $x^2 - x^3 + 4x^2 + 3x^3$ can be simplified by adding the coefficients of the variable x^3 (–1 and 3) together and the coefficients of x^2 (1 and 4) together:

$$2x^3 + 5x^2$$

Variables that have *different* exponential values are *not* like terms and can't be combined. Two terms that do not share a variable are also not like terms and cannot be combined regardless of their exponential value.

$$\text{You can't combine: } x^4 + x^2 =$$
$$y^2 + x^2 =$$

ALGEBRA, ABSOLUTE VALUE, AND EXPONENTS

The SAT covers a lot of Algebra II. In part, this means that the test asks more algebra questions that include absolute value, radicals, and exponents. All three mathematical concepts add certain complications to solving algebra equations.

Algebra and |Absolute Value|

To solve an equation in which the variable is within absolute value brackets, you have to follow a two-step process:

1. Isolate the expression within the absolute value brackets.
2. Divide the equation into two.

Divide the equation in two? What? Watch:

$$|x + 3| = 5. \text{ Solve for } x.$$

Since $x + 3$ has absolute value brackets around it, for the expression to equal 5, the expresion $x + 3$ when outside of the absolute value brackets can equal either $+5$ or -5. So you're actually dealing with two equations:

$$x + 3 = 5$$

$$x + 3 = -5$$

To solve the problem, you need to solve both of them. First, solve for x in the equation $x + 3 = 5$. In this case, $x = 2$. Then, solve for x in the equation $x + 3 = -5$. In this case, $x = -8$. So the solutions to the equation $|x + 3| = 5$ are $x = \{-8, 2\}$.

Here's another example with a much more complicated equation:

Solve for x in terms of y in the equation $3\left|\dfrac{x+2}{3}\right| = y^2 - 1$.

First, isolate the expression within the absolute value brackets:

$$\left|\frac{x+2}{3}\right| = \frac{y^2 - 1}{3}$$

Remember that in terms of PEMDAS, absolute value brackets are like parentheses—do the math inside them first. So solve for the variable as if the expression within absolute value brackets were positive:

$$\frac{x+2}{3} = \frac{y^2 - 1}{3}$$

Multiply both sides of the equation by 3:

$$x + 2 = y^2 - 1$$

Subtract 2 from both sides:

$$x = y^2 - 3$$

Next, solve for the variable as if the expression within absolute value brackets were negative:

$$\frac{x+2}{3} = -\frac{y^2 - 1}{3}$$

Multiply both sides of the equation by 3:

$$x + 2 = -(y^2 - 1)$$

Distribute the negative sign (crucial step, make sure you do this or you'll fall into a trap!):

$$x + 2 = -y^2 + 1$$

Subtract 2 from both sides:

$$x = -y^2 - 1$$

The solution set for x is $\{y^2 - 3, -y^2 - 1\}$.

Algebra, Exponents, and Radicals

Exponents and radicals can have devilish effects on algebraic equations that are similar to those caused by absolute value.

Consider the equation $x^2 = 25$. Seems pretty simple, right? Just take the square root of both sides and you end up with $x = 5$. But remember the rule of multiplying negative numbers?

When two negative numbers are multiplied together the result is a positive. In other words, -5 squared also results in 25: $-5 \times -5 = 25$.

This means that whenever you have to take the square root to simplify a variable brought to the second power, the result will be *two* solutions, one positive and one negative: $\sqrt{x^2} = \pm x$. The only exception is if $x = 0$.

Want an example?

If $2x^2 = 72$, then what is the value of x?

To solve this problem, you first simplify the problem by dividing 2 out of both sides: $x^2 = 36$. Now you need to take the square root of both sides: $x = \pm 6$.

BEAT THE SYSTEM (OF EQUATIONS)

So you're kicking butt and taking names on those old one-variable equations, huh? Good. But some SAT questions contain two variables. Lucky for you, those questions also always contain two equations, and you can use the two equations in conjunction to solve the variables. These two equations together are called a system of equations. We said earlier that manipulating equations isn't like manipulating your younger brother or sister. But solving systems of equations *is* like manipulating your younger brother and sister. You use one equation against the other, and in the end you get whatever you want.

There are two types of systems of equations that you'll need to be able to solve for the SAT. The first, easier model involves substitution, and the second type involves manipulating equations simultaneously.

Substituting into the System

You know substitution: Find the value of one variable and then plug that into another equation to solve for a different variable.

If $x - 4 = y - 3$ and $2y = 6$, what is x?

You've got two equations and you have to find x. The first equation contains both x and y. The second equation contains only y. To solve for x, you first have to solve for y in the second equation and substitute that value for y in the first equation. If $2y = 6$, then $y = 3$. Now, substitute 3 in for y in $x - 4 = y - 3$:

$$x - 4 = 3 - 3$$
$$x - 4 = 0$$
$$x = 4$$

Here's one that's more likely to give you trouble on the SAT:

Suppose $3x = y + 5$ and $2y - 2 = 12k$. Solve for x in terms of k.

In order to solve for x in terms of k, you have to first get x and k into the same equation. To make this happen, you can solve for y in terms of k in the second equation, and then substitute that value into the first equation to solve for x. (You could also solve this problem by solving for y in the first equation and substituting that expression in for y in the second equation.)

$$2y - 2 = 12k$$
$$2y = 12k + 2$$
$$y = 6k + 1$$

Then substitute $y = 6k + 1$ into the equation $3x = y + 5$.

$$3x = y + 5$$
$$3x = (6k + 1) + 5$$
$$3x = 6k + 6$$
$$x = 2k + 2$$

Solving Simultaneous Equations

Simultaneous equations are equations that both contain the same variables. You can use the equations to solve for the variables by using one of the equations to solve for one variable in terms of the other, and then substituting that expression into the other equation.

Suppose $2x + 3y = 5$ and $x + y = 7$. What is x?

In this particular problem, you need to find x. But in order to find the value of x, you need to get that pesky y variable out of one of the equations, right? Here's how to do it. First solve one of the equations for y in terms of x:

$$x + y = 7$$
$$y = 7 - x$$

Now substitute $7 - x$ for y in the equation $2x + 3y = 5$:

$$2x + 3(7 - x) = 5$$
$$2x + 21 - 3x = 5$$
$$-x = -16$$
$$x = 16$$

Here's what just happened. You manipulated one equation to separate the two variables on either side of the equal sign. Then you substituted one side of that equal sign into the other equation so that only the variable whose value you had to find was left. Bold move!

Another Way to Solve Simultaneous Equations

So that's how you can solve every simultaneous equation question on the SAT. But wait! There's another, even faster way to solve simultaneous equations.

Some students find this method tricky, but it is definitely faster, and it works. The choice of which method to use is up to you. Take a look at the following question:

$2x + 3y = 5$ and $-1x - 3y = -7$. What is x?

The amazing thing about simultaneous equations is that you can actually add or subtract the entire equations from each other. Observe:

$$2x + 3y = 5$$
$$\underline{+(-1x) - 3y = -7}$$
$$x = -2$$

Here's another example:

6x + 2y = 11 and 5x + y = 10. What is x + y?

Subtract the second equation from the first:

$$6x + 2y = 11$$
$$\underline{-(5x + y = 10)}$$
$$x + y = 1$$

In order to add or subtract simultaneous equations, you need to know what variable you want to solve for, and then add or subtract accordingly. But we've got to admit something: So far, we've purposely chosen very easy examples to show how this method works. You won't always have two equations that you can immediately add or subtract from each other to isolate one variable:

2x + 3y = –6 and –4x + 16y = 13. What is the value of y?

You're asked to solve for y, which means you've got to get rid of x. But how can you get rid of x if one equation has $2x$ and the other has $-4x$? Well, you can't. But remember, you can change the form of the equation without changing the actual equation, as long as you do the same thing to both sides of the equation. For instance, you could multiply both sides of $2x + 3y = -6$ by 2, which would give you:

$$2(2x + 3y) = 2(-6)$$
$$4x + 6y = -12$$

You can add this equation to $-4x + 16y = 13$ to isolate y.

$$4x + 6y = -12$$
$$\underline{+(-4x) + 16y = 13}$$
$$22y = 1$$
$$y = \frac{1}{22}$$

On the SAT, you will almost always be able to manipulate one of the two equations in a pair of simultaneous equations so that they can be added and subtracted to isolate the variable you want. The question is whether you can see how to do it. Our recommendation? Since it's faster, it always pays to take a second to try to see how to isolate the variable by adding or subtracting the equations. If you can't, then go ahead and solve the simultaneous equations using the first method we described.

INEQUALITIES

Life isn't always fair. That's why there are inequalities. An inequality is like an equation, but instead of relating equal quantities, it specifies exactly how two quantities are *not* equal. There are four types of inequalities:

1. $x > y$ — x is greater than y
2. $x < y$ — x is less than y
3. $x \geq y$ — x is greater than or equal to y
4. $x \leq y$ — x is less than or equal to y

Solving inequalities is exactly like solving equations except for one very important difference:

When both sides of an inequality are multiplied or divided by a negative number, the direction of the inequality switches.

Here are a few examples:

Solve for x in the inequality $\frac{x}{2} - 3 < 2y$.

$$\frac{x}{2} - 3 < 2y$$
$$\frac{x}{2} < 2y + 3$$
$$x < 2(2y + 3)$$
$$x < 4y + 6$$

Solve for x in the inequality $\frac{4}{x} \geq -2$.

$$\frac{4}{x} \geq -2$$
$$4 \geq -2x$$
$$-2 \leq x$$

Notice that in the last example the inequality had to be flipped, since both sides had to be divided by –2 between the second and third steps.

To help remember that multiplication or division by a negative number reverses the direction of the inequality, remember that if $x > y$, then $-x < -y$, just as $5 > 4$ and $-5 < -4$. The larger the number, the harder it falls (or the smaller it becomes when you make it negative).

Ranges

Inequalities are also used to express the range of values that a variable can take. $a < x < b$ means that the value of x is greater than a and less than b. Consider the following word problem:

A company manufactures car parts. As is the case with any system of mass production, small errors in production of every part occur. To make viable car parts, the company must make sure the unavoidable errors occur only within a specific range. The company knows that a particular part they manufacture will not work if it weighs less than 98% of its target weight or more than 102% of its target weight. If the target weight of this piece is 20.5 grams, what is the range of weights the part must fall within for it to function?

The car part must weigh between .98 × 21.5 = 21.07 grams and 1.02 × 21.5 = 21.93 grams. The problem states that the part cannot weigh *less* than the minimum weight or *more* than the maximum weight in order for it to work. This means that the part will function at boundary weights themselves, and the lower and upper bounds are included. The answer to the problem is $21.07 \leq x \leq 21.93$, where x is the weight of the part in grams.

Finding the range of a particular variable is essentially an exercise in close reading. Every time you come across a question involving ranges, you should carefully peruse the problem to pick out whether or not a particular variable's range includes its bounds. This inclusion is the difference between "less than or equal to"($\leq$) and simply "less than" ($<$).

Operations on Ranges

Ranges can be added, subtracted, or multiplied.

If $4 < x < 7$, what is the range of $2x + 3$?

To solve this problem, simply manipulate the range like an inequality until you have a solution. Begin with the original range:

$$4 < x < 7$$

Multiply the inequality by 2:

$$8 < 2x < 14$$

Add 3 to the inequality, and you have the answer:

$$11 < 2x + 3 < 17$$

And always remember the crucial rule about multiplying inequalities: If you multiply a range by a negative number, you *must* flip the greater-than or less-than signs. If you multiply the range $2 < x < 8$ by -1, the new range will be $-2 > -x > -8$.

Absolute Value and Inequalities

Absolute values do the same thing to inequalities that they do to equations. You have to split the inequality into two equations and solve for each. This can result in solutions to inequalities in which the variable falls between two values (as in a range) or a combination of two "disjointed ranges."

Single Range

If the absolute value is less than a given quantity, then the solution is a single range with a lower and an upper bound. An example of a single range would be the numbers between -5 and 5, as seen in the number line below:

On the SAT, you'll most likely be asked to deal with single ranges in the following way:

Solve for x in the inequality $|2x - 4| \leq 6$.

First, split the inequality into two. Remember to flip around the inequality sign when you write out the inequality for the negative number.

$$2x - 4 \leq 6$$

$$2x - 4 \geq -6$$

Solve the first:

$$2x - 4 \leq 6$$
$$2x \leq 10$$
$$x \leq 5$$

Then solve the second:

$$2x - 4 \geq -6$$
$$2x \geq -2$$
$$x \geq -1$$

So x is greater than or equal to –1 and less than or equal to 5. In other words, x lies between those two values. So you can write out the value of x in a single range, $-1 \leq x \leq 5$.

Disjointed Ranges

You won't always find that the value of the variable lies between two numbers. Instead, you may find that the solution is actually two separate ranges: one whose lower bound is negative infinity and whose upper bound is a real number, and one whose lower bound is a real number and whose upper bound is infinity. Yeah, words make it sound confusing. A number line will make it clearer.

An example of a disjointed range would be all the numbers smaller than –5 and larger than 5, as shown below:

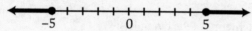

On the SAT, disjointed ranges come up on problems like the following:

Solve for x in the inequality $|3x + 4| > 16$.

You know the drill. Split 'er up, then solve each part:

$$3x + 4 > 16$$

$$3x + 4 < -16$$

Solving the first part:

$$3x + 4 > 16$$
$$3x > 12$$
$$x > 4$$

And the second:

$$3x + 4 < -16$$
$$3x < -20$$
$$x < -\frac{20}{3}$$

Notice, though, that x is greater than the positive number and smaller than the negative number. In other words, the possible values of x don't lie *between* the two numbers, they lie *outside* the two numbers. So you need two separate ranges to show the possible values of x: $-\infty < x < {}^{-20}/_3$ and $4 < x < \infty$.

BINOMIALS AND QUADRATIC EQUATIONS

The SAT asks quite a few questions on binomials. What is a binomial? Quite simply, it is an expression that has two terms: $x + 5$ and $x^2 - 6$ are both binomials.

Multiplying Binomials

The multiplication of binomials is its own SAT topic and a fundamental skill for dealing with the dreaded quadratic equations. Luckily, the best acronym ever made (other than SCUBA) will help you remember how to multiply binomials. This acronym is **FOIL**, and it stands for **F**irst, **O**uter + **I**nner, **L**ast. The acronym tells you the order in which you multiply the terms of two binomials to get the correct product.

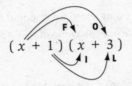

For example, let's say you were kidnapped by wretched fork-tongued lizard-men whose only weakness was binomials. Now what if the lizard-king asked to you to multiply the binomials:

$$(x + 1)(x + 3)$$

What would you do? Follow FOIL, of course. First, multiply the first terms of each binomial:

$$x \times x = x^2$$

Next, multiply the outer terms of the binomials:

$$x \times 3 = 3x$$

Then, multiply the inner terms:

$$1 \times x = x$$

And multiply the last terms:

$$1 \times 3 = 3$$

Add all these terms together:

$$x^2 + 3x + x + 3$$

Finally, combine like terms, and you get:

$$x^2 + 4x + 3$$

Here are a few more examples of multiplied binomials to use to test yourself.

$$(y + 3)(y - 7) = y^2 - 7y + 3y - 21 = y^2 - 4y - 21$$
$$(-x + 2)(4x + 6) = -4x^2 - 6x + 8x + 12 = -4x^2 + 2x + 12$$
$$(3a + 2b)(6c - d) = 18ac - 3ad + 12bc - 2bd$$

Quadratic Equations

Quadratics are the robots who return from the future to destroy humankind at the end of *Terminator 3*. Well, the future is now: The SAT forces you to take on quadratic equations. But the future also isn't that tough. Here's the first thing: A quadratic expression takes the form $ax^2 + bx + c$, where $a \neq 0$. And here's the second: Note how closely $ax^2 + bx + c$ resembles the products formed when binomials are multiplied. Coincidence? Fat chance.

A quadratic equation sets a quadratic equal to zero: $ax^2 + bx + c = 0$. The values of x for which the equation holds are called the roots, or solutions, of the quadratic equation. Some of the SAT questions on quadratic equations ask you to find their roots.

There are two basic ways to find roots: by factoring and by using the quadratic formula. Factoring is faster, but doesn't always work. The quadratic formula takes longer to work out, but works on every quadratic equation.

On the SAT, you'll be able to factor almost every quadratic expression or equation that appears, but every once in a while the test may throw in a quadratic that you need to know the quadratic formula to solve. In other words, you probably don't need to know the quadratic formula, and if you're pressed for time you could survive if you didn't spend time studying it. But if you want to slam dunk the SAT, memorize it.

Factoring Quadratics

Here's why quadratic expressions resemble the product of two binomials: Quadratic expressions *are* the product of two binomials. Factoring a quadratic means breaking the quadratic back into its binomial parts. Factoring might as well be called LIOF; it's FOIL in reverse. Check out this quadratic expression:

$$x^2 + 10x + 21$$

For starters, you know that the binomials have the form $(x + m)(x + n)$, where m and n are constants. How do you know this? Because of that x^2. When you FOIL to get the first term, you multiply the two first terms of the binomials. To get x^2, you have to multiply x by x. As for figuring out what m and n are, you have two clues to work with.

---

1. The sum of m and n is 10, since the $10x$ is derived from multiplying the OUTER and INNER terms of the binomials and then adding the resulting terms together ($10x = mx + nx$, so $m + n$ must equal 10).
2. The product of m and n equals 21, since 21 is the product of the two last terms of the binomials. The only pair of numbers that fit the bill for m and n are 3 and 7 ($3 + 7 = 10$ and $3 \times 7 = 21$), so $x^2 + 10x + 21 = (x + 3)(x + 7)$.

But what if this had been a quadratic *equation* rather than a plain old quadratic expression? Well, first of all, it would have looked like this: $x^2 + 10x + 21 = 0$. Second, once you'd factored it to get $(x + 3)(x + 7) = 0$, you could solve for its roots. Because the product of two terms is zero, one of the terms must be equal to zero. Since $x + 3 = 0$ or $x + 7 = 0$, the solutions (also known as the roots) of the quadratic must be $x = -3$ and $x = -7$.

Quadratics with Negative Terms

Once you get the hang of it, factoring a quadratic with negative terms is no harder than dealing with one with only positive terms.

Consider the quadratic equation $x^2 - 4x - 21 = 0$. Here's what we know about this equation: The first term of each binomial is x, since the first term of the quadratic is x^2; the product of m and n is -21; and the sum of a and b equals -4. The equation also tells you that either m or n must be negative, but that *both* cannot be negative, because only the multiplication of one positive and one negative number can result in a negative number. Now you need to look for the numbers that fit these requirements for m and n. The numbers that multiply together to give you −21 are −21 and 1, −7 and 3, −3 and 7, and 21 and −1. Of these, the pair that sums to −4 is −7 and 3. The factoring of the equation is $(x-7)(x+3) = 0$. So the roots of the equation are $x = 7$ and $x = -3$.

Two Special Quadratics

There are two special quadratics that pop up all the time on the SAT. If you know what they look like and can identify them quickly, you'll save time. These two quadratics are called the "perfect square" and the "difference of two squares."

Perfect square quadratics are the product of a term squared (multiplied by itself). There are therefore two kinds of perfect square quadratics: those formed by the squaring of a binomial of the form $(a + b)^2$ and those formed by the squaring of binomials that look like $(a - b)^2$.

---

1. $a^2 + 2ab + b^2 = (a + b)(a + b) = (a + b)^2$

Example: $a^2 + 6ab + 9 = (a + 3)^2$

---

2. $a^2 - 2ab + b^2 = (a - b)(a - b) = (a - b)^2$

Example: $a^2 - 6ab + 9 = (a - 3)^2$

Note that when you solve for the roots of a perfect square quadratic equation, the solution for the equation $(a + b)^2 = 0$ will be $-b$, while the solution for $(a + b)^2 = 0$ will be b.

The difference of two-squares quadratic equations follow the form below:

$$(a + b)(a - b) = a^2 - b^2$$
$$\text{Example: } (a + 3)(a - 3) = a^2 - 9$$

See how the middle term drops out? The disappearance of the middle term causes lots of students to fail to recognize when they're dealing with a difference of two-squares quadratic.

Practice Quadratics

Since the ability to factor quadratics relies in large part on your ability to "read" the information in the quadratic, the best way to sharpen your eye is to practice, practice, practice. Take a look at the following examples and try to factor them on your own before you peek at the answers.

$$x^2 + x - 2 = 0 \qquad \text{Roots}: \{-2, 1\}$$
$$x^2 + 13x + 42 = 0 \qquad \text{Roots}: \{-7, -6\}$$
$$x^2 - 8x + 15 = 0 \qquad \text{Roots}: \{3, 5\}$$
$$x^2 - 5x - 36 = 0 \qquad \text{Roots}: \{-4, 9\}$$
$$x^2 - 10x + 25 = 0 \qquad \text{Roots}: \{5\}$$
$$x^2 - 25 = 0 \qquad \text{Roots}: \{5, -5\}$$

VARIATION

One way that the SAT tests whether you understand an equation is to ask questions about the relationship between certain variables. For example,

If z triples while x doubles, what happens to y?

$$y = \frac{x}{z}$$

The easiest way to solve such problems is to just plug in:

$$y = \frac{2x}{3z}$$

So the value of y will be $2/3$ of what it was.

Essentially, these sorts of problems are testing to see if you understand how an equation works and how different variables interact. While in a simple equation like the first example, this is easy to see, it becomes a little more complicated as the equations get more complex:

> If z triples while x doubles, what happens to y?
>
> $$y = \frac{x^3}{2z}$$

Once again, you can still find the answer by plugging in $2x$ for x and $3z$ for z. You just have to do some additional math:

$$y = \frac{(2x)^3}{2(3z)} = \frac{8x^3}{6z} = \frac{4x^3}{3z}$$

The value of y will be $8/3$ of what it was. Since the original expression was $y = x^3/2z$, we must figure out what fraction times $1/2$ is equal to $4/3$:

$$\left(\frac{1}{2}\right)f = \frac{4}{3}$$

$$f = \frac{\frac{4}{3}}{\frac{1}{2}} = \left(\frac{4}{3}\right)\left(\frac{2}{1}\right) = \frac{8}{3}$$

It's also possible that you'll have to know some variation jargon for the SAT. There are two terms you need to know: *direct* and *inverse*. A direct relationship between two variables exists when, if one variable increases, the other variable increases. In the equation

$$y = \frac{x}{z}$$

y and x share a direct relationship, since if x increases, so does y.

An inverse relationship is just the opposite. In the same example, y and z have an inverse relationship, because if z were to increase, y would decrease.

HOW DO FUNCTIONS FUNCTION?

What's a function? A function describes a relationship between one or more inputs and one output. The inputs to a function are variables such as x; the output of the function for a particular value of x is usually represented as $f(x)$ or $g(x)$. In the function $f(x) = 2x$, the output of the function is always equal to two times the value of x. So, if $x = 1$, then $f(x) = 2$, and if $x = 12$, then $f(x) = 24$.

So far, it may seem as if a *function* is just another word for *equation*. Based on the way the SAT generally tests functions, it's fine to think of functions that way. However, all functions follow a special rule that you've got to know:

For every input x, a function can have only one value for f(x).

You might be asking yourself what this math babble means. Here's an example that should help translate. Take the equation $|y| = x$. Because y sits between absolute value brackets, if $x = 2$, then y could be equal to *either* 2 or –2. This equation can't be a function, because for each value of x, there are two possible values of y.

EVALUATING FUNCTIONS

Evaluating a function simply means finding $f(x)$ at some specific value x. To put it more bluntly, these are glorified substitution questions. We glorify them above all because they're easy. Here's an example:

If $f(x) = x^2 - 3$, what is $f(5)$?

See how that $f(5)$ substituted a 5 for the x in $f(x)$? Well, every time you see an x in the equation, replace it with a 5:

$$f(5) = 5^2 - 3 = 22$$

You almost don't even have to think at all when answering these questions. If the entire Math section was just a bunch of evaluating functions questions, amoebas could get 800s and Ivy League schools would welcome every well-rounded single-celled organism who applied.

Ah, but life and the SAT ain't that easy. Here's one wrinkle the new test may throw at you. You may have to evaluate a function at a variable rather than a constant. For example,

If $f(x) = \dfrac{3x}{4-x}$, what is $f(x + 1)$?

Okay, slightly harder than substituting in a number, but still not difficult. Search out all the occurrences of x in the function and replace it with $(x + 1)$:

$$\begin{aligned} f(x+1) &= \frac{3(x+1)}{4-(x+1)} \\ &= \frac{3x+3}{4-x-1} \\ &= \frac{3x+3}{3-x} \end{aligned}$$

As long as you remembered to distribute that negative sign across the $(x + 1)$ to make $-x - 1$ in that second step, you're all set.

Performing Operations on Functions

Functions can be added, subtracted, multiplied, and divided like any other quantities. A few key rules will make these operations easier. For any two functions $f(x)$ and $g(x)$:

	Rule	Example
Addition	$(f + g)(x) = f(x) + g(x)$	If $f(x) = x^2$ and $g(x) = 2x$: $(f + g)(x) = x^2 + 2x$
Subtraction	$(f - g)(x) = f(x) - g(x)$	If $f(x) = x^2 + 5$ and $g(x) = x^2 + 2x + 1$: $(f - g)(x) = x^2 + 5 - x^2 - 2x - 1 = -2x + 4$
Multiplication	$(f \times g)(x) = f(x) \times g(x)$	If $f(x) = x$ and $g(x) = x^3 + 8$: $(f \times g)(x) = x \times (x^3 + 8) = x^4 + 8x$
Division	$\dfrac{f}{g}(x) = \dfrac{f(x)}{g(x)}, g(x) \neq 0$	If $f(x) = 2x$ and $g(x) = x^2$: $\dfrac{f}{g}(x) = \dfrac{2x}{x^2} = \dfrac{2}{x}, g(x) \neq 0$

Here's a quick rule to follow for all of these operations on functions: Work out the value for both functions separately, and then perform the operation on those two values. Remember that any time you divide functions, $\frac{f(x)}{g(x)}$, the resulting function is undefined whenever the $g(x)$ in the denominator equals zero. Division by zero is always a no-no.

Wacko Symbols Questions (Algebra in Disguise)

The SAT seems to give itself a cooky thrill by creating odd symbols and then defining those symbols as mathematical functions. For example, a typical symbol SAT question might say,

> Let $a @ b$ be defined as $\frac{a^2}{b}$, where $b \neq 0$. What is the value of $4 @ 2$?

These symbols questions are just snazzy, dressed-to-kill, evaluating functions questions. Answer them by plugging in:

$$4 @ 2 = \frac{4^2}{2} = \frac{16}{2} = 8$$

Some students get frazzled when they see odd symbols in their test booklet, which is exactly what the SAT wants. Don't get tripped up on these otherwise easy questions.

COMPOUND FUNCTIONS

You know those Russian nesting dolls? Each doll has a smaller and smaller doll inside it? Compound functions are like that. A compound function is a function that operates on another function. It's written out like this: $f(g(x))$. To evaluate a compound function, first evaluate the internal function, $g(x)$. Next, evaluate the outer function at the result of $g(x)$. It's just double substitution: a classic SAT question that looks much meaner than it really is.

Try this example on for size:

> Suppose $h(x) = x^2 + 2x$ and $j(x) = |\frac{x}{4} + 2|$. What is $j(h(4))$?

First evaluate $h(4)$:

$$\begin{aligned} h(4) &= 4^2 + 2(4) \\ &= 16 + 8 \\ &= 24 \end{aligned}$$

Now plug 24 into the definition of j:

$$\begin{aligned} j(24) &= |\frac{24}{4} + 2| \\ &= |6 + 2| \\ &= 8 \end{aligned}$$

Just make sure you pay attention to the order in which you evaluate the compound function. Always evaluate the inner function first. If the question had asked you to evaluate $h(j(4))$, you'd get a completely different answer:

$$\begin{aligned} h(j(4)) &= h(|\tfrac{4}{4} + 2|) \\ &= h(|1 + 2|) \\ &= h(3) \\ &= 3^2 + 2(3) \\ &= 9 + 6 \\ &= 15 \end{aligned}$$

As with ordinary evaluating functions questions, the SAT doesn't always give you a constant with which to evaluate compound functions.

Suppose $f(x) = 3x + 1$ and $g(x) = \sqrt{5x}$. What is $g(f(x))$?

When you aren't given a constant, just substitute the definition of $f(x)$ as the input to $g(x)$. It's as if you're being asked to evaluate a signle function at a variable rather than a constant.

$$\begin{aligned} g(f(x)) &= g(3x + 1) \\ &= \sqrt{5(3x + 1)} \\ &= \sqrt{15x + 5} \end{aligned}$$

Compound Wacko Symbols Questions

The SAT also sometimes asks compound symbols questions. These are exactly the same as compound function questions.

Let $a\#b\#c\#d$ be defined for all numbers by $a\#b\#c\#d = ab - cd$. If $x = 6\#3\#5\#4$, then what is the value of $7\#x\#3\#11$?

Strange symbols are flying all over the place, and the question is asking you to calculate the value of a strange symbol with a variable in it?! No problem. The answer to this question is only two steps away:

1. Calculate the value of x.
2. Calculate the value of $7\#x\#3\#11$ (which won't be very hard, since by step 2, you'll know exactly what x equals).

Since:

$$a\#b\#c\#d = ab - cd$$
$$x = 6\#3\#5\#4 = (6)(3) - (5)(4) = 18 - 20 = -2$$
$$x = -2$$

Now plug $x = -2$ into $7\#x\#3\#11$:

$$7\#x\#3\#11 = 7\# - 2\#3\#11 = (7)(-2) - (3)(11) = -14 - 33 = -47$$

DOMAIN AND RANGE

Difficult SAT questions on functions test to see if you are the master of your domain and range. Here are the keys to the kingdom.

Domain of a Function

The domain of a function is the set of inputs (x values) for which the function is defined. Consider the functions $f(x) = x^2$ and $g(x) = {}^1/x$. In $f(x)$, any value of x can produce a valid result, since any number can be squared. In $g(x)$, though, not every value of x can generate an output: When $x = 0$, $g(x)$ is undefined. While the domain of $f(x)$ is all values of x, the domain of $g(x)$ is $x < 0$ and $x > 0$. The domain of the function $h(x) = \sqrt{x}$ is even more restricted. Since a negative number has no square root, $h(x)$ has a domain of $x > 0$.

Finding the Domain of a Function

To find the domain of a given function, first look for any restrictions on the domain. There are two main restrictions for function domain questions to look out for on the SAT:

---

1. **Division by zero.** Division by zero is mathematically impossible. A function is therefore undefined for all the values of x for which division by zero occurs. For example, $f(x) = {}^1/x\text{-}2$ is undefined at $x = 2$, since when $x = 2$, the function is equal to $f(x) = {}^1/0$.
2. **Negative numbers under square roots.** The square root of a negative number does not exist, so if a function contains a square root, such as $f(x) = \sqrt{x}$, the domain must be $x > 0$.

There are easy-to-spot warning signs that indicate you should look out for either division by zero or negative numbers under square roots. The division by zero warning sign is a variable in the denominator of a fraction. The negative number under square roots warning sign is a variable under a square root (or a variable raised to the 1/2 power). Once you've located the likely problem spots, you can usually find the values to eliminate from the domain pretty easily.

You must be itching for an example. Allow us to scratch that itch:

> What is the domain of $f(x) = \dfrac{x}{x^2 + 5x + 6}$?

$f(x)$ has variables in its denominator: red flag for the possibility of division by zero. You may need to restrict the function's domain to ensure that division by zero doesn't occur. To find the values of x that cause the denominator to equal zero, set up an equation equal to zero: $x^2 + 5x + 6 = 0$. A quadratic equation. Ahoy! Factor it: $(x + 2)(x + 3) = 0$. So, for $x = \{-2, -3\}$, the denominator is zero and $f(x)$ is undefined. The domain of $f(x)$ is the set of all real numbers x such that $x \neq -2, -3$. This can also be written in the form $\{x: x \neq -2, -3\}$.

Here's another example:

> What is the domain of $f(x) = \dfrac{2\sqrt{x-4}}{x-7}$?

This function has both warning signs: a variable under a square root and a variable in the denominator. It's best to examine each situation separately:

---

1. The denominator would equal zero if $x = 7$.
2. The quantity under the square root, $x - 4$, must be greater than or equal to zero in order for the function to be defined. Therefore, $x \geq 4$.

The domain of the function is therefore the set of real numbers x such that $x \geq 4$, $x \neq 7$.

The Range of a Function

A function's range is the set of all values of $f(x)$ that can be generated by the function. The easiest way to think about range is to visualize it on a graph. The domain, which is all the valid values of x in the function, is the x-axis, while the range, all the values of $f(x)$, is the y-axis. Take a look at the following two graphs:

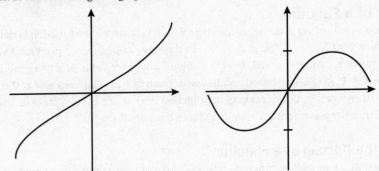

What values of the y-axis are reached on each graph? In the graph on the left, you can see that every possible value of y, from negative infinity to positive infinity, is included in the range. The range could be written as $-\infty \leq f(x) \leq \infty$. Contrast this with the graph on the right, where the range is quite limited: Only the values between -1 and 1 are part of the range. So the range is $-1 \leq f(x) \leq 1$.

There are two main warning signs of functions with limited ranges: absolute value and even exponents.

- **Absolute value.** The absolute value of a quantity is always positive. So, in a simple case, $f(x) = |x|$, you know that $f(x)$ must always be positive, and so the range includes only zero and positive numbers: $f(x) \geq 0$. Never assume that any function with an absolute value symbol has the same range, though. The range of $g(x) = -|x|$ is zero and all of the negative numbers: $f(x) \leq 0$.

- **Even Exponents.** Any time you square a number (or raise it to any multiple of 2) the resulting quantity will be positive.

Finding the Range

Calculating the range of a complex function is similar to finding the domain. First, look for absolute values, even exponents, or other reasons that the range would be restricted. Then adjust that range step by step as you run down the same checklist you use to find the domain.

> What is the range of $f(x) = \dfrac{|x-3|}{2}$?

In this case, the absolute value around $|x - 3|$ screams out that the range of $f(x)$ excludes all negative numbers: $f(x) \geq 0$. $|x - 3|$ is then divided by 2, so you have to divide the range by 2. But this division doesn't actually change the range, since both zero and infinity remain unchanged when halved.

Now for a more complicated example:

> What is the range of $\dfrac{\sqrt{|x-6|}+4}{2}$?

Tackle this example step by step.

1. The absolute value restricts the range to $0 \leq f(x) \leq \infty$.
2. Add 4 to each bound of the range. This action only affects the lower bound: $4 \leq f(x) \leq \infty$.
3. Taking the square root once again affects only the lower bound: $2 \leq f(x) \leq \infty$.
4. Finally, divide the bounds of the range in half to determine the range of the entire function: $1 \leq f(x) \leq \infty$.

Note that addition, subtraction, multiplication, division, and other mathematical operations don't affect infinity. That's why it's particularly important to look for absolute values and even roots. Once you can find a bound on a range that isn't infinity, you know that the operations on the function will affect that range.

The Range of a Function with a Prescribed Domain

Another way that the range of a function could be restricted is if the domain is itself restricted. If the SAT is feeling particularly nasty, it'll nail you with this kind of complicated domain and range question:

$f(x) = 2x^2 + 4$ for $-3 < x < 5$. What is the range of $f(x)$?

The first thing you have to realize is that there's no reason to assume that the range of the function will be at its high and low points at exactly the bounds of the restricted domain. If you assume that the range of $f(x) = 2x^2 + 4$ has its high point at 5 and its low point at -3, well, that's exactly what the SAT wants you to assume.

Here's where having a graphing calculator is immensely helpful on the SAT. If you graph $f(x) = 2x^2 + 4$, you'll see:

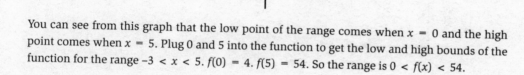

You can see from this graph that the low point of the range comes when $x = 0$ and the high point comes when $x = 5$. Plug 0 and 5 into the function to get the low and high bounds of the function for the range $-3 < x < 5$. $f(0) = 4$. $f(5) = 54$. So the range is $0 < f(x) < 54$.

FUNCTIONS AS MODELS

Functions as Models questions present information about a real-life scenario and then ask you to pick a function in equation or graph form that best describes the scenario.

A Function as Models question with graphs looks something like this:

If temperature is $f(x)$ and time is x, which of the following best describes a bucket of cold water left outside on a hot day?

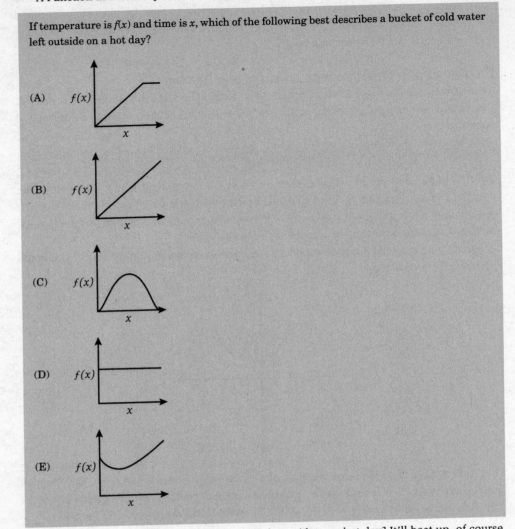

(A) $f(x)$

(B) $f(x)$

(C) $f(x)$

(D) $f(x)$

(E) $f(x)$

So, what'll happen to a bucket of cold water left outside on a hot day? It'll heat up, of course, so the answer's **B** . . . except that this is the real world and the question contains a trick. **B** shows that bucket heating up *forever*, when in fact, the water in the bucket can't actually get any hotter than the day itself. So at some point, that rise in temperature has to hit a plateau: **A** is the answer.

A Functions as Models problem that deals with written-out functions looks like this:

A bookstore is selling a particular book for $15 per copy. At this price it has been selling 20 copies of the book each day. The store owner estimates that for every dollar reduction in the selling price of the book, daily sales will increase by 20 copies. What is the daily sales, S, as a function of price, p?

(A) $S = -20p + 320$

(B) $S = 15p + 20$

(C) $S = \frac{3}{5}p$

(D) $S = -20p - 15$

(E) $S = p + 5$

The key to solving this sort of problem is to first define what kind of mathematical function this "real-world" scenario is describing. Take another look at the question: At $15, the book sells 20 copies, and for each dollar the price goes down, the book sells another 20 copies. In other words, for each dollar decrease in price, sales increase by a fixed amount. Sound like anything to you? How about a linear function, like $S = mp + b$, where m is the slope and b is the y-intercept. The "fixed increase" for every change of p is the slope. Since the slope *increases* 20 units for each dollar *decrease* in price, that slope must be negative: –20. You could now eliminate all the answers but **A** and **D**. To find the definitive right answer, though, you have to find b. You can do that by plugging in numbers from the question. You know that when the book costs \$15 dollars (p), it sells 20 copies (S). So, $20 = -20(15) + b$; $20 = -300 + b$; $b = 320$. There you go. **A** is the answer.

   If you're a little algebra-phobic, all this might seem very hard to you. But there's another way to go about it. Use the information in the question to build a graph. From the information in the question, you know that at the price of \$15, the store sells 20 copies, and that for each dollar less, the store sells 20 more copies. So, in other words, you know the points on this graph: (15,20), (14,40), (13,60). . .

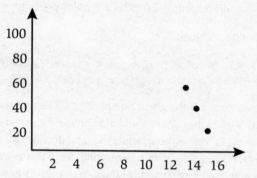

This graph doesn't give you the answer, but it does make it clear that you're dealing with a linear graph of slope –20, and that if you just keep on counting back to where $p = 0$, you'll get the y-intercept, or 320.

THE MOST COMMON WORD PROBLEMS

Word problems come in all shapes and sizes. But each and every year, the SAT includes certain particular varieties. We've got the skinny on 'em.

Rates

A rate is a ratio of related qualities that have different units. For example, speed is a rate that relates the two quantities of distance and time. Here is the general rate formula:

$$\text{quantity } A \times \text{rate } r = \text{quantity } B$$

No matter the specifics, the key to a rate word problem is in correctly placing the given information in the three categories: A, r, and B. Then, you can substitute the values into the rate formula. We look at the three most common types of rate: speed, work, and price.

Speed

In the case of speed, time is quantity A and distance is quantity B. For example, if you traveled for 4 hours at 25 miles per hour, then

$$4 \text{ hours} \times 25 \, \frac{\text{miles}}{\text{hour}} = 100 \text{ miles}$$

Usually, the SAT won't simply give you one of the quantities and the rate and ask you to plug it into the rate formula. Since rate questions are always in the form of word problems, the information that you'll need to solve the problem is often given in the befuddling complicated manner you've grown to know and hate.

Here's an example:

> Jim rollerskates 6 miles per hour. One morning, Jim starts rollerskating and doesn't stop until he has gone 60 miles. How many hours did he spend rollerskating?

This question provides more information than simply the speed and one of the quantities. You get unnecessary facts such as how Jim is traveling (by rollerskates) and when he started (in the morning). Ignore them and focus on the facts you need to solve the problem.

- **Quantity A:** x hours rollerskating
- **Rate:** 6 miles per hour
- **Quantity B:** 60 miles

$$x \text{ hours of rollerskating} = 60 \text{ miles} \div 6 \text{ miles per hour} = 10 \text{ hours}$$

Here's a more difficult rate problem:

> At a cycling race, the cyclist from California can cycle 528,000 feet per hour. If the race is 480 miles long, how long will it take her to finish the race? (1 mile = 5280 feet)

You should immediately pick out the given rate of 528,000 feet per hour and notice that the total distance traveled is 480 miles. You should also notice that the question presents a units problem: The given rate is in *feet* per hour, while the total distance traveled is given in *miles*.

Sometimes a question gives you inconsistent units, as in this example. *Always* read over the problem carefully and don't forget to adjust the units—the SAT makes sure that the answer you would come to if you had forgotten to correct for units appears among the answer choices.

For the cycling question, since the question tells you that there are 5,280 feet in a mile, you can find the rate for miles per hour:

$$528,000 \text{ feet per hour} \div 5,280 \text{ feet per mile} = 100 \text{ miles per hour}$$

Now you can plug the information into the rate formula:

- **Time:** x hours cycling
- **Rate:** 100 miles per hour
- **Distance:** 480 miles

$$480 \text{ miles} \div 100 \text{ miles per hour} = 4.8 \text{ hours}$$

Work

Work sucks. You're there from 9 to 5 and, at best, you get two weeks off per year, and you've got a boss constantly checking up on you. Work word problems on the SAT are a breeze in comparison. On work word problems, you'll usually find the first quantity measured in time (t), the second quantity measured in work done (w), and the rate measured in work done per time (r). For example, if you knitted for 8 hours and produced 2 sweaters per hour, then

$$8 \text{ hours} \times 2 \, \frac{\text{sweaters}}{\text{hour}} = 16 \text{ sweaters}$$

Here's a sample work problem. It's one of the harder rate word problems you might come across on the SAT:

> Four workers can dig a 40-foot well in 4 days. How long would it take for 8 workers to dig a 60-foot well? Assume that these 8 workers work at the same pace as the 4 workers.

First, examine what that problem says: 4 workers can dig a 40-foot well in 4 days. You know how much total work was done and how many people did it, you just don't know the rate at which the workers worked. You need that rate, since the 8 workers digging the 60-foot wells are working at the same rate. Since $r = w \div t$, you can get the rate by dividing 40 by 4, which equals 10. The workers together dig at a pace of 10 feet per day.

Now for that group of 8 workers digging a 60-foot well. The total work (w) done by the 8 workers is 60 feet, and they work at a rate (r) of 10 feet per day per 4 workers. Can you use this information to answer the question? Oh yeah. The rate of 10 feet per day per 4 workers converts to 20 feet per day per 8 workers, which is the size of the new crew. Now you can use the rate formula:

- **Time:** x days of work
- **Rate:** 20 feet per day per 8 workers
- **Work Done (in this case, distance dug):** 60 feet

$$60 \text{ feet} \div 20 \text{ feet per day per 8 workers} = 3 \text{ days of work for 8 workers}$$

This last problem required a little bit of creativity—but nothing you can't handle. Just remember the classic rate formula and use it wisely.

Price

In rate questions dealing with price, you'll usually find the first quantity measured in numbers of questions, the second measured in price, and the rate in price per question. If you have 8 basketballs, and you know that each basketball costs $25,

$$8 \text{ basketballs} \times \$25 \, \frac{\text{price}}{\text{basketball}} = \$200$$

Exponential Growth and Decay

Exponential growth and decay problems are like percent change problems on steroids: You must perform a percent change over and over again. You can use exponents on these repeated percent change questions. Here's an example:

> If a population of 100 grows by 5% per year, how large will the population be in 50 years?

You could do two things to solve this problem. You could multiply each successive generation by 5% fifty times to get the final answer, or you could use this formula:

$$\text{Final Amount} = \text{Original Amount} \times (1 + \text{Growth Rate})^{(\text{number of changes})}$$

The formula is probably the better bet. So, to solve this problem:

$$\text{final amount} = 100 \times 1.05^{50} = 1146.74 \approx 1147$$

Exponential decay only slightly modifies the formula:

$$\text{Final Amount} = \text{Original Amount} \times (1 - \text{Growth Rate})^{(\text{number of changes})}$$

Exponential decay is often used to model population decreases as well as the decay of physical mass.

We'll work through a few example problems to get a feel for both exponential growth and decay problems.

A Simple Exponential Growth Problem

A population of bacteria grows by 35% every hour. If the population begins with 100 specimens, how many are there after 6 hours?

You've got an original population of 100, a growth rate of .35 every hour, and 6 hours. To solve the problem, you just need to plug the appropriate values into the formula for exponential growth.

$$\text{final amount} = 100 \times 1.35^6 \approx 605 \text{ specimens}$$

A Simple Exponential Decay Problem

A fully inflated beach ball loses 6% of its air every day. If the beach ball originally contains 4000 cubic centimeters of air, how many cubic centimeters does it hold after 10 days?

Since the beach ball loses air, you know this is an exponential decay problem. The decay rate is .06, the original amount is 4000 cubic centimeters of air, and the time is 10 days. Plugging the information into the formula,

$$\text{final amount} = 4000 \times (0.94)^{10} \approx 2154 \text{ cubic centimeters}$$

A More Annoying Exponential Growth Problem

A bank offers a 4.7% interest rate on all savings accounts, per month. If 1000 dollars is initially put into a savings account, how much money will the account hold two years later?

This problem is a bit tricky because the interest rate is per month, while the time period is given in years. You need to make the units match up. In the two-year time period given by the question, there will be $2 \times 12 = 24$ months

$$\text{final amount} = 1000 \times 1.047^{24} \approx 3011.07 \text{ dollars}$$

Here's another compounding problem:

Ben puts $2000 into a savings account that pays 5% interest compounded annually. Justin puts $2500 into a different savings account that pays 4% annually. After 15 years, whose account will have more money in it if no more money is added or subtracted from the principal?

Ben's account will have $2000 $\times$ $1.05^{15} \approx$ $4157.85 in it after 15 years. Justin's account will have $2500 $\times$ $1.04^{15} \approx$ $4502.36 in it. Justin's account will still have more money in it than Ben's after 15 years. Notice, however, that Ben's account *is* gaining on Justin's account.

And with that, you've covered everything you need to know to rock SAT algebra. Turn the page for some practice.

PRACTICE SET 1: MULTIPLE CHOICE

1. If $3(x - 6) = 24$, what is the value of $(x - 6)^2$?

    (A) 8
    (B) 14
    (C) 30
    (D) 64
    (E) 196

2. If $12 + 5x > -7x - 24$, what must be true of x?

    (A) $x < -3$
    (B) $x \leq 3$
    (C) $x > -3$
    (D) $x \geq -3$
    (E) $x > 3$

3. What is the value of $\frac{3}{2}P$, when $\frac{3}{4}P = 72$?

    (A) 48
    (B) 60
    (C) 96
    (D) 120
    (E) 144

4. A retail outlet is having a clearance sale on all the shoes in its inventory over a period of four days. On the first day it sells 1/4 of its inventory, on the second day it sells 1/2 of the remaining inventory, and on the third day it sells 1/6 of the remainder. What fraction of the original inventory is left for the last day of the sale?

    (A) $^1/_{12}$
    (B) $^1/_{10}$
    (C) $^1/_8$
    (D) $^5/_{16}$
    (E) $^5/_8$

5. Which of the following lines accurately depicts the function $f(x) = -\frac{1}{4}x + 2$?

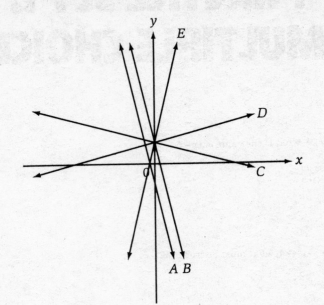

(A) line A
(B) line B
(C) line C
(D) line D
(E) line E

6. If $\frac{n}{p}$ is a positive, even integer, which of the following could be true?

    I. n and p are negative integers
    II. n and p are integers; n is an odd integer
    III. $n = p$

(A) I only
(B) II only
(C) III only
(D) II and III
(E) I, II, and III

7. If r is twice the value of p and p is 8 less than s, then in terms of p, what is the value of $r + s$?

(A) $2(p + 8)$
(B) $3p - 8$
(C) $p + 8$
(D) $3p + 8$
(E) $\dfrac{p + 8}{2}$

8. If $x + y = 8$ and $x - y = 2$, what is the value of the following expression?

$$\frac{x^2 - y^2}{x^2 - 2xy + y^2}$$

(A) 0

(B) $\dfrac{1}{2}$

(C) 1

(D) 2

(E) 4

9. Train A leaves Romeoville at 8:00 a.m., traveling at 55 mph toward Julietteville. Train B leaves Julietteville at the same time, heading toward Romeoville at 35 mph. If the distance between the two towns is 337.5 miles, what time do the two trains pass each other?

(A) 11:52 a.m.
(B) 11:45 a.m.
(C) 11:32 a.m.
(D) 11:15 a.m.
(E) 11:04 a.m.

10. Look at the following graph to answer the question below.

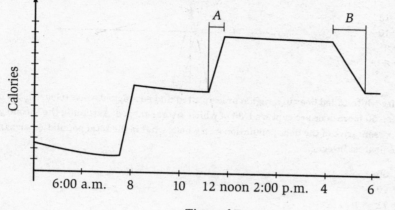

Time of Day

Which of the following activities best describes what occurred during time segments *A* and *B*, respectively?

(A) eating lunch and playing racquetball
(B) having a light nap and taking a brisk walk
(C) having a snack and eating a sandwich
(D) driving in a car and taking a slow walk
(E) jogging 4 miles and biking 12 miles

11. Holly goes to the store to buy peanut butter and jelly for a school picnic. Peanut butter costs $4 a jar, and jelly costs $2 a jar. If Holly spends a total of $28 and buys a total of 8 jars, how many jars of peanut butter did she buy?

(A) 12
(B) 8
(C) 7
(D) 6
(E) 2

12. Stephen is planning to take a two-day biking trip during which he will ride 122 miles. The distance he travels on the first day will be 40 miles less than twice the distance he travels on the second day. What is the distance he plans to travel the second day?

(A) 54
(B) 58
(C) 62
(D) 66
(E) 68

13. In the equation $3x^2 - 15x + 18 = 0$, what are the possible values of x?

(A) 2 and 3
(B) −2 and −3
(C) −2 and 3
(D) −1 and −3
(E) 1 and −3

SAT
Math
Workbook

14. Dana walks from home to school at a rate of 5 mph. It takes her 2 hours longer to walk home from school than it did to walk to school. If her total walking time to and from school was 8 hours, what was Dana's rate of speed walking home from school?

    (A) 3 mph
    (B) 4 mph
    (C) 5 mph
    (D) 8 mph
    (E) 15 mph

15. If the function of $f(x) = 2x - 3$ and $g(x) = x^2 - 1$, what is the function of $f(g(3))$?

    (A) 13
    (B) 10
    (C) 8
    (D) 6
    (E) 3

16. Fifty white-tailed deer in a region are captured and ear-tagged, then released. Six months later, 50 more deer are captured, 35 of which are ear-tagged. Assuming the second group is representative of the deer population as a whole, what is the total population size (rounded to the nearest integer)?

    (A) 35
    (B) 70
    (C) 71
    (D) 75
    (E) 85

17. Six years ago, June was twice the age of Sue and 8 years older than Bill. If Bill is now x years old, then in terms of x, what is Sue's current age?

    (A) $x + 8$

    (B) $\dfrac{x + 8}{2}$

    (C) $\dfrac{(x - 6) + 8}{2} + 6$

    (D) $\dfrac{x + 8}{2} + 6$

    (E) $\dfrac{(x - 6) + 8}{2x}$

18. Simplify $\dfrac{9^{90} - 9^{89}}{(3^2)^{89}}$

    (A) $-\dfrac{1}{3^{178}}$

    (B) 8

    (C) 9

    (D) 89

    (E) 9^{90}

19. Dweezle has $3,500 to invest. He places part of the amount in a stock option that yields 5% interest annually and the rest in a savings account that yields 8% interest annually. If Dweezle earns a total of $238 in interest for the year, what was the amount he placed in the savings account?

(*Interest = Original Amount* × *Interest Rate* × *Duration.*)

(A) $700
(B) $1,400
(C) $2,100
(D) $2,800
(E) $3,500

20. The cells of a certain culture of bacteria double every 6 minutes. If there are 3 cells in a petri dish, how many cells of bacteria will there be after one and a half hours?

(A) 16,384
(B) 24,576
(C) 49,152
(D) 98,304
(E) 196,608

ANSWERS & EXPLANATIONS

1. **D**

When you see that the question wants the numerical value of $(x - 6)^2$, bells should go off in your head that there will be a shortcut method to answering this question.

Divide both sides by 3 and you get: $3(x - 6) = 24$

If you square both sides at this point, you have your answer. $(x - 6) = 8$

There's **D**. $(x - 6)^2 = 64$

2. **C**

This one is a bit tougher than question 1 because this time there's an inequality instead of an equals sign.

$$12 + 5x > -7x - 24$$

$$12 + 5x + 7x > -7x + 7x - 24$$

$$12 + 12x > -24$$

$$12 - 12 + 12x > -24 - 12$$

$$12x > -36$$

$$x > -3$$

Because you divided with a positive 12 and not a negative one, there's no need to switch the signs. **C** is correct.

3. **E**

There are two ways to go about solving this problem. You can solve for P, then figure out what $\frac{3}{2}P$ equals, or you can try to figure out a way to convert $\frac{3}{4}P$ directly into $\frac{3}{2}P$. We'll skip the shortcut this time and do the legwork:

$$\frac{3}{4}P = 72$$

$$\left(\frac{4}{3}\right)\frac{3}{4}P = 72\left(\frac{4}{3}\right)$$

$$P = 96$$

$$\frac{3}{2}P = \frac{3}{2}(96) = 144$$

There's **E**. If you want to see the shortcut, look at the two fractions in front of P in the stem. Both have the same numerator (3), so only the dominator is different (2 and 4). If you multiplied $\frac{3}{4}p$ by 2, you would get the $\frac{3}{2}p$ fraction that the question wants.

$$\frac{3}{4}P = 72$$

$$(2)\frac{3}{4}P = 72(2)$$

$$\frac{3}{2}P = 144$$

E again. There's almost always a shortcut, but you don't have to find it. You can solve questions without it just as well.

4.   **D**

The word problem is pushing for you to create some wickedly convoluted algebraic formula involving all those fractions, but that's a sucker's game. Instead, make up a number for the amount of shoes in the inventory before it all goes down. We're going to use 80. In general, try to pick a fat, divisible integer, and if you have to go to fractions, so be it. Some numbers will work better than others, but if you do the math correctly, it won't matter what you started with. Now run through the computations:

80	number of shoes starting out
80 − 20 = 60	1/4 of 80 is 20, the amount sold on Day 1
60/2 = 30	1/2 the remaining number is sold on Day 2
30 − 5 = 25	1/6 of 30 is 5, the amount sold on Day 3

So we started with 80 and ended up with 25. This fraction works out to be: $\frac{25}{80} = \frac{5}{16}$, **D**.

Just for kicks, try starting out with a different number. Either way, do the math right, and you'll end up at **D**.

5.   **C**

If you have the geometry know-how about lines and slope, you can use that knowledge to solve this question. If not, just place x values into the function that you're given and see what comes out. The easiest number to plug in is $x = 0$ because this will knock out all the stuff in front of the x.

$$f(x) = -\frac{1}{4}x + 2$$

$$f(0) = -\frac{1}{4}(0) + 2$$

$$f(0) = 2$$

Your first point is at (0, 2). This eliminates **A** as an answer choice. Now put another number, such as 4, into the function.

$$f(x) = -\frac{1}{4}x + 2$$

$$f(4) = -\frac{1}{4}(4) + 2$$

$$f(4) = -1 + 2 = 1$$

Your second point is at (4, 1). Only line **C** goes through this point, so it is the answer to this coordinate grid function question.

6.   A

Here's a roman numeral question, and you might want to skip it until the very end. The reason is simple: You have to do the work of three questions to get credit for one. Here you would have to try different numbers for each roman numeral choice to see whether it could be true.

Let's start with roman numeral III, because it seems easiest. If $n = p$, then $\frac{n}{p}$ will always equal 1. Try a bunch of different numbers and see this for yourself. If roman numeral III is wrong, you can eliminate choices **C**, **D**, and **E** because they all contain choice III as an answer. It's down to a 50/50 shot. Roman numeral I doesn't seem as though it would work, but if $n = -14$ and $p = -7$, then:

$$\frac{n}{p} = \frac{-14}{-7} = 2$$

2 is a positive, even integer, so **A** must be the answer. What about roman numeral II? Who cares? Once you solve the question, move on.

7.   D

Here's another word problem. As usual, the key is to stop trying to work with abstract values and use real numbers instead. Let's make $r = 10$. The stem states that r is twice the value of p, so p must equal 5. Also, if p is 8 less than s, then s must equal 13, because 5 is 8 less than 13. Write this chart out next to the question:

$$r = 10$$

$$p = 5$$

$$s = 13$$

Now go through the answer choices, replace every p with a 5, and determine the numeric value of each answer choice. The value of $r + s$ is 23, and only answer **D** works out to be 23, so it is the correct choice.

8.   E

Here we enter the realm of the medium difficulty questions. There's no signpost announcing it, but you have to prepare yourself for questions that are a bit sneakier or more involved than the ones you've been working on thus far.

You have binomial terms in the stem and a quadratic expression in the denominator. What do you think the key to this question might be? You'll earn SAT savvy points if your mind jumps to, "There's going to be some factoring involved." If you don't get to this, don't sweat it. You will with some practice.

Once you factor, this question will split open like a sliced orange:

$$\frac{x^2 - y^2}{x^2 - 2xy + y^2} = \frac{(x+y)(x-y)}{(x-y)(x-y)} = \frac{(x+y)}{(x-y)} = \frac{8}{2} = 4$$

E is correct. If you don't factor, you can still solve this question if you take the two equations and solve them simultaneously. That gives you values for x and y, which you can then plug into the question. This takes a bit of time, but you can still get the question right.

9.　**B**

Oh, Romeoville Train, wherefore art thou on the rails? To solve this problem, take the answer choices and plug them in to find the right answer. Start with **C**. At 11:32 a.m., both trains have been chugging along for about 3.5 hours. In that time, the Romeoville express will have traveled (3.5 hours)(55 miles/hour) = 192.5 miles, and the Julietteville local will have gone (3.5 hours)(35 miles/hour) = 122.5 miles. Let's add these two distances. If they equal 337.5, the trains have passed each other:

$$192.5 + 122.5 = 315 \text{ miles}$$

C is a little too short. That crosses out **D** and **E** as well. The answer is either **A** or **B**, and because you need only a little more than **C**, you could guess **B** and feel pretty good about it. To prove it, however:

$$\text{Romeoville Train} = (3.75)(55) = 206.25 \text{ miles}$$

$$\text{Julietteville Train} = (3.75)(35) = 131.25 \text{ miles}$$

(We used the number 3.75 because that's 3 hours, 45 minutes in decimal form.)

206.25 miles + 131.25 miles = 337.5 miles. **B** is correct.

10.　**A**

Measuring calories is like monitoring the fuel consumption in a car because both relate to energy gained or lost. In time segment A, the calorie levels are rising, meaning Person A is "fueling up." What would account for this in a person? **B**, **D**, and **E** all start with activities that would burn calories, so they can be eliminated. It's either **A** or **C**. **C** has the person eating twice. This would lead to a graph showing two upward spikes, not one upward spike and one downward drop. **A** has the person playing racquetball in segment B, an activity that would burn calories and lead to the drop shown in the modeled function. **A** is correct.

11.　**D**

If you try to take the Math Path on this problem, you might mess up and get **A** as an answer. This would be quite foolish because the problem states that Holly purchased only 8 jars total. How could 12 be the answer? It couldn't, but it does work as a good trap for students who mess up the algebra.

Start with **C**, which is 7 peanut butter jars. This leaves one jelly jar at $2 apiece. Overall, the total for this mix would be

$$(7 \text{ peanut butter jars})(\$4) + (1 \text{ jelly})(\$2) = \$28 + \$2 = \$30.$$

We know this is incorrect because the problem states that everything together cost only $28. Too much peanut butter, but not by very much. Cross out **C** and run the question again using **D**, or take an educated guess and realize that because **D** is just slightly lower than **C**, it's going to be the right answer, which it is.

12.   **A**

Here's another word problem, and it earns its medium-difficulty badge by being a little strange in its wording. The statement "The distance he travels on the first day will be 40 miles less than twice the distance he travels on the second day" is intentionally confusing. Even Yoda makes more sense, and he says everything backward. Nevertheless, you can start with **C** and hammer away.

Suppose Day 2 equals 62 miles. Twice this is $(62)(2) = 124$, and 40 less than this number is $124 - 40 = 84$ miles. This is the Day 1 travel number. Add the two together and you get $62 + 84 = 146$, which is too much because the stem says the biking trip is 122 miles. You need a smaller number, so **C**, **D**, and **E** are all out.

Let's try **B**, 58 miles. Twice $58 = (58)(2) = 116$, and 40 less than this is $116 - 40 = 76$.

Day 1 + Day 2 = $58 + 76 = 134$. This is also too long. The answer must be **A**. You can check it if you like, but there's no real need. All other possibilities have been eliminated. Hooray for multiple-choice exams.

13.   **A**

A quadratic equation appears to test your reverse FOIL skills. Before plunging into the nightmare that is the quadratic formula, try to determine the two binomials. The answer choices will help you because you can get an idea of what the second term of each binomial might be by looking at what's listed. You can also do a little bit of factoring and take a 3 out of the left side. This makes things even more clear:

$$3x^2 - 15x + 18 = 0$$

$$3(x^2 - 5x + 6) = 0$$

Now factor the equation into binomials:

$$3(x - 3)(x - 2) = 0$$

For the entire equation to equal zero, one of the two binomials must equal zero. So x can be equal to 2 or 3. Circle answer **A**.

14.   **A**

Reading a word problem slowly can often give you insight into which answer choices are improbable. The story states, "It takes her 2 hours longer to walk home from school than it did to walk to school." If it takes 2 hours longer, she must be walking slower on the way back. That is, she's walking slower than 5 mph. Now look at your answer choices. What can you cross out? **C**, **D**, and **E** are all gone, simply because you took the time to understand the question instead of rushing off to devise the proper algebraic formula.

It's got to be either **A** or **B**. Again, the pull to create an algebraic equation is strong. Resist it. If her total walking time is 8 hours and it took 2 hours more on the way back, there's only one set of numbers that works: 3 and 5. Now maybe you an set up an equation, but only a small one:

(walking rate to school)(time spent) = (walking rate going back)(time spent going back)

$$(5 \text{ mph})(3 \text{ hours}) = (? \text{ mph})(5 \text{ hours})$$

$$(5)(3) = (?)(5)$$

The answer is **A**, 3 mph, because this makes the equation above match.

15. **A**

In this compound function, perform function g first, then take this answer and kowtow to function f.

$$g(x) = x^2 - 1$$
$$g(3) = 3^2 - 1$$
$$g(3) = 9 - 1 = 8$$
$$f(x) = 2x - 3$$
$$f(x) = 2x - 3$$
$$f(8) = 2(8) - 3$$
$$f(8) = 13$$

The answer is **A**.

16. **C**

From here on out, you have to earn it. The last five questions are going to be difficult, even if you do everything right. For this reason, don't break your head trying to ace all five of these. Getting two or three right and guessing on the rest will still give you a good score, provided you take your time and get the easy and medium questions right.

Determining what computations need to be done here is not an easy task. That's just how it is on some difficult questions. It's why they're *difficult*.

Fifty deer are caught, tagged, and released. The next time 50 deer are caught, 35 of them have tags. This group of deer—35 tagged and 15 untagged—is assumed to be representative of the deer population as a whole. So the deer population has grown, which means you can cross out at least **A**. If nothing else, take a guess from here. But if you have the time to do some math, stick with the question.

The deer ratio of $\frac{35 \text{ tagged}}{50 \text{ untagged}}$ is representative of the whole population. You know that there are 50 tagged deer total, so $\frac{35 \text{tagged}}{50 \text{ untagged}} = \frac{50 \text{ tagged-whole-population}}{\text{?-whole-population}}$. At this point, you can start plugging in answer choices where the question mark is or you can cross-multiply the ratio to find the answer. The ratio is very close to an algebraic equation, but that can't be helped.

$$\frac{35 \text{ tagged}}{50 \text{ untagged}} = \frac{50 \text{ tagged-whole-population}}{\text{?-whole-population}}$$
$$\frac{35}{50} = \frac{50}{n}$$
$$35n = (50)(50)$$
$$35n = 2500$$
$$n = 71.42 \approx 71$$

C is the answer.

17. **C**

Give June an age now, and you can figure everything out from there. Let's make her 20, so $J = 20$. Six years ago would make June age 14. If she was twice Sue's age at that time, $S = 7$. If June was 8 years older than Bill when she was 14, $B = 6$. We have:

$$J = 20$$
$$S = 7$$
$$B = 6$$

If x equals Bill's current age, then $x = 6 + 6 = 12$. Sue was 7 six years ago, so now she is 13.

Go through all the answer choices and replace each x with a 12. Then find the answer choice that works out to 13. **C**'s your answer.

18. **B**

This question illustrates how you can understand a concept such as factoring, but unless you really, really have a good understanding of it, you won't be able to utilize it on the difficult questions.

You might be able to use your calculator to muddle through this, but it won't be pretty. It also might not work simply because the numbers are too large. The real key is to see the hidden 9^{89}s. factor them out, then simplify. To do this, look at the following equation until you see why it makes sense:

$$9^{90} = 9^{89 + 1} = (9^{89})(9^{1}) = (9^{89})9$$

We pulled out one of the 9s from 9^{90} to make it $(9^{89})(9)$. This will allow us to take this unwieldy expression and whittle it down.

$$\frac{9^{90} - 9^{89}}{(3^2)^{89}} = \frac{9^{90} - 9^{89}}{9^{89}} = \frac{(9^{89})(9) - 9^{89}}{9^{89}} = \frac{9^{89}(9 - 1)}{9^{89}}$$
$$= (9 - 1) = 8$$

B is correct.

19. **C**

It's a word problem, but computations are going to be involved. Start with **C** and see what it brings. If Dweezle placed $2,100 in savings, then $3,500 – $2,100 = $1,400 is in a stock option. The interest on both these would be:

$$(0.08)(2,100) + (0.05)(1,400) = 168 + 70 = \$238$$

Hot diggity, it's **C**! Got it in one go.

20. **D**

This is another word problem, but working backward might be messier than going forward. The best approach to this question is to be ready and willing to start writing immediately. In 90 minutes (the hour-and-half time), the bacteria will double 90/6 = 15 times because there are 15 six-minute segments in 90 minutes.

Go low-tech for the toughest questions. The test-makers won't expect that route, which usually has its benefits. Write out the numbers 1 through 15 on a scratch sheet of paper. Then start figuring out how many bacteria there are. It's as simple as hitting the "times 2" function on your calculator.

Start	3 cells
1	6
2	12
3	24
4	48
5	96
6	192
7	384
8	768
9	1,536
10	3,072
11	6,144
12	12,288
13	24,576
14	49,152
15	98,304

There's your answer, **D**. The actual algebra would take some time to explain and would make your skull ache. Finding the answer is what's important, and that's what we did.

PRACTICE SET 2: GRID-INS

1. If $a + b + c = -350$ and $a = -725$, what is the value of $b + c$?

$$\sqrt{9} \le m \le \sqrt{49}$$
$$2^2 < n < 3^2$$

2. If m and n are integers that satisfy the conditions above, what is one possible value of $m + n$?

3. The Acme Industrial Technical College has fallen on hard times. Last year its enrollment dropped by 20%, and this year enrollment dropped another 15% from last year's. Next year the college expects to have 50% of this year's enrollment. What percent of enrollment can be expected to drop for all 3 years?

4. If $f(x) = x^2 - 2x$, what does $f(6)$ equal?

5. $(2x - 3)(5x + 14) = ax^2 + bx + c$, where $a, b,$ and c are numerical constants. Determine the value of b.

6. If 35% of 40% of x equals 70, what is the value of x?

7. $4x - 5y = 4$ and $2x - y = 8$. Using this information, determine the value of $(x - y)$.

8. The price of typewriters has increased by $10 per year over the past 5 years. If a typewriter currently retails for $165, by what percentage did the price of typewriters increase over the last 5 years?

9. If $x^2 - y^2 = 48$, and $x + y = 12$, what is the value of $x - y$?

10. Cindy currently has a balance of $240 on her credit card bill. She intends to pay 4% of the balance annually, but the debt has a 5% annual interest rate. After 4 years her debt will have increased by how much, in dollars?

11. The expression $\frac{6x - 2}{8} + \frac{2x + 5}{8}$ is how much greater than x?

12. If the function of $g(z) = az - b$, where a and b are constants, $g(12) = 83$, and $g(4) = 19$, what is the value of b?

13. It takes Ralph 4 hours to complete a certain job. Potsy can complete the same job in 3 hours. If Ralph and Potsy work together to complete $\frac{3}{4}$ of the job, how long in hours will it take Ralph to finish the job by himself?

14. If x and y are positive integers, $x > 30$, and $x - y > 25$, what is the LEAST possible value of $x + y$?

15. In the function $f(x) = \sqrt{x} \cdot x^2$, the domain is all positive numbers. What is one integer value of the range of this function?

ANSWERS & EXPLANATIONS

1. **375**

This is the easiest question—does it show?

$$a + b + c = -350$$
$$-725 + b + c = -350$$
$$-725 + 725 + b + c = -350 + 725$$
$$b + c = 375$$

Grid in the number 375.

2. **10**

Of the two integers, n is probably easier to figure out, so let's do that one first.

$$2^2 < n < 3^2$$
$$4 < n < 9$$

The variable n can be 5, 6, 7, or 8. One of the weird things about grid-in questions is that there isn't always one single answer. We can use any one of these integers and still get credit for this question, provided we determine the value of m correctly:

$$\sqrt{9} \leq m \leq \sqrt{49}$$
$$3 \leq m \leq 7$$

Because those are less than or equal to signs, m can be 3, 4, 5, 6, or 7. But don't spend time deciding which value to use. Both m and n can be 5, and $5 + 5 = 10$, so grid in 10 and move on. (Any integer value between 8 and 15 works.)

3. **66**

Poor Acme. Sob story aside, the key here is to come up with a number, then start chipping away at it with the appropriate percentages. Because percentages are involved, it may be very helpful to say that Acme started out with 100 students. Starting with 100 on percentage questions often makes it easier to calculate percentage change.

First year:	100 students
After a 20% drop:	20% of 100 is 20, so enrollment is now at $100 - 20 = 80$.
Another 15% drop:	15% of 80 = $(0.15)(80) = 12$ students. $80 - 12 = 68$. Only 68 remain.
Projected 50% drop:	50% of 68 is 34, so there are only 34 students left at Acme.

Because you start with 100 students, figuring out the percentage drop for all 3 years takes only a bit of substitution: 100 – 34 remaining students = 66 students gone = 66%. If you use a number other than 100, you have to do some more involved computing. So don't.

4. **24**

Simply follow the function:

$$f(x) = x^2 - 2x$$
$$f(6) = (6)^2 - 2(6)$$
$$f(6) = 36 - 12$$
$$f(6) = 24$$

5.   **13**

Here are two binomials begging to be FOILed. Once you send them through the FOILer, all you need to do is pick out b, the numerical value in front of the x variable.

$$(2x - 3)(5x + 14) =$$
$$10x^2 + 28x - 15x - 42 =$$
$$10x^2 + 13x - 42$$

This means that $b = 13$.

6.   **500**

If this were a multiple-choice question, we could head down to the answer choices and start trying different answers. But this isn't a multiple-choice section, is it? That's the whole nefarious point of the grid-in section. It limits the number of strategies you can use to find the right answer.

We have to set up a simple equation instead. If 35% of 40% of x equals 70, then:

$$(35\%)(40\%)(x) = 70$$

Of means "multiply" in Mathspeak.

$$(0.35)(0.4)x = 70$$

Here we convert the percentages to decimals by moving the decimal points two spaces to the left.

$$0.14x = 70$$

Dividing both sides by 0.14 leaves you with . . .

$$x = 500$$

The answer.

7.   **2**

You have two equations with two variables. Because the second equation is fairly basic ($2x - y = 8$), we're going to solve for y in that one, then place that value into the other equation.

$$2x - y = 8$$
$$2x = 8 + y$$
$$2x - 8 = y$$
$$4x - 5y = 4$$
$$4x - 5(2x - 8) = 4$$
$$4x - 10x + 40 = 4$$
$$-6x + 40 = 4$$
$$-6x + 40 - 40 = 4 - 40$$
$$-6x = -36$$
$$x = 6$$

There's x. You know that $2x - 8 = y$, so:

$$2x - 8 = y$$
$$2(6) - 8 = y$$
$$12 - 8 = y$$
$$4 = y$$

One last computation to go. The question asked for $(x - y)$—did you circle this?—so the answer is $6 - 4 = 2$.

All that work for a lousy 2.

8. **43.478**

This is another word problem that would be much simpler if we had answer choices to pick from. As it is, we'll have to take the Math Path, albeit reluctantly.

If the price of typewriters has increased by $10 per year over the past 5 years, then type-writers have gone up (5 years)($10 per year) = $50 in price. If they are currently at $165, then their price 5 years ago was $165 – $50 = $115.

We now must ask the question, "What percent of 115 is 50?" (Note that you use the original price to calculate percentage increase, not the current price of $165.) In Mathspeak, this question works out to:

$$x\% \text{ of } 115 = 50$$

$$\left(\frac{x}{100}\right)(115) = 50$$

$$\frac{115x}{100} = 50$$

$$\left(\frac{100}{115}\right)\left(\frac{115x}{100}\right) = 50\left(\frac{100}{115}\right)$$

$$x \approx 43.478\%$$

Here's one of the funky things about grid-in questions. You get credit if you grid in 43.478, 43.47, or 43.48. You don't have to fill in the entire grid, and you don't have to round up or down correctly. In general, though, try to make your answers as precise as possible—it's always best to err on the side of caution.

9. **4**

This is a quadratic problem, but it doesn't look that way at first because the middle bx term is missing. To be more precise, the middle term does not exist because it is canceled out.

$$x^2 - y^2 = 48$$

$$(x + y)(x - y) = 48$$

That's the key to this question. From there, you're given $x + y = 12$, so:

$$(x + y)(x - y) = 48$$

$$12(x - y) = 48$$

$$(x - y) = 4$$

10. **9.74**

If you understand percentages, you can take a shortcut on this question. Usually you can't add or subtract percentages because the base value (the value whose percentage is being taken) is different. But here, the base value for Cindy's balance payment and debt increase is the same, $240. This means you can combine the two percentages and uncover the net change in debt:

4% payments – 5% debt increase = 1% debt increase per year

1% of $240 is $2.40. After the first year, Cindy now owes $242.40. Now find out the increase for the second year, 1% of $242.40 is $2.424; for the third year, 1% of $244.824 is $2.44824; and for the fourth year. 1% of $247.27224 is $2.4727224. Now add up the four: $2.40 + $2.424 + $2.44824 + $2.4727224 = $9.7449624 or $9.74.

11. **3/8**

The brace of fractions makes this problem look much tougher than it really is. Because each fraction has an 8 in the denominator, they can be combined.

$$\frac{6x-2}{8} + \frac{2x+5}{8}$$
$$\frac{6x-2+2x+5}{8}$$
$$\frac{8x+3}{8}$$

We achieve what is needed by putting the two fractions together. Watch what happens when they are separated again:

$$\frac{8x+3}{8}$$
$$\frac{8x}{8} + \frac{3}{8}$$
$$x + \frac{3}{8}$$

There's your answer. The expression is greater than x by $\frac{3}{8}$.

12. **13**

This looks like a function question, and it is, but it's also something else. If you write out the two functions given, you have:

$$g(z) = az - b =$$
$$12a - b = 83$$

$$g(z) = az - b =$$
$$4a - b = 19$$

There are two equations with two variables. You have a simultaneous equation situation hiding out. It's tricky, but what did you expect, now that you're in the Land of the Hard Questions?

We solved the last simultaneous equation by one method, so we'll use the other method for this one. The b in the question above will cancel out as is, but b is the variable we're looking for. To get rid of the a terms, multiply the second equation by -3 and see what happens:

$$4a - b = 19$$
$$(-3)4a - (-3)b = (-3)19$$
$$-12a + 3b = -57$$

We can take this equation and add it to the first one:

$$+\begin{array}{r} 12a - b = 83 \\ -12a + 3b = -57 \\ \hline 2b = 26 \\ b = 13 \end{array}$$

It's an unlucky number, but a correct one.

13. **1**

Picking the right number will really help on this question. You have 4s and 3s abounding, so pick a number divisible by both, such as 12. Let's say the job Ralph and Potsy are working on is chair making. They need to make 12 chairs. It takes Ralph 4 hours to make 12 chairs, so he works at a rate of 3 chairs/hour:

Ralph: (4 hours)(3 chairs/hour) = 12 chairs

Potsy is faster. He takes only 3 hours to make 12 chairs, so his rate can be calculated in your head as 4 chairs/hour:

$$\text{Potsy: } (3 \text{ hours})(4 \text{ chairs/hour}) = 12 \text{ chairs}$$

Together, they complete $3/4$ of the job. What is $3/4$ of 12?

$$\frac{3}{4}(12) = 9$$

That means 3 chairs remain because $12 - 9 = 3$. The question asks how long in hours it will take Ralph to finish the job by himself. If Ralph completes 3 chairs/hour and there are 3 chairs left, it will take him 1 hour to finish the job.

14. **32**

Let's start small and take things from there. If $x > 30$, begin $x = 31$. Moving to the next inequality, $x - y > 25$, the largest number we can make for y is 5. This makes $x + y = 36$, but is this the least possible value? Keep in mind we're looking for the smallest number we can make, so using the largest value for y is not in our best interests. We want the smallest of y possible, and we can combine this with the smallest value of x that works.

If $x = 31$, the largest number we can make for y is 5, but the LEAST possible value for y is 1, because 1 is the smallest positive integer. (Zero is neither positive nor negative.) Having y equal to 1 still satisfies the second equation because:

$$x - y > 25$$

$$31 - 1 > 25$$

$$30 > 25$$

Therefore, the smallest value for $x + y$ is $31 + 1 = 32$.

15. **32**

The last question is quite often the weirdest. No exception here. You have to know about functions, and you have to understand the vocabulary to have a chance here. The question wants a range value, and you know the range is the set of all possible values of $f(x)$ that can be generated. You did know that, right? More so, the question wants "an integer value" of the range. This means you can't just plug in some positive x value and write the output down. You have to pick a number that will go into $f(x) = \sqrt{x} \cdot x^2$ and emerge an integer.

The key is the square root part. If you pick a perfect square, your number should emerge from under the square root sign unscathed. Some simple perfect squares are 4, 9, and 16. Let's use 4:

$$f(x) = \sqrt{x} \cdot x^2$$
$$f(4) = \sqrt{4} \cdot 4^2 = 2 \cdot 16 = 32$$

32 is one integer value for the range of this particular function and will work just fine as our answer.

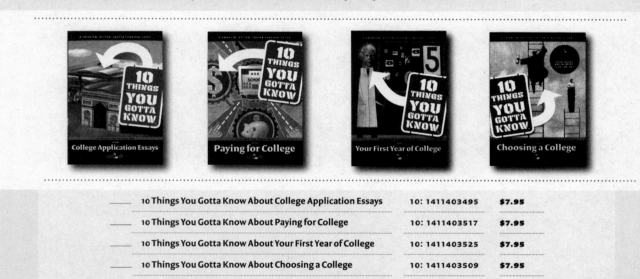